语言学论丛

书面纠错与第二语言学习
Written Error Correction and Second Language Learning

姜 琳 著

图书在版编目(CIP)数据

书面纠错与第二语言学习/姜琳著.—北京：北京大学出版社，2014.4
（语言学论丛）
ISBN 978-7-301-24694-8

Ⅰ.①书… Ⅱ.①姜… Ⅲ.①第二语言－研究 Ⅳ.①H003

中国版本图书馆 CIP 数据核字(2014)第 193548 号

书　　　名：	书面纠错与第二语言学习
著作责任者：	姜　琳　著
组稿编辑：	黄瑞明
责任编辑：	刘　虹
标准书号：	ISBN 978-7-301-24694-8/H · 3561
出版发行：	北京大学出版社
地　　　址：	北京市海淀区成府路 205 号　100871
网　　　址：	http://www.pup.cn　新浪官方微博:@北京大学出版社
电子信箱：	zpup@pup.cn
电　　　话：	邮购部 62752015　发行部 62750672　编辑部 62754382
	出版部 62754962
印　刷　者：	三河市博文印刷有限公司
经　销　者：	新华书店
	650 毫米×980 毫米　16 开本　16 印张　300 千字
	2014 年 4 月第 1 版　2014 年 4 月第 1 次印刷
定　　　价：	50.00 元

未经许可，不得以任何方式复制或抄袭本书之部分或全部内容。
版权所有，侵权必究
举报电话：010-62752024　电子信箱：fd@pup.pku.edu.cn

本书的研究和出版得到了广东省高等学校高层次人才项目(批准号:312-GK131036)、教育部人文社会科学重点研究基地重大项目(批准号:12JJD740006)的共同资助。

前　言

自20世纪七八十年代,随着过程写作法的推广,二语写作教学的侧重点由传统的篇章结构、语法、词汇,转向了对写作内容和写作过程的关注。不言而喻,在这场教学范式转变的潮流中,传统的语法纠错受到了极大的冲击。与此同时,在二语习得领域,要求摒弃对语言错误纠正的呼声也是越来越高:外语学习的进步是靠对大量正确语言输入的吸收,而不是对错误的纠正,纠错只会提升学习者的情感过滤(affective filters),从而妨碍语言学习(Krashen 1982,1984;Truscott 1996)。此番言论一出即引起学界的广泛争鸣,有关书面纠错的书籍、评述性文章和实证研究如雨后春笋般涌现出来。

目前,学界对书面纠错的研究基本分为两派:二语写作派和二语习得派。虽然两派考察的对象相同,但兴趣出发点、研究方法和研究结论却截然不同,逐渐形成各自为政的局面。首先,二语写作派探讨书面纠错对全面提升学习者写作水平的影响,因此,他们是抱着"有错必纠"的态度评改作文。然而,二语习得派只关注纠错对学习者习得特定语言结构的影响,因此,他们的纠错是有重点、有针对性的,如这次纠正"时"的错误,下次纠正"体"的错误。其次,二语写作派通常采用"学生初稿→教师反馈→学生修改"的实验设计,而二语习得派则采用"前测→干预→后测→延迟后测"的设计理念,对学习者的语言发展作长期跟踪。最后,二语写作派认为间接反馈比直接反馈更益于提高学习者作文语言的准确性(如 Ferris 2002),这是因为间接反馈可以鼓励学习者做假设验证(hypothesis testing),继而进入深层次的内部加工,固化正确的语言形式。但二语习得派对此却并不认同:间接反馈需要更多的认知加工,从而推迟了对假设的证实;相反,直接反馈可以帮助学习者更富有成效地内化正确的语言形式(如 Chandler 2003)。

整合迄今的研究成果,人们还不能提供没有异议的证据来说明什么形式的纠错反馈更有效,这主要是因为不一致的实验设计让以往的研究根本没有可比性,而解决这一问题的关键就是将两个阵营的研究结合起来,通过科学的实验方法找出答案。该领域研究前景光明,极有可能为外语写作和二语习得学科的后续发展奠定新的理论基础。

本书从理论、研究和教学三个层面对书面纠错进行了细致的分析。笔者认为,外语学习者的知识结构和经验基础与母语学习者不同,他们除了会犯和母语学习者类似的错误之外,还会犯下更多由于母语负迁移和外语知识缺失所造成的错误。因此在外语学习中,他们需要不同的教学方法、额外的知识补充和恰当的纠错反馈。虽然学习者的语言错误常常会出现"屡纠不绝"的现象,但这并非意味着纠错是在浪费时间,相反,我们应该反思是不是在提供反馈的方式和时机上出了问题。纠错反馈研究既是一项结合我国外语环境特点而开展理论创新的课题,又是一项具有较高应用价值和较大推广潜力的课题,它对于提高我国外语教学质量具有重要的现实意义,同时也为我国学者在国际外语教学研究领域迎头赶上积蓄力量。

本书分为四个部分:第一部分(第一章)简要介绍纠错研究的意义、国内外研究现状和纠错反馈的类型,使读者对该领域研究有一个初步的了解,同时深化认识纠错反馈研究的理论与实践价值。

第二部分(第二、三章)分别概述了不同时期二语习得理论和写作理论对于错误和纠错的认识。本书在前人研究成果基础上,通过融合最新的二语习得理论,根据时间发展顺序与核心理念的异同,将二语习得理论划分成七大流派,即行为主义流派、生成语言学流派、加工流派、基于使用流派、交互流派、社会文化流派和动态系统理论流派,并悉数每一流派的主要内容、代表性理论以及他们对于错误和纠错的认识。此外,对二语写作理论的介绍则追溯到19世纪70年代哈佛大学开设的"新生写作"课。本书系统地分析和比较了各理论、模型、假说的纠错观,交叉阅读相关内容有助于读者全面认识不同理论间的联系与差别。

第三部分(第四、五、六章)首先简要回顾了口头纠错研究的发展,随后按照研究性质和内容将书面纠错研究分成两个大类,11个小类,并对每一类别的发展现状作了细致的介绍与评价,仔细研读可增强对于整个纠错研究领域的宏观把握能力。

第四部分(第七章)从理论、研究和教学三个角度,具体分析了书面纠错领域的未来发展趋势。理论上构建了纠错反馈促学理论模型,并对模型中的关键要素进行了剖析。研究部分包括实验方法和研究内容。实验方法上特别强调考察个体变异性特征、归纳和分析学习者语言错误、充分发挥同伴反馈作用的必要性;研究内容上,本章从反馈目标、反馈形式、反馈量、教辅活动、个体因素和反馈效果六个方面,提出了未来研究亟待解决的问题。最后,本章从教学角度提出了培训新手教师有效运用反馈的七个步骤。

  本书的研究和出版得到了广东省高等学校高层次人才项目(批准号:312—GK131036)、教育部人文社会科学重点研究基地重大项目(批准号:12JJD740006)的共同资助。本书部分内容曾在《现代外语》《当代外语研究》《英语教师》等期刊上发表,收入本书时已作了必要的修订和更新。本书讹误和纰漏恐在所难免,敬请读者批评指正。

  北京大学出版社外语编辑部为本书的出版做了大量细致的工作,感谢刘虹、黄瑞明女士校订本书稿,并提出了宝贵的修改意见。最后,要特别感谢我的家人对我一直以来的支持和爱护,你们是我努力工作的精神支柱和强大动力。

姜 琳

2014 年 1 月

目 录

第一章 绪论 …………………………………………… (1)
　1.1 研究意义 …………………………………………… (1)
　1.2 研究现状 …………………………………………… (3)
　1.3 书面反馈的类型 …………………………………… (6)
　1.4 小结 ………………………………………………… (14)

第二章 二语习得理论对于错误及纠错的认识 ……… (15)
　2.1 引言 ………………………………………………… (15)
　2.2 行为主义学习理论 ………………………………… (16)
　2.3 基于生成语言学的二语习得理论 ………………… (21)
　2.4 二语学习加工理论 ………………………………… (26)
　2.5 基于使用的二语习得理论 ………………………… (33)
　2.6 二语习得社会文化理论 …………………………… (38)
　2.7 二语习得互动假说 ………………………………… (41)
　2.8 二语学习动态系统理论 …………………………… (48)
　2.9 小结 ………………………………………………… (52)

第三章 写作理论对于错误及纠错的认识 …………… (54)
　3.1 引言 ………………………………………………… (54)
　3.2 一语写作理论对于错误及纠错的认识 …………… (54)
　3.3 二语写作理论对于错误及纠错的认识 …………… (60)
　3.4 Truscott 的纠错论 ………………………………… (64)
　3.5 小结 ………………………………………………… (71)

第四章 反馈研究综述 ………………………………… (73)
　4.1 引言 ………………………………………………… (73)
　4.2 口头反馈与书面反馈的区别 ……………………… (74)
　4.3 口头反馈研究综述 ………………………………… (75)
　4.4 书面反馈研究综述 ………………………………… (83)
　4.5 小结 ………………………………………………… (105)

第五章 观察性和调查性书面反馈研究 (106)
  5.1 引言 (106)
  5.2 观察性反馈研究 (106)
  5.3 调查性反馈研究 (110)
  5.4 小结 (113)

第六章 准实验性书面反馈研究 (115)
  6.1 引言 (115)
  6.2 反馈对于习得二语语法结构的作用 (115)
  6.3 反馈对学生修改作文的短期影响 (119)
  6.4 反馈对学生写作语言发展的长期影响 (129)
  6.5 反馈形式与效果 (135)
  6.6 错误类型、纠错数量与反馈效果 (146)
  6.7 个体和环境因素对反馈效果的影响 (149)
  6.8 小结 (153)

第七章 反馈研究未来展望 (155)
  7.1 引言 (155)
  7.2 反馈理论展望 (155)
  7.3 实验方法展望 (163)
  7.4 研究内容展望 (167)
  7.5 教师培训 (173)
  7.6 小结 (182)

附录1 (184)
附录2 (192)
附录3 (195)
参考文献 (208)

第一章　绪论

1.1　研究意义

二语习得作为一门独立的学科始于中介语错误分析,在其四十余年的发展历程中,研究者对于错误的热衷程度一直有增无减,甚至将其视为"探究大脑黑箱的切入点"(王初明 2009:54)。然而,与之形成鲜明对比的是他们对于纠错的困惑和迟疑。二语学习者的语言错误是否需要纠正以及如何纠正,学界对此意见不一。有些学者(如 Krashen,Truscott)不主张纠错,甚至建议完全摒弃纠错。对此,他们的理由是:(1)语言学习关键在于接触大量正确的可理解性输入,因此二语习得的内在机制应在正确的语言输入过程中探寻;(2)纠错不能提升学习者实际运用语言的能力,相反还会造成诸多不利的影响,如提升学习者的焦虑感,迫使学习者使用简单的语言结构等等。

与此同时,也有一批学者(如 Bitchener,Ferris,Long)支持纠错,他们的理由可归纳为以下两点:(1)错误经过多次重复会成为习惯性的自觉行为,从而阻碍学习者对于新目标结构的掌握,所以要及时、坚决地纠错,以免妨碍外语学习;(2)纠错可引发学习者关注语言形式,并通过认知比较,意识到自己当前的中介语水平与目标语之间的差距(noticing the gap),一旦注意到这种差距,他们就会在接下来的语言输出中自觉修正语误,从而促进第二语言的发展。

解决上述争议的有效方法就是开展实证研究。书面纠正性反馈(written corrective feedback(CF),以下简称反馈),又称语法纠错(error/grammar correction),是针对学习者写作中的语言错误而提供的书面反馈信息(Keh 1990)。长期以来,对于"反馈促学"问题如火如荼的探讨(如 Bitchener 2008;Chandler 2003;Ellis et al. 2008;Sheen 2007,2010;Truscott 1996),成就了其在二语习得领域的一席之地。目前,对于反馈的研究形成了两派阵营:二语习得派和二语写作派。虽然两派研究的对象相同,但研究问题、方法和结论不同,逐渐形成各自为政的局面。反馈研究发展至今,若要继续保持良性发展态势、实现更大的突破,两派间的交流与整合尤显重要。正是在这样的情况下,作者决心编写这本书,尝试将反馈研究的两条相互独立且又十分重要的脉络(即二语习得与二语写作)整合在一起,力图全面、系统、清晰地呈现出反馈研究所取得的成果和存在的问题。概括起来,本书主要有以下三大特色:

第一,本书内容充实,对于开阔视野、提高认识有着重要的作用。首先,作者梳理了二语习得和二语写作的诸多理论,涵盖了认知心理、先天论和社会文化等不同范畴。书中对二语习得理论的介绍追溯到了20世纪30年代的行为主义学习观,对二语写作理论则追溯到了19世纪70年代哈佛大学开设的"新生写作"课。本书系统地分析和比较了各理论、模型、假说的纠错观,交叉阅读相关内容可帮助读者全面认识不同理论间的联系与差别。此外,本书称得上是反馈研究的"大观园"。经粗略统计,所涉及的研究百余个,时间跨度长达80年(1930—2013),包括观察性、调查性、实验性和综述性等类型研究。作者按照研究性质和内容,将这些研究进一步分成两个大类,11个小类,并对每一类别的发展现状进行了细致的介绍与评价,仔细研读可增强对于反馈研究领域的宏观把握能力。

第二,本书内容具有前瞻性,对反馈研究的发展具有指导意义。作者单独使用一个章节分析了反馈研究的未来发展趋势。在理论方面,拟建了一个融合学习者内在心理认知因素和外在环境因素的综合性理论模型。根据该模型,所有影响反馈效果的变量都将依托于学习者而发生关联,它们相互作用、相互制约,形成了一个动态的、复杂的交互系统。在实验方法方面,本书对于完善和创新实验设计提出了一些可行性措施,建议未来研究在关注群体普遍性特征的同时,加强对于个体变异性特征的考察,将定量与定性分析有机融合。在研究内容方面,作者提出了一些突破性的研究问题,从中可以洞察出未来反馈研究的几点动向:(1)关注学习者的个体差异;(2)强调学习环境与条件;(3)加强教学辅助活动以促进反馈的效果;(4)强调语言发展的动态特征;(5)关注各研究变量之间的交互作用;(6)注重实证研究的教学现实性。上述理论、方法和内容上的展望对反馈领域的健康发展有着重要的意义。

第三,本书对于完善教师培训、提高教学质量具有现实意义。外语教师常常会发现:通过纠错只能使错误改正一时,学生日后仍然可能犯同样的错误,这些"屡纠不绝"的错误使得很多教师对纠错持怀疑和犹豫的态度。而另有一种情况:有些教师笃信纠错,见错便纠,他们甚至将写作课变成了改错课,为了便于改错,规定作文字数的上限,让学生写短作文,课内限时写(王初明 2011b)。上述两种情况都不同程度地损害了教学质量。要摆脱这一尴尬局面,关键是要帮助教师熟悉反馈的理论和研究成果,并且接受科学、理性的培训指导。而本书最大的价值就在于其将反馈的理论、研究与实践有机结合而形成的强大效力,通篇阅读必会受益匪浅。此外,本书在实践部分的细致演绎也不失为一个亮点:在充分吸收前期理论和研究成果的基础上,为帮助新手教师有效运用反馈,本书提供了一系列具体的建议,包括操作步骤、注意事项及材料样本等,还推荐了一些教师参考书目。

当然,一本书的内容是有限的,而一个领域的发展是无限的,作者旨在抛砖引玉,激发更多反馈研究者的深入思考。同时,也希望外语教师通过研读本书,对纠错问题有更为理性的认知,不再盲从教学潮流的钟摆而左右不定了。

1.2 研究现状

输入是促成语言习得的必要条件,它包括正面证据和负面证据。正面证据为学习者提供了目标语模式(target language models),即什么样的语言形式符合目标语要求,它是语言学习最直接的途径,这一点没有异议。负面证据,又称负面反馈或纠正性反馈,是针对学习者的语误而提供的信息,它对二语发展有着怎样的影响,不同的二语习得理论有着不同的看法。20 世纪 50—60 年代,在行为主义语言学习观的影响下,语言学习强调外部环境在习惯形成中的重要性,通过强化学生的合适行为、消除不合适行为来塑造外语的发展;具体地说,就是要及时纠正学生的语言错误,以免妨碍语言发展。到了 70—80 年代,Chomsky 的语言天赋论盛极一时;该理论认为,正面证据可触发学习者的语言习得机制(Language Acquisition Device),使其通过参数重设(parameter resetting)习得第二语言,而负面证据对于二语习得没有任何实质性的作用。进入 21 世纪,语言天赋论逐渐淡出了人们的视野;此时,二语习得理论受认知心理学和社会文化理论的交叉影响,对纠错有了更为理性的认识,即在肯定纠错作用的同时,更加关注纠错的效率问题。伴随着人们对于纠错理论认识的不断深入，相关的实证研究也取得了长足的进步。接下来，我们分别对国内外反馈研究现状进行概述。

1.2.1 国外研究现状

Chaudron(1977)对于口头反馈的描述性研究掀开了反馈研究的新篇章。此后，反馈研究所取得的成果无论是对于建构二语习得理论，还是拓展外语教学法都发挥了重要的作用。20年后，Lyster & Ranta(1997)在浸入式课堂(immersion classrooms)环境下开展的口头反馈研究具有里程碑式的意义，为全面、系统地开展口头反馈研究奠定了基础，同时也激发起人们去探索反馈形式与教学效果之间的关系。

与口头反馈研究相比，书面反馈研究的发展相对滞后。有关书面反馈的争议源自 Truscott 发表于 1996 年的一篇文章(The case against grammar correction in L2 writing classes. *Language Learning*)，该文从理论、研究和教学三个层面论述了二语写作中的语法纠错不仅完全没有必要，还非常有害，呼吁写作教师彻底摒弃对语言错误的纠正。此后十余年，Truscott 又陆续发表数篇文章来捍卫自己的观点(Truscott 1999, 2001, 2004, 2007, 2010; Truscott & Hsu 2008)，其言论在学界引起了广泛的争鸣，有关这方面的书籍、评述性文章和实证研究如雨后春笋般涌现出来，与此同时，反馈作为一种形式教学的重要手段在国际上引起了普遍关注。

纵观几十年的研究成果，反馈对于外语发展的作用基本上得到了证实，同时，很多认知理论和心理语言学理论对反馈的促学价值提供了坚实的理论基础，如互动假说(Interaction Hypothesis)(Long 1983, 1996)、语言输出假说(Output Hypothesis)(Swain 1985, 1995)、注意假说(Noticing Hypothesis)(Schmidt 1995, 2001)、技能习得理论(Skill Acquisition Theory)(如 Dekeyser 1998, 2007)、迁移适当学习理论(Transfer Appropriate Learning Theory)(如 Segalowitz & Lightbown 1999)、平衡化假说(Counterbalance Hypothesis)(Lyster & Mori 2006)等。这些理论普遍认为，反馈可以引起学习者的注意，而这种注意能够激发认知比较，使学习者意识到自己当前的语言发展水平与目标语之间的差距，一旦注意到这种差距，学习者便有动力在接下来的语言输出中修正自己的语言错误,从而提升自己的外语水平。但是,就什么形式的反馈更能有效促进外语学习,现有理论所持的观点并不相同。例如,Long(1991,1996)强调在意义协商(negotiation for meaning)过程中所提供的"输入型反馈"(input-providing feedback)(如 recast)的促学价值,而其他研究(如 Ammar 2008;Ammar & Spada 2006;Lyster 2004)则强调在形式协商(negotiation of form)过程中所提供的"输出推动型反馈"(output-promoting feedback)的作用。与认知语言学和心理语言学理论不同,社会文化理论认为,没有任何一种反馈是万能的,只有当它的形式充分符合外语学习者所处的发展阶段时,才能最大程度地发挥其脚手架式(scaffolding)的作用(Sheen 2010)。

口头反馈研究主要基于二语习得理论和假设而开展,书面反馈研究则多基于一语和二语写作理论而开展,尽管如此,两类研究所关心的问题是相通的,例如:(1)反馈能否促进外语学习;(2)什么形式的反馈更有效;(3)个体差异和环境因素对于反馈效果的影响;(4)如何完善反馈研究的实验方法。本书将对过去几十年所开展的口头和书面反馈研究进行系统性的梳理,以加深我们对于反馈促学机理和促学价值的认识,从而提升外语教学质量。

1.2.2 国内研究现状

与国外的火热局面相比,国内反馈研究却非常匮乏。此外,我国外语写作教学长期处于高耗低效的尴尬局面,学生怯写、教师怕改的现象日趋严峻。然而,写作能力是一个人交际能力的重要组成部分,是知识素养的综合体现。在某些行业中,具有较强的写作能力已经成为选拔精英人士的重要标准。本人作为一线教师,身处英语写作教学的最前沿,深深体会到语言评改是写作教学的重要一环,改什么、怎么改直接关系到学生写作水平的发展。虽然,国外同行对此已进行了积极的探索并取得了一些宝贵经验,但我们绝不能将国外的研究成果简单地应用到我国的外语写作教学和研究中,主要有以下两点原因:

首先,国外研究多针对英语作为第二语言的写作教学。在这样的环境里,学习者必须使用英语来生活、工作和完成学业。然而在我国,英语只是一门外语,学习者用英语写作的机会有限,这便造成了他们小觑写作、漠视反馈的无奈局面。这两种写作环境的本质区别决定了我们不能生搬硬套,而是要以国外的研究成果为指导,以中国的课堂教学为基础,探索适合中国学生的外语写作反馈模式。

其次,国外现有的实证研究在方法上存在诸多纰漏,从而造成实验结果大相径庭,不利于指导外语写作教学,同时也导致了许多外语教师对反馈持怀疑和犹豫的态度。因此,我们必须在整合国外研究成果的基础上改进和创新实验方法,深入系统地考察适合我国外语写作教学环境的最佳反馈策略。

1.3 书面反馈的类型

为便于读者更好地理解本书的内容,同时为反馈研究提供类型学基础,本节将介绍书面反馈的主要形式。Hyland & Hyland(2006)曾指出,尽管反馈是二语写作教学的重要组成部分,但它的促学价值并没有在实证研究中得到充分的证实;同时,写作教师也没有很好地开发出它的促学潜能。导致这一结果的原因主要有两方面:一是反馈研究没有系统性地比较不同类型反馈的促学价值;二是反馈研究没有对一些潜在的干扰因素做严格的控制(Guenette 2007)。有鉴于此,对书面反馈做系统的类型学分析实属必要,这不仅有利于开展相关的科学研究,而且对于制定教学方案和教学手段也非常有益。

Ellis(2009)对书面反馈的类型做了系统的概述(见表1.1),本书在此基础上具体介绍8种反馈类型。

表 1.1 书面反馈的类型

反馈类型	具体形式	代表性研究
1) 直接反馈(Direct feedback)	针对语言错误提供正确形式	Lalande (1982) Robb et al. (1986)
2) 间接反馈(Indirect feedback)	提示有错误发生,但不提供正确形式	
A. 定位错误	标出错误的位置	Chandler(2003) Ferris & Roberts (2001)
B. 不定位错误	在页边空白处说明对应行有语言错误,但不给出错误的具体位置	Robb et al. (1986)

续表

反馈类型	具体形式	代表性研究
3）元语言反馈（Metalinguistic feedback）	对错误的性质提供元语言解释	
A. 使用错误代码（error code）	通过错误代码说明错误的性质，如 WW＝wrong word；Art＝article	Chandler (2003) Ferris & Roberts (2001) Lalande (1982)
B. 简要的语法描述	给错误编号，然后在文章结尾处，对每种类型的错误做简要的语法描述	Sheen (2007)
4）反馈的焦点	指全面纠正学生的语言错误，还是聚焦于几类错误，该标准适用于以上三种分类	
A. 非聚焦反馈（Unfocused feedback）	全面纠正学生的语言错误	Chandler (2003) Ferris (2006)
B. 聚焦反馈（Focused feedback）	有针对性地纠正一类或几类语言错误（如冠词、介词、一般过去式等错误）	Sheen (2007)
5）电子反馈（Electronic feedback）	将错误链接到包含了正确用法样例的电子资源库	Milton (2006)
6）重述（Reformulation）	在保证原文内容不变的情况下，对学生的作文作通篇的目标语重述	Sachs & Polio (2007)

1.3.1 直接反馈

直接反馈是指对语言错误直接提供正确形式，具体作法包括：划掉多余的词、短语或语素，插入遗漏的词或语素，在错误之处给出正确形式，如图 1.1 所示。直接反馈提供了显性的语言信息，这对于那些不知该如何改正错误的学生来说非常有帮助，尤其是对于低水平的学习者，直接反馈的效果要好于间接反馈（Ferris & Roberts 2001）。但是，由于直接反馈不需要学习者作出太多的认知加工，因此其长效性还有待进一步考证。

```
                    a         a                                    the
A dog stole∧ bone from∧ butcher. He escaped with ~~having~~ bone. When the dog
          over       a                     a              a
was going ~~through~~ bridge over ~~the~~ river, he found∧ dog in the river.
```

图 1.1　直接反馈

1.3.2　间接反馈

间接反馈会提示有错误发生,但不予纠正,具体形式包括:在错误之处画线,在有遗漏发生的地方画一个插入号,或者在错误发生行的页边空白处画一个错号(即页边反馈),如图1.2所示。可见,间接反馈可提示或不提示错误发生的位置。

```
A dog stole∧ bone from∧ butcher. He escaped with having∧ bone. When the dog
was going through bridge over the river, he found dog in the river.       ×
```

图 1.2　间接反馈

间接反馈能激发学习者去发现学习(discover learning),并在发现问题、解决问题的过程中内化正确的语言形式,促进外语发展(Ferris & Roberts 2001)。但是,间接反馈的促学价值并没有得到普遍的证实。例如,虽然 Lalande(1982)发现间接反馈比直接反馈更能有效促进学习者修改错误,但 Ferris & Roberts(2001)却发现,直接反馈与间接反馈的促学效果没有显著差异。

此外,根据间接反馈的促学机理(Ferris & Roberts 2001),不定位错误的间接反馈应该比定位错误的间接反馈更利于外语学习,因为前者需要学习者开展更深层次的内部加工,但事实并非如此。Robb et al.(1986)考察了包括直接反馈和(不定位错误的)间接反馈在内的四种反馈类型的效果,结果发现,他们的促学效果并不存在明显差异。Lee(1997)比较了不同形式间接反馈的作用,结果发现,定位错误比不定位错误更利于学习者修改原文错误。以上研究主要通过让学习者写修改稿来观察之前的反馈是否帮助他们改正了原文的错误。然而,即便学习者修改了原文的错误,也不能充分说明反馈对二语习得有促进作用。事实上,考察语言知识是否被习得,关键要看学习者能否将在当前学习任务中所掌握的语言知识有效应用于新任务(如 Luria 1961)。因此,未来研究可以考察学习者在新作文中的语言使用情况,从而检验不同形式间接反馈的促学效果。

1.3.3 元语言反馈

元语言反馈是指对错误性质作出解释,主要包括两种形式:错误代码和元语言解释。错误代码是最常见的元语言反馈形式,它可以出现在错误之处(如图1.3)或者页边空白处(如图1.4)。对于后者,学习者需要先对错误进行定位,然后根据代码再将错误改正过来。目前,有关错误代码的使用还没有统一标准,例如,是否可以使用Art.表示所有的冠词错误,还是针对定冠词和不定冠词错误分别采用不同的代码?事实上,我们在研究和教学领域使用错误代码的标准还是比较宽泛的。

有研究考察了错误代码的促学效果。Lalande(1982)发现,接收错误代码反馈的德语二语学习者在新作文中的语言准确性要好于接收直接反馈的学习者,但二者的差异没有达到显著程度。Robb et al. (1986)发现,接收错误代码反馈的实验组与其他三个反馈实验组(包括一个直接反馈组和两个间接反馈组)的表现没有明显差异。Ferris (2006)考察了四类语言错误,包括动词错误、名词错误、冠词错误、句子错误;通过比较学生的第一和第四次作文的错误率,Ferris发现,错误代码反馈只对动词错误有效。Ferris & Roberts(2001)发现,错误代码反馈可以鼓励学习者开展自我编辑(self-editing),其效用与间接反馈相仿。总之,有关错误代码反馈的研究还非常有限,现有结果还不能证实此种反馈具有长期的促学效应。

```
              Art.        Art.                  ww  Art.
A dog stole∧ bone from∧ butcher.  He escaped with having∧ bone.  When the dog
         Prep.     Art.         Art.       Art.
was going through∧ bridge over the river he found∧ dog in the river.
```

图1.3 元语言反馈(定位错误)

```
Art. x3 ; WW     A dog stole bone from utcher.  He escaped with having bone.
Prep. ; Art. x2  When the dog was going through bridge over the river he
Art. x1          found dog in the river.
```

图1.4 元语言反馈(不定位错误)

除了使用错误代码外,元语言反馈还可以提供元语言解释,如图

1.5所示。这种反馈形式在现实教学中不太常见,一方面它比较耗时,另一方面需要教师具有丰富的语法知识,以保证对错误性质给出清晰、正确的解释。Sheen(2007)比较了直接反馈和元语言解释反馈的作用,结果表明,两种反馈在短期内的促学效果相当,但从长期看,后者比前者更具促学优势。

```
           (1)        (2)                    (3)
A dog stole bone from butcher. He escaped with having bone. When the dog
         (4)      (5)         (6)          (7)
was going through bridge over the river he found dog in the river.

(1),(2),(5),(6) and (7)—— you need 'a' before the noun when a person or thing is mentioned for the first time.
(3) —— you need 'the' before the noun when the person or thing has been mentioned previously.
(4) —— you need 'over' when you go across the surface of something; you use 'though' when you go inside something (e.g. go through the forest).
```

图 1.5 元语言反馈(元语言解释)

1.3.4 聚焦和非聚焦反馈

面对学生作文中的语言错误,我们可以选择全面纠正(即非聚焦反馈),也可以只针对其中的几类错误提供反馈(即聚焦反馈)。这种聚焦/非聚焦(即全面/针对性纠错)的区分标准适用于前面三种反馈类型。图1.1—1.5中的例子都是非聚焦反馈,当然,我们也可以只针对其中的冠词错误提供反馈,在这种情况下,就变成了聚焦反馈。

对于非聚焦反馈,由于学习者的注意资源和加工能力有限,他们很难消化和吸收全部反馈,故容易造成"高耗低效"的教学局面。相比之下,聚焦反馈的效果可能会更明显,学习者反复接触针对同一类型错误的反馈,当接触量累积到一定程度时,外语学习就会发生质的变化,即学习者不仅理解了犯错的原因,同时也掌握了正确的用法形式,并将其逐步内化为自己的二语知识。如果对语言形式的注意(attention to form)是习得语言的第一步,那么我们有理由相信:当注意越集中时,学习效果越好。这也就是说,聚焦反馈通过强化学习者对于语言形式的注意,从而促进其外语学习的进步。另一方面,非聚焦反馈也具有促学潜质:它可以较为全面地反映学生的语言水平,满足学生语言的个性发展,尽管它不能像聚焦反馈那样可以在短期内促进学习者对于某一语言结构的习得,但从长远角度看,它的长效性会更理想。迄今为止,有关聚焦反馈与非聚焦反馈的对比研究还非常有限(Ellis et al. 2008;Sheen et al. 2009),未来研究可对此作深入探讨。

1.3.5 电子反馈

如今,各式各样的英语语料库可以为学生的英语写作提供帮助。Milton(2006)使用一种名为"Mark My Words"的软件程序协助教师批改学生的作文。这个软件中的数据库包含了中国英语学习者作文中最常见的100种词汇/语法错误以及对每种错误的分析;同时,这个软件还可以链接到一个包含了正确语言形式的电子资源库(electronic resources)。教师通过这个软件对学生作文中的语言错误提供反馈,然后将作文反馈发回给学生,学生通过链接进入到电子资源库,并将自己产出的句子和资源库中的正确句子进行比对,从而修正自己的语言错误。此外,这个软件还可以为每篇作文生成错误日志(error log),从而激发学生关注语言形式。Milton没有通过实证研究检验电子反馈对于外语学习的作用,但是,他通过个人的经历证实了这种方法很有效。有一次,一个学生发给了Milton一篇长达十页的文章,Milton通过"Mark My Words"软件在文章中查找出了100个语言错误。随后,他让这个学生通过查找电子资源库将文中的错误改正过来,结果显示,学生的修改非常成功。

电子反馈有很多优点。首先,它改变了教师作为评判语言唯一标准的现状。教师在判断语言正误时,难免会出错,而电子反馈所归纳出的100种语法错误是基于对大量语料的分析和总结基础上得来的,可以说是一种基于使用的(usage-based)、相对客观的纠错方法(Ellis 2009),因此电子反馈具有较高的可信度。此外,提供有效纠错的前提是要辨识出学生的文本意图(textual intention)。虽然电子反馈协助教师找到了学生的语言错误,但至于如何修改,则是由学生通过电子资源库找到最符合自己文本意图的目标语形式,这不仅提高了反馈效率,同时也培养了学生的学习独立性。

1.3.6 重述

重述是对学习者的语言产出做目标语重写(rewriting),这为他们修改原稿错误提供了样板,但至于要不要改正以及如何改正错误则由学习者本人决定。事实上,辨识错误的第一步就是重建(reconstruction);换言之,为了辨识学习者的语言错误,教师应首先建立起一个目标语范文(native-speaker version),然后将其与学生的语言产出进行对比,从而确定错误。重述的设计初衷就来自于这一理念。对学生的作文进行重写需要在保证原文内容不变的基础上尽量使语言接近目标语(Cohen 1989)。随后,学生通过比对原稿和教师的重写稿,找出有变化的地方,并决定是否接受这些重述。

原文:	As he was jogging, his tammy was shaked.
重述:	As he was jogging, his tummy was shaking.
	tummy shaking
直接反馈:	As he was jogging, his ~~tammy~~ was ~~shaked~~.

图 1.6 重述

Sachs & Polio(2007)比较了重述和直接反馈的作用,如图 1.6 所示。实验中,一组学生的作文接受重述反馈,一组接受直接反馈,还有一组不予任何反馈(即对照组)。两个实验组学生有 20 分钟的时间阅读教师的反馈,且可以在有需要的地方做笔记。第二天,三组学生被要求修改自己的作文,但不能参阅之前教师的反馈及自己所做的笔记。实验结果显示,两个实验组的修改稿语言准确性均好于对照组,同时直接反馈组好于重述组。研究指出,重述作为一种反馈,不仅仅局限于表面的语言错误,还会引起学习者对于文体和结构方面错误的注意,因此该研究结果不应该被看作是重述促学价值的反例。

1.3.7 尾注反馈

尾注反馈由 Bean(1996)首次提出,具体形式为:教师只对作文某一段中的错误以画线方式指出,不提供正确形式和解释,同时在作文结尾处作简要总结,归纳出学习者在作文修改时所要注意的语言问题。图 1.7 给出了尾注反馈的具体样例。

> Everyone have been a liar once in their life. People who lie intentionally to harm others are bad people and their lies are harmful too. However, there are lies that are done with good intention. So, there are times that lies are appropriate. A lie is either a good or bad one base upon the liar's intention. Only one person can really tell whether a lie is intended to harm or do good.
>
> Dear Student,
> I enjoyed your interesting essay about good and bad lies. As you revise your paper, you should pay attention to several language issues:
> • *Be sure to check the forms of your verbs and of your pronouns to see that they agree in number (singular/plural) with the subject noun they refer to.*
> • *Be sure that your word choice is accurate. You might ask someone to read your paper to let you know if any words sound wrong or are confusing.*
> • *Don't forget that you need a comma before a coordinating conjuction such as 'and' that connects two sentences.*
> I have underlined examples of problems in these areas in the first paragraph of your essay, but you should read the whole paper carefully because there are similar errors in other paragraphs. Be sure to let me know if you have any questions!
> Good luck,
> Teacher

图 1.7　尾注反馈（Bithener & Ferris 2012：169）

1.3.8　最小批改

最小批改（Minimal Marking）由 Haswell(1983)首次提出，具体形式为：在错误发生行的页边空白处打个对号，以提示学生此行有错误，最小批改实际上就是一种页边反馈。Haswell 通过研究证实，这种反馈方法不仅能够帮助学生有效修改原文错误，而且对于其写作语言准确性的长期发展也具有显著的促进作用。图 1.8 给出了最小批改的具体样例。该反馈方法不仅形式独到，而且促学效果也得到了一定的证实，因此 Haswell(1983)的文章虽然只有短短的五页，但影响非常深远，不仅被多次引用，而且还被教师培训书目收录（如 Bean 1996）。

√ √ √	Everyone have been a liar once in their life. People who lie intentionally to harm others are bad people and their lies are harmful too. However, there are lies that are done with good intention. So, there are times that lies are appropriate. A lie is either a good or bad one base upon the liar's intention. Only one person can really tell whether a lie is intended to harm or do good.

表 1.8　最小批改（Bitchener & Ferris 2012：170）

1.4　小结

长期以来,错误的性质和作用,以及纠错对外语学习的影响等问题,始终受到二语习得界的高度重视,盖因这些问题对于认识二语习得机制、发展二语习得理论、提升外语教学质量均至关重要。虽然国外学者对反馈问题已进行了积极的探索并取得了一些宝贵经验,但由于现实教学环境的不同,我们绝不能将国外的研究成果简单地应用到我国的外语教学和研究中。此外,国外现有的实证研究在方法上存在诸多纰漏,从而造成实验结果大相径庭,不利于指导外语教学,同时也导致了许多外语教师对反馈持怀疑和犹豫的态度。因此,本书从理论、研究和教学三个层面对错误和纠错问题进行了系统的分析,归结起来主要有三大特色:(1)内容充实,对于开阔视野、提高认识有着重要的作用;(2)内容具有前瞻性,对反馈研究的发展具有指导意义;(3)对于完善教师培训、提高教学质量具有现实意义。

希望通过阅读本书,外语教师对纠错问题有了更为理性的认知,不再盲从教学潮流的钟摆而左右不定;同时,反馈研究人员能在整合国外研究成果的基础上,改进和创新实验方法,深入系统地考察适合我国外语教学环境的最佳反馈策略。

第二章 二语习得理论对于错误及纠错的认识

2.1 引言

二语习得研究历经四十余年的发展,如今已具备相对独立和稳定的学科地位,一批跨领域、多视角的研究理论逐步出现并稳步发展,他们的共同目标是要回答一个问题:人类如何习得第二语言。在探寻答案的过程中,他们对学习者的语言错误产生了浓厚的兴趣,将其视为"探究大脑黑箱的切入点"(王初明 2009:54),从不同方面开展了系统的研究。同时,在现实教学中,外语老师也是笃信纠错,认为只有将错误消灭掉,外语水平才能提高(王初明 2009)。综上可见,错误及纠错问题无论是对于二语习得研究还是外语教学实践,都有着不同寻常的意义。我们应该如何看待学习者的错误?是从负面角度将其定义为阻碍语言发展,应及时消灭的有害物,还是从正面角度将其看作为二语习得过程中的必然现象,反映了学习者当前的中介语水平?要回答此问题,我们有必要了解不同时期二语习得理论对于错误及纠错的认识。这样做,一方面可方便读者把握不同理论流派在纠错问题上的联系、交叠、差异、甚或冲突,另一方面可为本书系统介绍反馈研究提供广阔的理论背景。

Norris & Ortega (2003) 将二语习得理论综合成四类:生成语法观、互动观、浮现观和社会文化观。Mitchell & Myles (2004) 则把二语习得理论划分为六类,即普遍语法视角、认知视角、功能/语用视角、输入与互动视角、社会文化视角和社会语言学视角。VanPatten & Williams (2007) 的理论划分更为细致,共计九类:普遍语法导向、概念导向、认知-联结理论、技能习得理论、输入加工导向、可加工性理论、自主归纳理论、互动假说和社会文化理论。本书在上述划分基础上,通过融合最新的二语习得理论,根据时间发展顺序与核心理念的异同,将二语习得理论归结为七大流派:行为主义流派(Behaviorist Perspective)、生成语言学流派(Generative Approach)、加工流派(Processing Approach)、基于使用流派(Usage-based Approach)、互动流派(Interactionist Perspective)、社会文化流派(Sociocultural Approach)和动态系统理论流派(Dynamic Systems Theory)。接下来,我们将悉数每一流派的主要内容、代表性理论以及他们对于错误和纠错的认识。

2.2 行为主义学习理论

2.2.1 早期行为主义学习理论

行为主义学习理论又称刺激—反应理论,产生于20世纪初的美国。该理论认为,学习是人类思维与外界环境相互作用的结果;环境是刺激,伴而随之的有机体行为是反应,学习就是刺激与反应的联结。俄国心理学家巴甫洛夫用狗做了一个著名的刺激—反应实验:每次给狗送食物前打开红灯、响起铃声,这样经过一段时间以后,铃声一响或红灯一亮,狗就开始分泌唾液。

行为主义关注客观的、可观察到的行为,而不是内部的心智活动(胡壮麟2008)。他们把人的心智看成一个"黑匣子",由于看不到黑匣子里面发生的情况,就通过定量观察有机体对于刺激的反应,从外部来推测其学习过程,因而不需要了解内部的心理活动(Mergel 1998)。从事行为主义研究的主要代表人物有John B. Watson和Burrhus F. Skinner等。

根据行为主义的观点,学习语言与学习其他行为没有区别,是由经验或实践在行为上产生相对恒定的变化(Huitt & Hummel 2006),是一种习惯的形成(habit formation)。行为主义有关语言学习最完整的理论见于Skinner(1957)的《言语行为》(*Verbal Behavior*)一书。根据行为主义学习理论,由于新行为经过多次重复会成为习惯性的自觉行为,因此错误是不可容忍的,它一旦成为一种习惯性行为,会阻碍学习者对于新目标行为的掌握。所以,语言学习要最大程度地强化学生的正确行为,同时消除不正确行为,换句话说,教师要及时、坚决地纠正学生的语言错误,以免妨碍语言发展。

虽然行为主义看重纠错,但它认为预防错误比纠正错误更重要。

第二章
二语习得理论对于错误及纠错的认识

为了帮助学习者产出没有错误的句子,外语教学应该反复提供学生观察和练习正确语言模式的机会,缩短错误语言产出与提供相应正确模式之间的时间间隔(Brooks 1960)。恰逢行为主义鼎盛之时,美国因二战需要大量的外语人才协助军事业务。为了在短时间内训练军事人员学会外语,结合直接教学法①(Direct Method)、结构语言学②(Structural Linguistics)和行为主义学习理论的听说教学法(Audio-lingual Approach)应运而生,因其特殊的产生背景,又被称之为军事教学法(Army Method)。

听说教学法以外语直接教学,听说教学先于读写教学,重视结构与形式、忽视意义为其基本特征。由于该方法将外语学习视为一种习惯形成的过程,因此背诵对话、操练句型及学习语法规则便成了该教学法的主要内容。但是,这种在机械性操练中所获得的语言知识不仅容易忘记,而且也难于迁移到日常语言使用中(Hendrickson 1978)。另外,听说教学法虽然能够促进学习者听说能力的提高,但由于缺少读写训练,因此外语技能难以实现全方位的发展。

行为主义学习理论在20世纪50年代达到顶峰,并广泛应用于外语教学。然而,Chomsky(1959)对Skinner(1957)的《言语行为》一书进行了深刻的批判,一时震撼了美国语言学和心理学界,被称为"语言学的革命"。从此,行为主义一落千丈。Chomsky(1959)的主要观点(详见胡壮麟2008)包括:(1)人类语言行为中的"刺激"不像动物行为那样有严格的定义,如对人名可以在该人不在场时回想起,无需相应的刺激—反应等操作来巩固;(2)语言使用是一个创造性的活动,我们所接触到的合乎语法的句子是没有限定的,几乎每一个句子都是词的新组合,因此有关"语言学习是刺激—反应联结"的说法是不现实的;(3)正常儿童的语言发展非常快速,且发展轨迹、范式相似,因此人类一定具有某种特殊的机能来习得语言,一定有一种内在的普遍语法来引导他们归纳所接触的语言输入。

---

① 直接教学法是指在课堂上直接使用目标语言做沟通工具,不借助任何母语翻译,训练学生用目标语去思考,给学生实地使用语言的机会,尽量鼓励学生多说话,以语境为主,同时学习附带的文化背景。该方法可协助学生融入外语实境中,不必通过教师的翻译和文法解析就可学成一口流利的外语。直接教学法在小班教学中推行得非常成功,但在大班教学的效果就不那么理想了。

② 结构语言学在20世纪上半期成为语言学的主流,它重视共时语言研究,分析、描写语言的结构系统,不孤立地看待语言要素,认为语言的一切都建立在关系的基础上。

Chomsky 一方面抨击行为主义关于语言学习的简单机械的模式,另一方面强调人类固有的语言习得机制和天赋的普遍语法。两派在语言及语言习得方面的争论,逐渐构成了二语习得研究的两派不同阵营,即基于认知学的二语习得研究和基于语言学的二语习得研究[③]。

2.2.2 对比分析

对比分析(Contrastive Analysis)是基于行为主义理论派生出的一种方法,是对两种或更多语言的选定结构的系统比较,目的是为教师和教材编写者提供信息,从而促进教材编辑、课程设计、课堂教学技巧的发展(Hammer & Rice 1965)。对比分析盛行于 20 世纪 50—60 年代,代表人物有 Charles Fries 和 Robert Lado[④]。

对比分析研究主要受到移民双语现象研究的启发,但方向不同。后者研究第二语言对母语使用及保持的影响,而前者关注母语对第二语言学习的影响。对比分析借用了心理学的"迁移"和"干扰"两个概念,认为第二语言学习的主要障碍是母语干扰,所以要将母语和第二语言做科学、系统的对比分析,找出二者的不同,预测学习者在第二语言学习过程中可能会出现的错误,从而阻止母语负迁移的发生。对比分析的核心思想是:母语和第二语言相似之处可产生正迁移,而不同之处则产生负迁移,即干扰。

对比分析在近 20 年的发展中形成了强式和弱式两个版本(Wardhaugh 1970)。前者对两种语言进行对比,并预测第二语言学习中可能出现的困难和错误;后者虽认为语际差异和语际干扰即为学习困难之所在,但不主张对第二语言学习过程进行预先的估测,而是强调对错误出现之后的分析解释,找出错误产生的根源并予以纠正。

强式版本过高地估计了对比分析的预测能力。研究发现,有些预测会出现的错误并未在学习者的语言产出中出现(Dulay & Burt 1973),而有些没有预测到的错误却出现了(Hyltenstam 1977);此外,说不同母语的学习者有时会犯一些非常相似的错误(Lightbown &

---

③ Chomsky 同样主张研究人类的认知能力和认知过程,但他认为认知是天赋的,句法是一个自足的系统。这一观点在 20 世纪 60 年代后期引起了一些语言学家,而且主要是生成语言学阵营内部一些成员的质疑。

④ Lado 在 1957 年出版的《跨文化语言学》(*Linguistics Across Culture*)一书被认为是对比分析的标志。

Spada 2008),说明有些错误不能归因于母语干扰。以上发现使得人们开始质疑强式版本的预测能力(Wardhaugh 1970)。弱式版本虽然比强式版本更为实用,但由于仍将语际差异视作第二语言学习的困难所在,忽视了来自同一语言系统内部的语内障碍,故仅能解释那些源于母语干扰的错误,而对其他类型的错误则显得无能为力。

此外,学界对对比分析的批评还包括以下三个方面。首先,束定芳、庄智象(1996)指出,对比分析将差异与困难等同起来,而差异是语言形式上的概念,困难是心理学上的概念,没有任何心理学依据可以将这两个概念等同起来。其次,对比分析主要集中于音系、语素和句法三个层面,也就是说,只局限于结构主义所描述的表层结构来对比不同语言,缺乏对其他语言认知层面的考察。最后,对比分析没有明确在什么情况下,母语知识会对目标语学习产生干扰;事实上,干扰主要会受到两种非语言因素的影响:一是环境,自然环境中的母语负迁移比课堂环境中的影响要小;二是学习阶段,初学阶段的负迁移影响大,而中高级阶段的影响小。

Oller & Ziahosseiny(1970)根据强、弱两个版本的不足之处,提出了温和版本的对比分析,作为前两个版本的折衷。温和版本认为,依据所观察到的两种语言间的相似与差异,对具体和抽象的语言模式进行分门别类,这才是学习的基础。因此,无论是在一个语言系统内部,还是多个语言系统之间,只要这些模式存在形式或意义上的细微差别,就会产生混淆。换言之,第二语言学习的最大困难,并非源自母语和第二语言表层间的差异,而是存在于两种语言之间以及各语言内部的细微差别。温和版本放弃了前两种版本的"差异即为困难"的观点,强调了人类认知模式的实质,即人们容易忽略细枝末节,因而也就容易忽略事物间的细微差别,从而导致学习困难。此外,在探寻错误根源方面,温和版本跳出了语际干扰的苑围,将目光投向语内干扰,拓宽了语言学家对错误根源的查找范围。

尽管温和版本更切中问题的要害,但依然不能解决语言学习的很多问题。事实上,语言学习涉及了语言、认知、情感和社会等诸多因素,而对比分析的三个版本仅仅是对语言本体的分析,并试图以分析的结果来解决外语学习中的困难,他们忽视了与语言学习密不可分的认知、情感和社会因素的影响。

总之,对比分析虽不完善,但已成为语言学研究的一个重要手段。大量研究显示,迁移是学习新知识的一个重要途径,迁移的范畴、内容、条件及方法必须通过对比分析才能认识清楚(王月平 1999)。根据目前的外语教学理论发展趋势,人们越来越强调跨文化意识的培养,对比分析仍不失为培养这种意识的最佳方法之一。进入 20 世纪 80 年代,人们开始重新审视和评价对比分析对语言研究和外语教学的重要贡献,探索对比分析的新领域,因此对比分析研究又有所活跃(王月平 1999)。

2.2.3 错误分析

随着对比分析局限性的日益凸显,20 世纪 60 年代末、70 年代初,错误分析(Error Analysis)应运而生,它是对二语学习者的错误进行系统性的分析研究,最早倡导者是 Pit Corder。Corder(1967)指出,错误在第二语言学习过程中是不可避免的,它为我们了解学习者的发展过程提供了有用的信息,是好事情。而在此之前,错误一直被认为是有害的,应尽量消除。

错误分析的产生有其语言学及心理学的基础。在语言学领域,此时只描述语言表层特征的结构语言学正逐渐被生成语言学所取代,后者认为语言既受规则支配,又具有创造性。在心理学领域,Skinner 有关"环境对儿童语言及行为发展具有决定性作用"的观点,正逐渐被 Piaget 的心理发展论所取代(Piaget 1970;Piaget & Inhelder 1966);后者认为,知识能力先受认知发展的影响,再受社会互动的影响,认知发展论为语言习得研究奠定了基础。

根据错误分析,二语学习者的很多错误并非源自母语或第二语言,而是一种内在错误(learner internal),为了认识这些错误,不仅要对错误进行分类,还要将二语习得中的错误与母语习得中的错误进行对比。错误分析与对比分析的区别在于:前者不预测因母语干扰而出现的错误,而是去努力揭示和描述各种类型的错误,目的是想了解学习者如何处理二语信息。错误分析的一般步骤为:(1)选择语料;(2)确认错误;(3)对错误加以分类;(4)解释错误产生的原因;(5)评价其对教学的意义。

错误分析使人们意识到对比分析在外语教学实践中的局限性,改变了人们对错误本质及其作用的认识,形成了一套有效的错误分析方法和操作程序,是继对比分析之后二语习得领域的又一重要发展阶段(Larsen-Freeman & Long 1991)。此外,错误分析研究引出了重要的中介语(interlanguage)概念。

根据错误分析,学习者的错误具有动态性和系统性,说明了学习者自身在积极构建目标语的使用规则,其语言系统自成一体,并遵循一定的原则。在这一点上,它与学习母语的幼儿所使用的语言系统相类似,Selinker(1972)称二语学习者的语言为中介语。中介语是二语学习者建立起来的目标语知识系统,介乎于母语和目标语之间,且随着语言输入的增加而不断发生变化,它具有开放性、系统性和灵活性三大特点。中介语与母语、目标语的关系如图2.1所示。

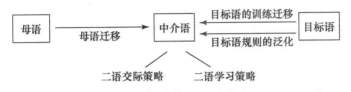

图 2.1 中介语、母语与目标语的关系

Selinker认为,学习者在构建中介语的过程中主要使用以下手段:(1)语言迁移;(2)目标语规则的过度泛化;(3)训练迁移;(4)二语学习策略;(5)二语交际策略。中介语研究有助于了解学习者所处的阶段和所采用的学习策略,这为揭示二语习得规律,设计外语教学计划和方法提供了理论依据。同时,中介语研究也改变了教师对学生言语行为的态度,放弃了对低水平学习者目标语行为的不合理期望。

当然,错误分析也存在局限性,例如,错误的定义及分类缺少统一标准,"回避现象"在错误分析里不好处理等等。上世纪70—80年代,出现了大量有关错误分析的论文,但随着学界对于错误分析批评声音的不断增多,人们对它的热情开始减退,注意力移至语言运用分析和其后出现的语篇分析。

2.3 基于生成语言学的二语习得理论

2.3.1 生成语言学及其在二语习得研究中的应用

20世纪50年代后半叶,美国语言学界出现了一种全新的理论——转换生成语言学(简称生成语言学),它猛烈地冲击了当时在美国占主导地位的结构语言学。生成语言学的研究对象是语言能力而不是语言行为。1957年,Chomsky出版了《句法结构》(*Syntactic Structure*)一书,标志着生成语言学正式形成。

生成语言学对语言的认识包括以下三个方面。首先,语言是创造的。习得语言并不是去学会特定的句子,而是利用组句规则去理解和创造句子,句数是无限的。其次,语法是天赋的。儿童天生就具有一种普遍语法,其实质是一种大脑所具有的、与语言知识相关的特定状态,一种使儿童能学会人类任何语言的生理及相应的心理机制。儿童凭借普遍语法去分析和理解后天语言环境中的语言素材,语言的习得过程就是由普遍语法向个别语法转化的过程,转化通过先天的语言习得机制实现。最后,每个句子都有两个结构层次——深层结构和表层结构。深层结构显示基本的句法关系,决定句子的意义;表层结构表示用于交际的句子形式,决定句子的语音等;句子的深层结构通过转换规则变为表层结构,从而被感知和传达。

基于生成语言学的二语习得理论承认普遍语法在二语习得中的存在及作用,即"成人二语习得者能继续利用由生物基因决定的语言学习能力,包括高度抽象的句法原则与参数天赋知识、普遍语义知识"(戴曼纯 2007:444)。但至于普遍语法能在多大程度上发挥作用,二语习得领域还存在争议。例如,最小树假说(Minimal Tree Hypothesis)(Vainikka & Young-Scholten 1996)认为,成人习得第二语言时,依然还有天赋的语言知识;中介语出现屈折形态缺失现象,是因为成人二语习得者只能利用实义语类投射,二语发展初期缺少功能语类特征及其相关的特征值,而这些不会从母语迁移过来。然而,充分迁移/充分可及假说(Full Transfer/Full Access Hypothesis)(Schwartz & Sprouse 1994,1996)认为,形态缺失不是因为二语学习者没有功能语类知识,而是由于形态向音系映射时出现了问题。

此外,基于生成语言学的二语习得理论认为,正面证据可触发学习者的语言习得机制,使其通过参数重设习得第二语言,而负面证据(即纠错)不能帮助参数重设(如 White 2003)。Schwartz(1993)指出,负面证据包含了有关语言的信息(information about language),但这种信息不是语言输入,不会渗透进语言能力,对二语习得没有实质性作用。20世纪90年代,White 及其同事开展了一系列实证研究(Trahey 1996;Trahey & White 1993;White 1990/1991,1991,1992;White, Spada, Lightbown & Ranta 1991)来检验负面证据的作用,结果均证实负面证据无效。

2.3.2 Krashen 的监控模型

Krashen 作为生成语言学二语习得研究的代表人物,于 20 世纪 80 年代提出了著名的监控模型(Monitor Model),其中包括五大假说(见图 2.2)(Krashen 1981,1982,1985):习得—学得假说(The Acquisition-learning Hypothesis)、监控假说(The Monitor Hypothesis)、输入假说(The Input Hypothesis)、自然顺序假说(The Natural Order Hypothesis)及情感过滤假说(The Affective Filter Hypothesis)。这些理论对于二语习得研究的发展起到了极大的推动作用,对于揭示二语习得机制、提高外语教学质量具有重要的现实意义。

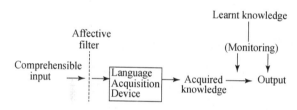

图2.2 监控模型五大假说(Gregg 1984;Krashen 1982)

习得—学得假说

该假说认为,习得与学得是两个分开独立的概念。习得是潜意识的学习过程,是以意义为核心的自然交际的结果,在很多方面与儿童学习母语的过程相似。相反,学得是有意识的学习过程,即通过课堂讲授并辅之以练习,从而达到对所学语言的了解和对语法概念的掌握。习得和学得的知识分别存储于大脑的不同区域。只有习得的知识才能促进第二语言能力的发展,才是人们运用语言的真正机制,而学得的知识只对语言使用起监控作用,不能被视为语言能力的一部分。此外,语法教学和纠错只能帮助学习者学得语言知识,而且学得的知识不能转化为习得的知识。但是,有些研究认为,学得的知识和习得的知识之间存在接口,前者通过适当的练习可转化为后者(如 DeKeyser 2001,2007;McLaughlin 1978,1980,1987)。

然而,该假说与心理学研究发现相悖。有关记忆的研究表明,大脑内的信息加工过程是平行进行的,无论是以何种途径摄入的信息,一旦进入到大脑网络,大脑就会把其他相关信息与之比较、鉴别、排列、匹配,这些活动是以多层面平行的方式进行。心理学家认为,以任何方式获得的知识都会不断与已有的知识进行交流,新知识会对已存在的知识进行修改,有意识学得的知识在经过一定的练习使用后,可以转化成无意识的自动化知识。

监控假说

监控假说与习得—学得假说密切相关,认为习得和学得作为两个不同的体系,所产生的知识在语言使用时起不同的作用。习得的知识才是真正的语言能力,而学得的知识只在使用第二语言时起监控或编辑作用,这种监控功能既可发生在语言输出(说、写)前,也可发生在其后。监控功能要发挥作用取决于三个条件:(1)有足够的时间,即语言使用者必须要有充足的时间才能有效地选择和运用语法规则;(2)注意语言形式,即语言使用者的注意力必须集中于语言形式的准确性;(3)了解语言规则,即语言使用者必须具有相关的语法概念及语言规则知识。基于上述分析,我们不难想象,纠错能激发学习者关注形式,从而促进监控功能发挥作用。

输入假说

输入假说认为,学习者是通过接触可理解的语言输入(comprehensible input),按照自然顺序习得第二语言。可理解的语言输入只略高于学习者现有语言水平的输入。如果用 i 代表学习者现有的水平,1 代表学习者的下一个发展阶段,那么 i+1 即为可理解的语言输入。当学习者接触到大量的可理解输入后,语言结构会自然习得,这也就意味着,语法教学及纠错没有促学价值。

输入假说面临精确界定和验证学习者的 i 与 i+1 阶段的问题。"概念不精确、不利于实验,就会造成理论停滞不前"(戴曼纯 2007:79)。另外,Krashen 虽然强调语言习得机制是二语习得的根本,但输入假说似乎只关注外部输入,忽视了语言习得机制的内在作用。

自然顺序假说

自然顺序假说认为,人们是按照一定的可预见顺序来习得第二语言,有些规则先被习得,有些后被习得。"这个习得顺序不由这些语言规则的难易程度来决定,也不依赖于课堂上所授语言内容的次序"(Krashen 1985:1)。自然顺序假说源于对语素和语法结构输出准确度的研究。Brown(1973)考察了三名英语儿童对 14 个英语语素的习得情况,结果发现,虽然受试的习得速度不同,但习得顺序相同。受此启发,二语习得领域也开展了类似的语素研究(如 Dulay & Burt 1973,1974,1975;Dulay, Burt & Krashen 1982),结果显示,处于不同教育环境下的不同母语背景的儿童,会以相同的顺序习得11个英语语素,而且成人学习者的习得顺序与之相似。Krashen认为,上述研究的结果虽然存在一些差异,但总体上具有很强的一致性,足以证实习得顺序假说的可预见性。课堂教学和纠错不能改变自然的习得顺序,对于学习者习得目标语没有帮助。

自然顺序假说的证据来自于对学习者在某一特定时刻的语言产出准确性的研究,众所周知,语言产出具有极大的变异性,因而能否将语言产出准确性作为判定语言习得的依据,还需进一步的理论与实践探索。

情感过滤假说

情感过滤假说认为,二语习得过程受到很多情感因素的影响,它们对语言输入起过滤作用,语言输入必须通过情感过滤才有可能变为摄入(intake),学习者的情感过滤强度因人而异。影响语言习得的情感因素包括:(1)学习目的是否明确直接影响学习效果,目的明确则动力大、进步快,反之则收效甚微;(2)自信、外向、乐于置身于不熟悉的学习环境、自我感觉良好的学生在学习中进步较快;(3)焦虑感较强者,情感屏障高,获得的输入少;反之,则容易得到更多的输入。鉴于以上分析,纠错可能会提高学习者的情感过滤,打击其自信心,从而影响学习效果。

虽然情感因素在二语习得中的作用已得到广为认可,但是情感过滤假说还是受到了一些批评。例如,有些学生比较敏感,情感过滤高,但不见得就不是个好的语言学习者;相反,有些学生比较自信、外向,情感过滤低,但不一定是个好的语言学习者。另外,该假说对于情感过滤工作机理的解释还远不够充分。

总之,Krashen的二语习得理论引起了诸多争议,也正是这些争议所激发的讨论,为二语习得研究提供了新的视角,使我们对于当前研究的成果及所存在的问题、争议、局限性等有了进一步的认识,为在教学中借鉴性地使用二语习得理论提供了指导。

2.3.3 二语习得研究范式的转变

在20世纪与本世纪交替之际,二语习得研究经历了一次范式转变(paradigm shift),早期基于行为主义、生成语言学的二语习得研究逐渐淡出视野,取而代之的是一批基于认知心理、社会文化因素的二语习得理论逐渐受到追捧并有新的发展。为了弄清楚人脑是如何加工和学习新信息、如何习得第二语言,认知心理视角的二语习得研究将注意力投向了具有自主性(autonomous)的学习者本人,他们认为,尽管学习者需要从社会环境中获取语言输入,但最终决定其习得路径的还是学习者本人。认知心理流派关注语言学习的认知心理过程,以及学习者所处的社会环境与其认知过程间的交互作用,相关理论包括:二语学习加工理论(如 Anderson 1983;DeKeyser 2007;McLaughlin 1987)和基于使用的二语习得理论(如 Ellis 2005)。社会文化视角的二语习得研究以 Vygotsky 的社会文化理论与实践为基础,关注语言学习过程中的社会调节和社会构建的本质,代表性理论为二语习得的社会文化理论(Lantolf & Thorne 2006)。此外,还有一些二语习得理论,如互动假说(如 Long 1996)、外语学习的学伴用随原则(如王初明 2009),强调社会文化视角与认知心理视角的整合,主张认知植根于社会互动,强调学习者内部认知与外部环境的协同。接下来,我们具体介绍这些二语习得理论的新发展,尤其关注他们对于语言纠错的认识。

2.4 二语学习加工理论

二语学习加工理论是关于不同的记忆存储方式(短时记忆、长时记忆)如何处理二语信息的理论,即如何通过反复的激活实现信息提取的自动化,具体包含四个理论模型:(1)信息加工模型(Information Processing Model)(McLaughlin 1987,1990);(2)思维适应性控制模型(Adaptive Control of Thought Model)(Anderson 1983,1985);(3)可加工性理论(Processability Theory)(Pienemann 1998,2003);(4)技能习得理论(Skill Acquisition Theory)(如 DeKeyser 2007)。

2.4.1 信息加工模型

20世纪50年代,认知心理学领域发展形成的信息加工模型,将人脑和计算机进行类比,把人脑看成类似于计算机的信息加工系统。McLaughlin(1987)首先把信息加工模型应用于二语习得研究,提出了二语学习的信息加工模型。该模型的基本理念是:"复杂行为源于简单过程"(McLaughlin & Heredia 1996:213),语言作为一种复杂的认知技能，其习得过程同样建立在简单的过程之上。自动化（automotization）和重建（restructuring）是该模型的两个核心概念。

根据信息加工模型，语言信息是以受控或自动形式被加工，语言学习就是从受控加工向自动加工的转换过程。人的记忆是各种信息结点（node）的集合，通过学习，这些结点相互连接构成了一张记忆网。二语学习始于受控加工，涉及特定信息结点的暂时激活，此过程需要占用学习者大量的注意资源，并会受到短时记忆局限性的制约。然而，通过反复激活，这些语言信息由受控加工逐步向自动加工转化，并最终以单位（units）的形式储存于长时记忆。在长时记忆中，大多数信息结点都是静止的，每当接触到外部语言输入的刺激，最近的结点就会被自动激活，而后扩散至相应的结点，这就是信息的自动加工。由此可见，一旦信息被存储于长时记忆，无论何时需要，学习者都能以最少的注意资源成功提取。练习和纠错可刺激相关信息被反复激活，从而推动受控加工向自动加工转化。

受控加工向自动加工的转化过程是伴随着二语系统持续性重建而实现的。重建不仅涉及学习者大脑中的知识表征，还有对学习策略的运用。表征重建是指例子（examplar-based）表征转化为规则（rule-based）表征（McLaughlin & Heredia 1996）。具体说来，二语学习始于记忆一些没有分析过的语块（chunk），随着语言水平的不断发展，这些语块会逐步得到分析，并具有创造性。学习策略重建是指学习者在习得复杂的技能时，往往设计一些新框架来储存新知识，并将已有的旧知识也安排到这个框架中。学习的过程是主动建构的过程，是对既有知识体系不断进行再创造、再加工以获得新意义、新理解的过程。练习对于重建有着重要的作用。

信息加工模型存在两点不足。首先，它虽然强调练习的重要性，却没有明确定义哪些练习可以促进受控加工向自动加工转化。此外，表征重建的概念过于笼统，没有具体分析哪些语言结构何时被重建，什么因素会促进重建等（李俏 2005）。

2.4.2 思维适应性控制模型

思维适应性控制模型与信息加工模型的理念相同，均认为二语习得过程是一个知识系统不断累加（step-by-step nature of learning），并最终为学习者可以自动使用的过程，练习有利于实现自动化。但是，思维适应性控制模型涉及的范围更广,旨在解读人类对于所有技能的学习。

Anderson 把知识分为两类:陈述性知识(declarative knowledge)和程序性知识(procedural knowledge)。二者获得的心理过程、在头脑中的表征形式,以及保持激活的特点都有很大差异。陈述性知识是有关是"什么"的知识(knowledge *that*),包括有意识掌握的事实、概念、观点等。程序性知识是有关"怎么办"的知识(knowledge *how*),是无意识掌握的知识。二者的区别主要体现在以下三个方面:(1)陈述性知识的掌握是有或无(all-or-none)的状态,必须被完整地获得,而程序性知识可以被部分掌握;(2)学习者通过教学可快速获得陈述性知识,而程序性知识是要通过练习来逐渐获得;(3)陈述性知识可以被学习者意识到,可用语言表述出来,而程序性知识一般不被学习者意识到,难以用语言表述出来。Anderson(1983)指出,所有知识的学习都始于陈述性知识,但该言论随即受到了反驳(DeKeyser 1997)。Anderson也意识到了其问题所在(Anderson & Fincham 1994;MacWhinney & Anderson 1986),例如,母语习得就并非开始于陈述性知识。

思维适应性控制模型区分了三种记忆:工作记忆(即短时记忆)、陈述性的长时记忆和程序性的长时记忆。Anderson 认为,陈述性知识与程序性知识是两类不同的知识,故要存储于不同的记忆形式中。陈述性知识转化为程序性知识要经历三个阶段(Anderson 1985),如表 2.1 所示,接下来,我们以学习英语动词单三形式为例,具体阐释每个学习阶段的内容。

表 2.1 思维适应性控制模型的三个学习阶段

1.	认知阶段(the cognitive stage)	学习语法规则
2.	联合阶段(the associative stage)	找到可以练习使用该规则的方法,把普遍的规则运用到具体的例子中
3.	自动化阶段(the automatic stage)	自动使用该规则

在认知阶段,学习者需要有意识地学习语法规则,即当主语为单数第三人称时,谓语动词的形式为:动词原型＋s 或 es。我们常会发现,即便学习者已经熟知了该规则,但在实际使用时,却不能自如运用。这说明,学习者虽然掌握了相关的陈述性知识,但这一知识尚未

得以程序化。在联合阶段,学习者要学会将知识与运用联合起来,即在什么样的语境下,如何给动词原型加 s 或 es;偏误最有可能发生在此阶段。在自动化阶段,学习者通过大量练习,可以实现流利正确地使用动词单三形式。

综上可见,思维适应性控制模型中的陈述性知识就相当于监控模型中的"学得的知识",以及信息加工模型中的"受控的知识";而该模型中的程序性知识就相当于监控模型中的"习得的知识",以及信息加工模型中的"自动化的知识"。在之前的论述中我们提到,监控模型与信息加工模型的主要区别在于:陈述性知识能否转化为程序性知识;前者认为不能转化,后者认为可以转化。思维适应性控制模型同样支持"转化观",而且强调练习在转化中的重要作用。

事实上,有不少研究赞同"转化观"(如 DeKeyser 1997,2001,2007; Hulstijn 1995; Schmidt 1990, 1994, 1995; Schmidt & Frota 1986; Swain 1985; Swain & Lapkin 1995)。例如,DeKeyser(1997)详细分析了二语显性知识(即陈述性知识)如何通过长期、系统性的训练转化为自动化的隐性知识(即程序性知识)。但这些分析推理仅限于理论层面,缺少实验证据的支持。目前,只有非常少量的证据可以说明,在二语习得过程中,陈述性知识通过长期练习可以转化为程序性知识,但实验证据的缺失不等于两种知识转化的缺失(DeKeyser 2003)。

2.4.3 可加工性理论

可加工性理论(Pienemann 1998, 2003)将语法理论和信息加工理论有机融合,因而可以更为有效地解释二语习得过程。其中,所涉及的语法理论是词汇功能语法[5](Lexical Functional Grammar)(Kaplan & Bresnan 1982),它与普遍语法有着本质区别:前者的目的是要拥有心理现实性,力图与语言加工的认知特征相吻合;后者是纯粹的语言

---

[5] 词汇功能语法产生于 20 世纪 70 年代后期,由句法学家 Joan Bresnan 和计算语言学家兼心理语言学家 Ronald M. Kaplan 共同提出,起先在麻省理工学院教授。随着 Bresnan 在 1983 年改至斯坦福大学任教,词汇功能语法就以斯坦福大学为根据地继续发展,并在 90 年代吸收了理论音韵学的优选理论,出现了优选词汇功能语法。到了 21 世纪前十年,Bresnan 教授将统计学的方法融入进了词汇功能语法,目前正逐步从传统形式语法学派的质化、范畴性研究转为量化、连续性研究。

学理论。可加工性理论的核心观点是：二语学习者只能产出和理解当前语言处理器(language processor)可以处理的语言形式。根据该理论,第二语言发展主要涉及六个加工程序(见表2.2),从低到高构成了一个序列等级：词条提取程序→范畴程序→词组程序→简单句子程序→句子程序→从句程序。

表2.2　加工序列等级(Pienemann 1998：87)

Level 1：	Lemma access; words; no sequence of constituents.
Level 2：	Category procedure; lexical morphemes; no exchange of information-canonical word order.
Level 3：	Phrasal procedure; phrasal morphemes.
Level 4：	Simplified S-procedure; exchange of information from internal to salient constituents.
Level 5：	S-procedure; inter-phrasal morphemes; exchange of information between internal constituents.
Level 6：	Subordinate clause procedure.

在词条提取程序阶段,学习者的语言能力十分有限,仅能处理一些孤立的语言成分,使用的词汇缺乏形态变化。第二阶段为范畴加工程序,涉及数、时、体等范畴概念的形成,词汇开始出现形态变化,句子语序为SVO典型顺序。在词组加工程序阶段,学习者主要处理词组内部信息,句法特点表现为状语前置和DO前置等。在句子程序阶段,形态和句法的复杂性明显增强,学习者开始习得主谓一致、倒装语序等。最后一个阶段为从句程序,学习者的句法加工能力进一步提高,已经掌握主句与从句的关系,从句不再使用倒装语序。Pienemann开展了大量的实证研究检验可加工性理论的有效性,所涉及的目标语言包括德语、英语、瑞典语和日语。其中最为著名的是对德语语序习得的考察,结果显示,无论是在自然环境还是课堂环境,该语法结构的习得均遵循相似的发展路径。

Pienemann根据可加工性理论的教学启示,提出了可教性假设(Teachability Hypothesis)(Pienemann 1981, 1987, 1989, 1998),基本观点包括：如果语言教学超前于学习者所处的语言发展阶段,他们将无法习得所教内容;只有当所教的语言结构接近学习者该阶段在自然环境中有能力习得的语言结构时,教学才有效。可教性假设并不是一种教学技巧,而是一个为外语教学建立心理语言学基础的理论,它强调语言的可教性受限于学习者是否已经"做好了准备",Stage X+2 阶段的有效输入需以 Stage X+1 为基础,如果学习者处于 Stage X+1 阶段,他们将无法有效接受 Stage X+3 阶段的语言输入。

根据可教性假设,纠错可以促进二语习得,但前提是不能超前于学习者所处的发展阶段,否则学习者可能会采用回避策略,对语言习得产生消极影响。例如,Pienemann(1987)发现,三名处于初级阶段的成年德语学习者已经在课堂上学习了现在完成时,但仍然用"情态动词+动词"的结构来代替现在完成时。Pienemann 认为,现在完成时处于较晚的习得阶段,超前教学并不能帮助学习者掌握该结构,相反刺激了他们的回避行为,阻碍了语言的正常发展。

2.4.4 技能习得理论

技能习得理论是在思维适应性控制模型基础上发展起来的,它认为语言学习与其他技能(如象棋、钢琴、数学)学习本质相同,都是从最初的改变,不断发展到熟练的、自动化行为的过程,任何技能的学习都需要通过不断的练习(同一活动的反复操练)而取得进步。与前期的加工理论相比,技能习得理论更为系统和完善,DeKeyser(2007)对该理论作了详细的介绍。

技能习得理论认为,人类习得各种技能要经历三个阶段:陈述性阶段、程序性阶段和自动化阶段。第一阶段是掌握有关技能方面的知识,包括相关的概念和规则,即关于事物本身的陈述性知识。现代认知心理学认为,大部分陈述性知识在人脑中是以命题网络的形式表征并储存,其层次结构的好坏决定了其质量的高低。高质量的知识,不仅保存时间长,而且有利于准确、快速地提取和迁移。在解决问题时,只要知识一受到刺激,就能顺利地产生联想,提取出一个相关的知识群。

第二阶段是执行该技能,把知识变成行为的阶段。学习者通过自己的理解,运用长时记忆,把所获得的陈述性知识转化为执行任务所需的程序性知识,程序性知识是关于如何做事的知识。使知识由陈述性形式向程序性形式转化的过程并非特别耗时耗力,假使学习者已经具备了相关的陈述性知识,并在不断地向靠近既定目标而努力,那么这个转化过程很容易就能完成。

第三阶段是自动化阶段。学习者通过练习可以减少每次执行任务的时间(即反应时)、犯错误的比率(即错误率)和执行任务所需的注意量。因此,学习者一旦获得了程序性知识,要想使相关行为表现得流畅自如、几乎没有错误,还需要大量的练习来减少反应时,降低错误率。这个阶段遵循学习幂定律(the power law of learning),该定律是指,通过一段时间的练习会使行为发生质的变化。反应时、错误率及所需注意量的降低,反映了知识的提取机制发生了质的改变,改变在初始阶段会比较突然,但随着时间的发展会逐渐稳定下来。

在二语习得领域,技能习得理论研究的代表人物是 Robert DeKeyser。根据他的观点,技能习得理论并不能解释二语学习的全部,而是更适合于初始阶段的学习情况,具体说来,就是高语能的成人学习者在早期教学中对简单语言结构的学习。此外,他强调练习和纠错的作用。练习可以让技能在一定时间内发生质变,由陈述性知识转化为程序性知识,然后转化为程序性知识自动化。因此,大量有意义的练习对于推动知识使用自动化非常有帮助。纠错可以提供显性知识,使学习者意识到自己的问题之处,从而避免错误被程序化后发展成为一种自动化行为,但至于如何反馈以及提供多少反馈才能高效纠错,还需深入探讨。

DeKeyser(2007)考察了 61 名本科生在 11 周的时间里学习一种人工语言的情况。实验中的教学、练习和测试都借助于计算机,通过让受试反复选择与人工语言相对应的图片来测量他们理解的反应时和产出的错误率。实验结果显示,理解的反应时与产出的错误率会随着练习的增多呈下降趋势,研究结果支持了技能习得理论。

Hartshorn et al.(2010)在技能习得理论的框架下考察了纠错反馈的促学效果。Hartshorn 等人认为,大量集中性的练习可以推动语言使用自动化,所以当写作任务和纠错反馈是意义丰富、及时、持续并可操控时,就会产生促学效应。实验中,受试每天都要进行 10 分钟的写作,实验人员批改作文的语法错误,并在第二天返还。受试根据反馈修改作文,直至没有任何语法错误。终结性单位(T-unit)检验显示,实验组的语言准确性要明显好于对照组,而语言的流利性、复杂性及修辞能力与对照组没有显著差异。Evans et al.(2011)在不同的学习环境下复制了这个研究,并得到了相似的实验结果。

以上四种加工理论,即信息加工模型、思维适应性控制模型、可加工性理论和技能习得理论,均关注学习者的认知发展,将学习者视为自主的个体,而非存在于社会互动环境中的一分子。接下来,我们要介绍的基于使用的二语习得理论,虽然也属于认知流派,但更准确地说,应该是社会认知流派,因为他们关注学习者所处的社会环境与其认知过程的交互作用。

2.5 基于使用的二语习得理论

基于使用的二语习得理论认为,语言习得是通过使用,从输入中归纳语言型式(pattern)与规则(regularities),并在大脑中建立相互间关联的过程,该过程会受到社会环境、学习者个体差异和输入频率等因素的影响。众多理论聚集在该理论流派大旗下,对二语习得研究形成前所未有的冲击,具体包括:联通论(Connectionism)(如 Christiansen & Chater 2001)、功能语言学(Functional Linguistics)(如 Bates & MacWhinney 1981)、浮现论(Emergentism)(如 Elman et al. 1996)、认知语言学(Cognitive Linguistics)(如 Langacker 1987)、构式语法(Construction Grammar)(如 Goldberg 1995;Tomasello 2003)、计算语言学(Computational Linguistics)(如 Bod 1998)、联结-认知原则(Associative-Cognitive CREED)(Ellis 2007)及频率理论(Frequency-based Approach)(Ellis 2012)。代表人物有 Nick C. Ellis 和 Michael Tomasello 等。

该阵营流派众多,比较复杂,他们重在说明语言习得的过程,而对语言本体性质的解释相对较弱。但值得一提的是,构式语法和浮现论将语言学和语言习得理论有机融合,对"语言知识由什么构成"和"语言知识如何习得"这两个根本问题给出了自己的答案,本节会对这两个理论做详细论述,而在此之前,我们先介绍一下基于使用的二语习得理论的核心观点。

2.5.1 理论综述

基于使用的二语习得理论犹如一面旗帜,召集了多个语言学和语言习得理论。虽然这些理论的具体内容不同,但核心理念是相通的。接下来,本节在王初明(2011a)研究成果的基础上,归纳该流派的四个核心观点。

首先,基于使用的二语习得理论建立在基于使用的语言学理论之上,包含五个核心理念:(1)语言存在的根本目的是为了交际;(2)任何自然语言总是在语境中使用,受语境因素的影响,如说话者与听者之间的关系影响词语的选择;(3)语言是后天学会的,不存在先天的语言习得机制;(4)意义不仅仅来自于词项,语法结构本身也有意义;(5)不划分句法、词法等语言层次,每个句法结构有其独特意义,相互之间不存在转换关系,如被动句不由主动句转换而来。

其次,语言知识源于语言使用体验,在交际使用的过程中习得。学习者最初以语块的方式逐一接触语言的具体实例,进而从实例体验中抽绎出带规律性的语言型式。这个由具体到抽象的过程与语言接触频率有直接关系。语言接触频率可分为两类,一是实例频率(token frequency),一是类型频率(type frequency)。实例频率指一个具体语言表达式在语言体验中出现的次数,它可以是一个音、一个单词、一个短语或一个句子。类型频率指一个语言型式在语言使用中的具体表现个数。例如,以[tr]开头的英语单词是一个语言型式,所有以[tr]开头的英语单词便构成了它的类型频率。语言型式都有其类型频率,有的类型频率大一些,有的小一些。例如,双宾结构 V NP_1 NP_2 是一个语言型式,能用在双宾结构中的动词不是很多,远少于能够用在与格结构 V NP_1 NP_2 中的动词数。Tomasello(2003)指出,在语言体验过程中,一个表达式的实例频率决定其固化程度(entrenchment)和被提取使用的流利程度,而类型频率则决定一个语言型式使用的可生成性(productivity),一个语言型式的类型频率越高,此型式的可生成性越强。Bybee(2008)认为,涵盖众多实例的语言型式,其大脑表征更加巩固,自然也更有可能用于创造新的语言表达式。因此,与实例频率相比,类型频率更有助于生成新的语言表达式。但是,两种频率都利于语言能力的发展。

再次,基于形式的学习(form-focused learning)对于语言习得必不可少。二语习得的很多方面仅仅依靠隐性学习是难以实现的,即使能,也需要相当长的时间;而基于形式的学习通过将学习者的注意力引向语言形式,从而推动显性学习,其结果会产生显性知识,并存储于外显记忆。显性知识的积累与巩固是隐性知识发展的前提(Ellis 2005),如果外界提供有针对性的语言输出练习,学习者可在反复操练的过程中,有意识地从外显记忆筛选出那些受外界刺激、反复激活的显性知识,将其转化为隐性知识后存储于内隐记忆(DeKeyser 2003;陈亚平 2011)。纠错作为一种显性干预手段,可促使学习者关注形式,从而有助于显性知识的积累,为随后隐性知识的发展提供"抓手"

(Ellis 2008)。

最后,基于使用的二语习得理论与 Chomsky 的语言天赋论形成了鲜明对比。Chomsky 认为,儿童生来具有一种表现为普遍语法的语言习得机制,后天只需少量语言输入设定该语言所特有的参数,便可熟练掌握目标语言。然而,基于使用的语言习得理论则认为,不存在什么先天的语言习得机制,语言知识是学习者主动积极建构起来的,语言习得主要依靠认知能力以及学习者与周围环境的互动。

2.5.2 构式语法

构式语法理论创立至今只有十几年的时间,但已发展成为一种比较完善的语言学理论,包含系统的语言观和一套分析语言习得的程序,在国际语言学界产生了重要的影响(邓云华、石毓智 2007),代表学者为 Adele E. Goldberg。构式语法的理论基础是认知语言学(Langacker 1987,1991),它认为语言由构式组成,构式是指任何形式—意义的结合体,而且意义不能由组成成分来解释(Goldberg 1995)。该定义实际上把各种大小的语言单位都囊括进来,包括最小的音义结合体(即语素)和各种复杂的句式。

构式语法是对生成语法理论反思的结果,是生成语法最大的挑战。第一,生成语法认为语法是多层的,表层结构的背后还有隐含的深层结构或者逻辑形式、语音形式等,它们通过各种规则生成表层形式,不同的语法结构之间可以转换等等。这些看不见的东西大大增加了分析的随意性,降低了分析的客观性和准确性。相反,构式语法认为,形式就是表层所看到的内容,不存在隐含形式,也不承认零形式(即没有语音形式的语法标记)的存在,这样就可以把分析建立在直观而可靠的经验事实之上,从而大大提高了研究的客观性、科学性和准确性。

第二,在研究对象上,构式语法与生成语法形成互补。生成语法认为语法是一个演绎系统,可以靠少数几条规则推演出无数合乎语法的句子,他们感兴趣的是使用频率最高的结构,并把它们看成语言的核心(core);而对于解释不了的语法结构,则被认为是不值得研究的特例,将他们看作边缘(peripheral)而加以忽略。然而,构式语法认为,语法结构不论常见与否,都有相同的理论价值和研究价值,尤其是那些生成语法解释不了的、不值得研究的特例,正是构式语法优越性最强有力的佐证。

第三,生成语法很少关注结构的意义,尤其是除去词汇的语法结构本身的意义。而构式语法认为,不同的语法形式一定对应不同的语义。例如,下面两个句子的含义并不一样,(1)a 可以理解为"因为 Zach 太忙,Liza 帮他买了一本书",(1)b 则只能理解为"Liza 有意给 Zach 买了一本书"(Goldberg 2003)。既然不同的结构具有不同的语义,那么它们之间就不存在形式推演问题。

(1) a. Liza bought a book for Zach.
　　b. Liza bought Zach a book.

第四,生成语法承认语言共性的存在,但采用了一种"先天说",即人类具有一种与生俱来的普遍语法,可惜这种假设迄今既未找到生理基础,又未发现心理现实性。构式语法则认为,语法是一个开放的系统,可以用可观察到的经验事实来说明不同语言的共性,其中一些语言之外的因素起着重要的作用(邓云华、石毓智 2007),例如,不同的语言都有双宾结构的原因在于:物体传递是每个民族经常进行的日常活动之一,这种事件结构反映到语言中就成了双宾结构。

第五,生成语法认为,儿童拥有与生俱来、专门用于习得语言的机制,因此从一开始就有和成人一样的语法知识,这必然导致"儿童语言与成人语言有语法一致性"的假设(袁野 2010)。然而大量研究显示,很多情况下儿童的语言表现与成人不一致(Tomasello 2003)。相反,构式语法的观点是:儿童在社会生活中与他人进行交流,通过一般的认知技能和社会认知技能,主动地模仿、建构、使用语言,最终能够由此及彼,从以项目为基础的儿童语言转入抽象的语言结构(赵芳 2009)。

当然,构式语法也存在不少局限性,邓云华、石毓智(2007)归纳了七点不足:(1)对构式概念的不合理扩张掩盖了本质上极不相同的语言现象,不利于对语言的探讨;(2)分析十分繁琐,不反映语言使用者的理解过程;(3)尚未解决语法结构的多义性问题;(4)无法解释一个构式的跨语言差异;(5)适用的结构类型有限;(6)确立语法结构的标准不明确;(7)语言哲学观模糊不清。

2.5.3 浮现论

浮现论认为,"语言现象应由大脑中的非语言因素及其之间的互动来解释,如生理、感知、加工、工作记忆、语用、社会交往、输入特征、学习机制等"(O'Grady 2008a:448)。浮现论不承认天生的语法原则,但承认语法特征的存在,如主谓一致、约束原则等。它赞同联通论,反对模块论,认为语言知识是以神经元网路的形式存储于大脑,网络的各个结点处于不同的激活状态,结点之间连接强度不同,大脑处理语言时采取的是并行加工模式而不是串行加工模式(贾光茂 2011)。

浮现论又分为输入浮现观(Input-based Emergentism)和天赋浮现观(Nativist Emergentism)。输入浮现观以 Nick C. Ellis 等为代表,否认天生语言习得机制的存在,认为语言习得是学习者通过一般的学习机制,分析输入语言的频率和分布特征,从而归纳出语言规则的过程,与人类一般的学习行为没有区别。输入浮现观不承认"刺激贫乏",强调语言学习者在语言输入基础上足以提取出抽象的语法规则。由于以构式语法为基础,输入浮现观对双宾结构、致使结构等做了较为成功的研究,但对于生成语言学的主要课题如约束、提升、控制、一致等现象基本没有涉及(贾光茂 2011)。

天赋浮现观又称基于处理器的浮现观(Processor-based Emergentism),以 William O'Grady 为代表,是一条"激进的中间道路"(O'Grady 2003:1),承认存在先天的语言习得机制,但这种机制不是由普遍语法规则构成,而是人类具有学习和使用语言的能力。O'Grady(2008b)赞同频率、分布特征和联想学习的重要性,但认为输入浮现观所倡导的归纳学习不能完全解释语言习得的逻辑问题[⑥],一些抽象的语法结构,如缩略形式、约束、控制、一致等,不可能完全从语言经验中归纳出来,演绎的方法以及先天的语言学习和运用能力也应该起重要作用。另外,天赋浮现观承认存在"刺激贫乏",但语言经历和语言知识间的缺口可以在内部处理器的帮助下予以补足,无须借助任何天赋的语言规则。最后,根据天赋浮现观,输入频率的重要性次于处理器对工作记忆负荷的运算和评估。内部处理器固然对输入频率高度敏感,但是当频率和运算成本相悖时,语言处理器更关注的是

---

⑥ 语言习得中的逻辑问题是指,儿童可以在有限、残缺、不足的语料输入基础上,迅速而一致地获取丰富的语言能力这一似乎有悖于逻辑的现象。先天论者相信二语习得中同样存在逻辑问题,特别是在外语学习环境下,语言输入及刺激比较贫乏,但二语习得中又不乏优秀的成功者,他们获得的语言能力同样也非他们所接触的语言输入、感觉经验及认知参与所能解释,换句话说,他们所接收到的语言知识并不足以决定他们最后获得的语言能力。

后者。语法是效率优先的线性加工模式与语言输入互动的结果。

输入浮现观和天赋浮现观互相补充,共同成就了语言浮现论的整体性与合理性,目前正被越来越多地应用于语言研究,如词汇(Meara 2006)、句法(Mellow 2006)和隐喻(Cameron & Deignan 2006)研究等。浮现论加深了我们对语言现象的理解,但它只是观察和了解世界的一种方法,对其作用不应片面夸大,至于其在应用语言学领域的实用价值,还有待时间来检验(杨梅 2009)。

2.6　二语习得社会文化理论

二语习得社会文化理论是在 Vygotsky(1962,1978)的文化历史心理学的基础上发展起来的,它强调社会文化因素在人类独特的高级认知功能发展中的核心作用。高级认知功能是人类在参与社会文化活动的过程中,通过人类社会文化构建的工具的调节而发展起来的(牛瑞英 2007)。Vygotsky 的社会文化理论早在 20 世纪 60 年代就被西方心理学所关注,然而应用于二语习得研究还是在 20 世纪最后十年才得以实现,代表人物是 James Lantolf。《社会文化理论与第二语言发展起源》(*Sociocultural Theory and the Genesis of Second Language Development*)正是 James Lantolf 与 Steven Thorne 合作的一部从社会文化理论视角研究二语习得的专著。该书全面、系统、清晰地呈现了社会文化理论所涵盖的主要内容,以及该理论应用于二语习得研究 20 年来的主要研究成果和现状。牛瑞英(2007)对此书作了详细的评介。

二语习得社会文化理论有三个核心概念:调控理论(Regulation Theory)、最近发展区(Zone of Proximal Development)理论、活动理论(Activity Theory)。下面,我们分别概述每个理论的主要内容。

2.6.1　调控理论

调控理论是社会文化理论的核心思想,基本观点如下:人类独特的高级认知功能(如记忆、注意和理性思维等)是依靠人类文化构建的辅助工具的调节而发展起来的,语言是最基本的调节工具(牛瑞英 2007)。语言在调节人类活动的同时,从根本上改变了人类的心理结构,从而形成了人类特有的、高级的、被调节的心理机能——认知发展

(余震球 2004)。儿童的认知发展经历三个阶段。在成长初期,儿童处于"它物调控"(object-regulation)阶段。例如,父母叫他们去拿远处的一个玩具,在去拿玩具的过程中,他们往往会被其他事物所吸引而忘记了父母的指令。随着年龄的增长,他们可以完成某些任务,但必须在父母、照料者或者能力更强的同伴的帮助下才能实现,这些帮助是由恰当的语言作为中介,该阶段被称为"他人调控"(other-regulation)阶段,他人调控的功能主要通过对话来实现。随着儿童高级心理活动能力的增强,他们最终会发展其独立完成某一任务的能力,即达到"自我调控"(self-regulation)阶段(姜孟 2012)。因此,Lantolf & Appel (1994)认为,儿童的认知发展过程,就是儿童通过符号的中介作用来获得对策略性心理活动的调控过程。在这一过程中,语言的作用经历了从社会语言(social speech)、自我中心语言(egocentric speech)、个体语言(private speech)到内在语言(inner speech)的发展转化。

在二语习得领域,错误通常被认为是学习者中介语发展的标志,是由诸如过度概括、母语迁移等学习者内在心理行为所造成的,但社会文化理论对错误给出了不同的解释。根据该理论,错误可能反映了不同形式的个体语言(Frawley & Lantolf 1985),是学习者在执行某个颇具难度的任务时,设法进行自我调控的表现。当学习者面临特别困难的任务时,他们往往会求助于自己以前所获得的、完全内化了的结构形式,从而出现"倒退"(regression)或"滑坡"(backsliding)现象,这被称为"连续可及原则"(the principle of continuous access) (Frawley & Lantolf 1985)。"倒退"之所以出现,是因为学习者失去了控制而需要重新建立起自我调控。因此,从这一角度看,错误反映的不是知识的欠缺,而是学习者正在从事的特定学习活动的性质(姜孟 2012)。

2.6.2 最近发展区理论

"他人调控"向"自我调控"的转化发生在最近发展区。最近发展区概念源于 Vygotsky 的文化发展遗传规律(genetic law of cultural development),是指个体实际发展水平与潜在发展水平之间的距离 (Lantolf & Thorne 2006)。实际发展水平是个体当前能独立完成某些活动的能力,它反映了个体已经建立起了某些智力过程或者功能;潜在发展水平是指个体在成人、专家或能力更强的同伴的帮助下能够达到的智力水平或执行某项行动的能力。人们在最近发展区内所得到的协助被称为"支架"(scaffolding)。随着与他人的交互以及个体认知能力的发展,当前的潜在发展水平就会变成下一个实际发展水平。

在二语习得领域,最近发展区理论已被用于研究师生改错、互动和同伴合作等学习活动对二语习得的作用,结果发现:支架作用不仅存在于不同语言水平的合作者之间(如教师和学生、本族语者和外语学习者、高水平和低水平的学生之间),还存在于相同语言水平的合作者之间,甚至低水平者可以为高水平者提供帮助(牛瑞英 2007)。以口头互动为例,外语学习者通过与本族语者交互协商,可以使用本族语者产出的语言形式来表述自己现有二语水平还无法表述的概念。由于学习者在互动中不是被动的接收者,而是主动的参与者,因此这种支架式的帮助可以促进二语发展(姜琳 2011)。

2.6.3 活动理论

活动是指心理发展得以实现的社会实践,它包括一系列用于阐释人类行为和认知以及了解人类发展过程的概念工具。活动理论重点研究人类认知的社会起源以及导致认知形成的实践活动。活动理论的发展经历了三个阶段。第一阶段是 Vygotsky 的文化调节理论。Vygotsky 根据这一理论建立了反映人类活动中主体、客体和调节工具之间关系的三角模型。第二阶段是 Leontiev 的活动调节论。Leontiev 承认文化调节的重要性,同时强调是活动把外部的社会物质活动和个人的发展联系起来。他提出活动有三个层次:活动(activity)、行动(action)和操作(operation),分别表现为活动的动机、取得目标的过程和行动的手段。第三阶段是 Engestrom 的集体活动系统,他在 Vygotsky 和 Leontiev 理论的基础上,在人类活动的三角模型中加入集体活动的层次,形成了集体活动系统模型(牛瑞英 2007)。

活动理论在二语习得研究中的应用包括:主体性研究、词汇学习、互动活动分析和教育变革。活动和任务是不同的概念,任务是活动的计划蓝图,活动是任务执行者对任务的构建。由于主体性的作用,学生在完成同一任务中所从事的活动和任务完成的结果会不同。目前实证研究的结果表明:主体性是一个关系建构,与动机关系密切,对二语发展产生正面或负面的影响;单词的偶然记忆取决于它在活动完成中所起的作用;可以用活动理论分析课堂上的教学活动(如同伴修改作文活动),发现问题并改进教学(牛瑞英 2007)。

综上所述,社会文化理论将二语习得看作是一个二语语言结构(即二语形式与功能)逐步内化的过程。在这一过程中,学习者对语言结构的使用由起初的"它物/他人调控"逐步发展到"自我调控"。Lantolf & Thorne(2006)认为转化的过程可能会利用到诸如重复、简化、示范和纠错反馈等策略。在学习之初,学习者通过参与各种学习活动,在各种外部中介的帮助下(如听录音或听他人谈话),以模仿的方式使用某个语言结构。这时,学习者处于"它物调控"或"他人调控"阶段,外部中介对他十分重要,离开了外部中介,他将无法使用这些语言结构。随着水平的发展,二语结构逐步由外部环境进入学习者大脑,学习者开始能够凭借个体话语的中介作用来使用这些结构,但还没有达到随意自如的程度。随着二语学习的继续进行,最终,学习者达到了在不需要借助任何外部中介的情况下,仅靠自己内部语言就能使用这些结构的能力,即达到了"自我调控"阶段。正是从这一观点出发,社会文化理论特别强调对话互动在二语习得中的作用,互动不仅提供了输入,还是二语习得发生的根本条件,构成了二语习得过程的一部分(姜孟 2012)。

2.7 二语习得互动假说

在二语习得研究中,"互动"有两层含义,一种是认知互动,即学习者内在机制之间的互动,如大脑内不同模块的相互作用以应对或理解外部语言输入。另一种是社会互动,即在面对面的交流中所出现的人与人之间的活动,它可以通过口头媒介面对面的进行,也可以通过书面媒体的形式发生(顾伟勤 2010)。互动假说(Interaction Hypothesis)(Long 1983,1996)作为认知互动与社会互动的有机融合,关注外语学习者与本族语者(或高水平学习者)之间的口头互动,尤其是基于意义协商的负面反馈(即纠错)对于外语学习的影响,其研究成果对于书面反馈研究有着重要的指导意义。互动假说研究的代表人物为 Michael H. Long。

2.7.1 早期的互动假说

Long(1983)的互动假说是对 Krashen 的输入假说的进一步拓展

和延伸。输入假说认为,语言习得的根本在于接触大量的可理解性输入,互动只是促使输入被理解的三种手段之一(另外两种分别是简化输入和运用上下文),具体说来,在互动中,语言输入越是被询问、解释、修正,其可理解性越高,越能促进语言习得。根据输入假说,虽然互动是获取可理解性输入的一个重要途径,但并非必需,更没有任何特别优势。

根据互动假说,可理解的语言输入是习得发生的必要条件,尤其是发生在意义协商中的互动调整式的语言输入特别有益于语言习得,因为它是针对学习者感到困难的语言形式、有的放矢地提供所需要的信息。意义协商是指在会话过程中,当出现理解障碍时,会话双方通常使用意义协商手段,从而使讲话人对先前的话语进行调整修正,使得不理解的话语为听者理解。意义协商的手段包括:理解校验(comprehension check)、确定核准(confirmation check)、澄清请求(clarification requst)、重述(reformulation)和重铸(recast)等,详见表2.3所示。

表 2.3 意义协商的主要手段

Comprehension check (from Varonis & Gass (1985a)):对话一方检验另一方是否理解了自己的意思。 　　$NNS[⑦]_1$: And your family have some ingress. 　　NNS_2: Yes ah, OK OK. 　　NNS_1: More or less OK? ←
Confirmation check (from Mackey & Philp (1998)):对话一方检验自己是否理解了另一方的意思。 　　NNS: *What are they (.) What do they do your picture? 　　NS: What are they doing in my picture? ← 　　NS: There's just a couple more things. 　　NNS: A sorry? Couple?
Clarification request (from Oliver (1998)):对话一方请求另一方澄清意思,以克服理解上的障碍。 　　NNS_1: Where do I put? 　　NNS_2: What? ← 　　NNS_1: The plant. 　　NNS_2: The plant. 　　NNS_2: What's that plant? ←

[⑦] 本书中,NNS 代表 non-native speaker,NS 代表 native speaker。

续表

Reformulation (from Varonis & Gass (1985b)): 对话一方将另一方的语言改述成"or choice"问句,以克服理解上的障碍。 　　NS: What did you want? A service call? 　　NNS: Uh 17 inch huh? 　　NS: What did you want a service call? Or how much to repair a TV? ←
Recast (from Phip (1999)): 对话一方(本族语者或高水平外语学习者)就另一方语言输出中的错误而提供的部分或全部目标语重述。 　　NNS: *Why he want this house? 　　NS: Why does he want this house? ←

为便于其他学者对互动假说进行检验,Long(1985)提出了"三步曲"建议:第一步,证明意义协商中所发生的结构/对话调整(linguistic/conversational adjustments)能促进学习者对语言输入的理解;第二步,证明理解能促进二语习得;第三步,推断出结构/对话调整有助于二语习得。在当时,实证研究大都集中在第一步,而直接验证理解是否促进习得(第二步),以及互动式调整的输入是否有助于习得发生(第三步)的实证研究则非常有限。

针对互动假说"第一步"所开展的实证研究所得结论一致。Pica, Young & Doughty(1987)比较了三组不同条件下的学习者对于指令的理解。第一组是对照组,学习者听到的是本族语者之间正常对话时的指令。第二组是预先调整的输入组,学习者听到的是本族语者与非本族语者对话时所使用的简化指令。第三组是互动式调整的输入组,学习者在不理解指令时可以与下达指令者进行意义协商。实验结果显示,互动式调整的输入组对指令的理解最佳,对照组最糟糕。由此可见,当学习者有机会进行意义协商时,他们能更好地理解语言输入。Loschky(1994)也发现,互动式调整的输入比预先调整的输入更能促进语言理解。

在上述实验中,互动式调整的输入往往比预先调整的输入花费更多的时间,这样就无法确定互动式调整输入对理解的促进作用是因为提供了更多的输入,还是有了更长的输入处理时间。针对这一情况,顾伟勤(2008)严格控制和统一了各实验组的时间,结果发现,互动式调整输入组对指令的理解程度确实好于预先调整输入组,尽管二者之间的差异没有达到显著程度。

针对互动假说的"第二步",有研究提出了异议。例如,顾伟勤

(2010)指出,学习者完全可能理解某些超越他们现有语言知识的输入,但这种理解很大程度上依赖于语言之外的环境或个人常识等,而语言外的信息不可能促进语言规则的内在生成。因此,对语言输入的理解并不一定保证习得发生,习得发生的关键在于处理输入而不是理解输入,当然在有些情况下二者可以同步进行。

2.7.2 新版互动假说

Long(1996)在前期研究成果的基础上提出了新版的互动假说,具体内容为:"意义协商,尤其是可以激发互动式调整的意义协商,有助于习得,因为它将输入、学习者的内在能力(特别是选择性注意)及输出有机地融合在一起(Long 1996:451-452)……外部环境的促学作用要借助于学习者的选择性注意以及不断发展的二语处理能力来实现,而这些认知资源可以在意义协商中被有效粘合,尽管意义协商不是其形成合力的充要条件"(Long 1996:414)。新版假说有以下五点发展。

第一,新版假说的解释力更强。互动中的输入、选择性注意和输出皆有促学作用。具体表现在,输入可为学习者提供正面证据或负面反馈。正面证据指正确、恰当的语言输入,若为学习者采用,可内化为二语知识;负面反馈指关于目标语语误的信息,若为学习者注意,可助其修正错误(Gass 2003)。选择性注意被认为是二语学习的先决条件(Schmidt 1990,2001;范烨 2009)。输出则有验证二语假设、促进二语使用自动化和促使学习者关注形式等功能(Swain 1995)。互动假说的解释力就在于其将上述三者有机结合而形成的强大合力(Long 1996;王启 2012)。

第二,新版假说在某种程度上与信息加工模型相通(顾伟勤 2010)。学习者的处理能力有限,很难同时关注意义和形式。Van Patten(1990)发现,学习者,尤其是初学者,在关注意义时很难再关注形式;同样,当他们关注语言形式时就很难获取其意义。而意义协商为学习者提供了他们所需要的时间,使他们能在处理信息内容的同时关注语言形式。

第三,新版假说肯定了负面反馈对于二语习得的作用。正面证据是学习者接触到的一系列口头或书面形式的、符合目标语要求的句子,它是学习者获取语言材料、形成语言假设的最直接途径。然而,仅仅依靠正面证据难以帮助学习者建立完整的语言体系。负面反馈可激发学习者的认知比较，使其意识到自己当前的中介语水平与目标语之间还存在差距，从而会有意识地学习目标语言形式。截至目前，已出现了大量的实证研究来考察口头负面反馈的促学效果，本书的第四章会对此作详细介绍。

第四，新版假说强调了修正输出（modified output）的重要性。修正输出指学习者在意义协商中，根据对方的反馈，对自己之前的错误所做的修正。修正输出的过程有助于学习者关注二语形式，并实现语言使用的自动化（Swain 1995）。Krashen 的输入假说特别排斥输出的作用，尤其是修正的语言输出根本不足以促学（Krashen 1998）。然而，Krashen 却忽视了一点，尽管修正输出数量有限，但可促使学习者注意到自己的问题之处，并为语言质变的发生提供机会。

第五，新版假说融合了社会互动和认知互动的理念。社会互动，即人际间的互动，帮助学习者注意到输入中的语言形式，随后再通过认知互动，即大脑内部模块间的相互作用，来进一步处理和内化语言输入，促进二语习得。

2.7.3 补缺假说

王初明（2003，2006，2007，2010）是国内研究"人际互动促进二语习得"的第一人，他提出的补缺假说从语用的角度阐释了人际互动对二语发展的作用。该假说认为，一般的外语学习往往未将语言形式的学习融入到情景语境中，这样一来，由于目标语语境知识的缺失，导致母语语境知识的补缺，进而激活母语表达式，导致母语迁移。人就是语境，本族语者就是真实语境。因此，同本族语者互动，可使学习者置身于目标语语境中，语言形式与情景语境之间的正确交互时刻发生，从而可以促进二语习得。

另外，在互动过程中，"对话双方相互协调，交互启发，默契配合，自动对焦，无意识地不断构建相互趋同的情境模式，从而促进彼此间的理解。这种说话者因互动而产生的大脑认知状态契合就是协同"（王初明 2010：297）。协同（alignment）不仅能够促进话语理解，确保对话顺畅进行，还是第二语言能被习得的关键。对话者之间的互动配合促使他们在语言的选择上相互适应并利用，因而会常常重复自己或对方用过的语言结构。对于外语学习者而言，这种语言使用的协同过程能够极大地促进其二语能力的发展。

2.7.4 互动假说研究的不足及展望

二语习得领域对互动假说的研究已经走过了30多个年头,其间的大量研究表明,不论是在课堂环境还是实验室环境,不论是儿童二语学习者还是成人二语学习者,和本族语者交流互动都能促进其二语能力的发展。可见,互动对二语习得的促进作用已经成为一种不争的事实,而不再是一种假说。因此,研究者们认为已经到了将"互动假说"更名为"互动模型"(Interaction Model / Interaction Approach)的时候了。随之,互动研究的重心也从"互动能否促学"转向"互动何以促学"。在新的研究重心引导下,研究者开始关注人的认知过程,尤其是注意和工作记忆,并开始与其他领域的学者合作,以便更好地揭示互动与二语习得之间的关系。研究重心的转移使得进一步发展实验方法成为必然:在数据收集方面,从先前的"前测—干预—后测"发展到当前的内省法;在数据分析方面,研究者们借鉴其他二语研究领域的编码方法,尝试着将语言的流利性、准确性和复杂性作为编码的标准,并且有意识地将编码的范围扩充到"有关语言的谈论"(language-related episodes)。当然,互动假说研究也存在一些问题亟待解决,下面归纳出了五个主要问题,并在此基础上指明未来研究的方向。

第一,一些重要概念的操作定义不统一。以重铸为例,其定义涉及了长/短、隐性/显性、陈述/疑问等方面的差异,而这些差异会直接影响实验结论。法语浸入式教学研究(如 Lyster 1998;Lyster & Ranta 1997;Panova & Lyster 2002)发现,重铸不能促使学习者修正错误的语言输出,因而对二语发展没有太大帮助。但是,Doughty & Varela(1998)却发现了相反的结果。导致这一矛盾的原因在于:后者在研究中先使用升调来重复学习者语言输出中的错误以引起对方的注意,然后再提供重铸,故这样的重铸更显性,更容易引起学习者的注意,因而促学效果更加。针对这一情况,未来研究有必要对一些重点概念统一操作定义,这有利于减少不必要的研究分歧。

第二,互动研究主要通过测量学习者对于目标结构的掌握情况,从而判定互动的促学价值。但是,语言习得究竟意味着什么?认知心理学将知识区分为显性和隐性两类。前者是有意识的知识,对语言的使用起监控作用,后者是潜意识的知识,有助于语言使用自动化,二者相互依存、相互交叉，共同构成了语言学习复杂的动态系统（Ellis 2005）。所以想要全面、客观地反映外语学习的全貌，就需要对两种知识的习得情况分别作考察。然而，现有的互动研究大多只测量学习者的显性知识，而忽视了其隐性知识的习得情况。事实上，有些语言特征的显性知识很容易掌握，但相应的隐性知识却很难，而有些语言特征则刚好相反。因此，未来研究有必要系统考察学习者对显性、隐性知识的习得情况，从而全面评估互动的促学价值。

第三，忽视了社会因素的影响。目前，互动研究更多关注于学习者的认知能力对互动效果的影响，而忽视了社会因素在这一过程中的作用。例如，Oliver & Mackey（2003）发现，不同的课堂环境会激发不同形式的互动，从而产生不同的学习效果。然而，目前有关环境因素的研究还非常有限，因此未来的互动研究可对环境作进一步的细化，如互动双方的情况、互动任务的性质、互动环境等等，并将这些因素纳入研究框架。

第四，考察的语法结构非常有限。互动研究所涉及的语言不外乎英语、西班牙语、法语和日语。为了从更广阔的视角验证互动促学的效果，未来研究可以考察其他目标语言和结构，考察与规则学习相悖的套语（formulaic language）学习，考察显性、隐性知识在互动中的转化情况，如比较学习者对其显性知识有一定了解的语言结构和对其隐性知识完全不了解的语言结构的习得，在哪种情况下互动的效果更突出？如果是前者，那么学习者需要提前掌握多少相应的显性知识才能使互动最大程度地发挥作用？

第五，互动研究主要聚焦于负面反馈，很少涉及正面证据。根据常识，互动中的负面反馈为数甚寥，正面证据才是输入的主体。因此，要想全面揭示互动促学的机理，正面证据的作用不容忽视。互动中的正面证据分为显、隐性两种。显性正面证据是指，在以语言练习为导向的互动中提供的、明确提醒学习者注意的正面证据，如句型操练中的目标结构；隐性正面证据是指，在意义磋商为导向的互动中提供的、未提醒学习者注意的正面证据。王启（2012）采用同盟者脚本技术（confederate scripting technique），以英语主、被动结构为目标结构，考察了互动中的隐性正面证据能否为中国英语学习者采用。实验结果显示，此类证据能为学习者采用，但采用情况受到学习者二语水平的影响，学习者须达到一定水平才能采用之，水平越高，采用几率越大。姜琳、易慧文（2013）首次考察了书面形式的正面证据与负面反馈对于中国学生习得英语动词第三人称单数形式的作用。实验采用"前测—干预—后测—延迟后测"的设计模式,结果显示,两种输入形式都能有效促进受试对于英语动词单三形式的掌握,但促学机理不同:正面证据通过融合形式、意义、语境,直接促进学习者与目标语形式的协同,从而增进他们对于动词单三形式的掌握;负面反馈可引起学习者注意到中介语和目标语之间的差距,并在随后的语言输出中修正相关的语言错误,从而实现流利、正确地使用动词单三形式。正面证据是互动促学的一个重要方面,值得未来研究作深入的探讨。

为更好地探究互动促学的机理,研究者应该在自我创新的同时加强同其他领域的合作,如心理学、社会学、神经科学等。研究领域的拓宽、研究方法的创新必然会导致更多研究问题的出现。我们相信,未来的互动研究一定会焕发更大的光彩。

2.8　二语学习动态系统理论

2.8.1　二语学习动态系统理论概述

动态系统理论(以下简称 DST)是一种纯数学范式,用来研究时间流逝中的复杂系统,目前已广泛应用于数学、物理学、经济学、气象学、海洋学等多个领域(李兰霞 2011)。应用语言学领域对动态系统理论的研究始于 Larsen-Freeman(1997),当时使用的是"复杂自适应系统"(Complex Adaptive Systems)这一术语,还有学者使用混沌论(Chaos)、动态复杂系统、非线性系统等名称(de Bot 2008)。虽然上述叫法不同,但他们关注的问题相同,即如何动态、系统地研究语言发展。DST 研究的代表人物有 Kees de Bot 和 Diane Larsen-Freeman 等。

传统的二语习得理论把二语发展描绘成:以渐变连续的步骤、从零到近似母语的线性发展过程(de Bot et al. 2005)。而 DST 认为,第二语言学习是基于使用、基于项目的学习,是一个动态、非线性、混沌、不可预测的学习过程,习得和磨蚀(attrition)是语言发展不可分割的两个方面(de Bot 2008)⑧。DST 作为一门新兴理论,试图超越传统科学一直尊奉的简化论(reductionism)理念和均值分析法(means analysis),研

---

⑧　DST 倡导避免使用传统术语—"第二语言习得",因为语言不但会增长,也会衰退,第二语言学习过程是一个布满了峰与谷、进步与倒退的曲线过程(Larsen-Freeman 1997)。

究真实的、充满变异性的第二语言发展(李兰霞 2011)。

根据 DST,语言发展对初始条件和反馈非常敏感。初始条件的细微变化会影响到未来行为的发展。具有不同初始条件的系统行为,不管开始多么相似,都会随时间流逝以指数方式歧变,即通常所说的"蝴蝶效应"(李兰霞 2011)。反馈是语言发展的另一个关键条件。达尔文认为反馈敏感是自然的内在属性:积极反馈促使进化向前,消极反馈使得螺旋上升中的变异出局(Briggs 1992)。

DST 认为语言发展是在使用中,通过自下而上浮现出来的,而频率是引起语言系统自我重组的重要因素,这与基于使用的二语习得理论一致;DST 强调在时间和语境中研究真实语言,这与社会语言学的理念相通;DST 倡导以统一的方式看待语言和语言学习,摒弃了结构主义对言语和语言,以及生成语言学对表现和能力的二元区分。综上可见,DST 是认知语言学、社会语言学、历史语言学、语言演变等研究的整合与升华。

2.8.2 外语学习的学伴用随原则

国内二语习得领域对 DST 研究最有代表性的学者首推王初明。王初明(2009)提出了外语学习的学伴用随原则,其核心观点与 DST 不谋而合。该原则认为,"第二语言学习终究发生在学习者身上,所有影响中介语发展的变量,包括外在的社会文化因素和内在的心理因素,势必依托于学习者而发生变化和形成关联,关联的变量也就自然成为一个复杂的交互系统。此系统因学习者的社会、认知、心理活动而总是处于动态变化之中,当中的一个变量发生变化,会对系统中所有其他变量产生影响,制约着中介语的发展"(王初明 2009:54)。学过的语言知识能否用得出来,用出来的是对还是错,取决于语言知识在学习过程中与什么变量相伴。王初明(2009)将上述语言学习中的关联现象称为"学相伴、用相随"原则,简称学伴用随原则。

在学伴用随原则基础上,王初明(2011b)又提出了语言习得有效路径:互动→理解→协同→产出→习得。"有效的语言习得植根于互动,经历理解、协同、产出等环节,得益于产出与理解紧密结合所产生的协同效应,是学习者经历所有前列四个步骤的自然结果"(王初明 2011b:542)。语言变量(如词、短语、句子、语篇)和非语言变量(如认知、情感、情境、母语文化背景知识)在互动中交互融合,促进理解,引发协同,制约产出。王初明根据互动因素相伴多寡,将语言习得有效路径分成两部分,在协同和产出之间隔开,如图 2.3 所示。他将产出之前有各类互动因素相伴的环节,包括互动、理解和协同称为"学相伴",将产出和产出之后的习得环节称为"用相随",反映了"学相伴"的后效。他进一步指出,所有与所学语言结构互动或相伴的变量可视为学习此结构的背景,影响其后续产出。因此,语言学过能否用出来,关键要看是否与正确的语境变量相伴而学,生成可理解的语言输入,从而促进习得。

$$\underbrace{互动 \rightarrow 理解 \rightarrow 协同}_{学相伴} \rightarrow \underbrace{产出 \rightarrow 习得}_{用相随}$$

图 2.3　语言习得有效路径(王初明 2011b:543)

根据学伴用随理念,犯错的源头多半出现在"学相伴"部分,要使纠错生效,不应只关注产出一个环节。王初明(2011b:544)指出,"在互动中提供正确用法,结合上下文或丰富的语境进行纠错,使得正确用法与语境融合,加深正确用法的理解和协同,纠错可能更易奏效"。然而在现实教学中,教师通常只在产出环节对学生的错误提供反馈,在句子或短语层面上纠错,以纸质方式传递反馈信息,较少利用上下文等语境信息与学生互动沟通,协同效应弱,纠错效果差。"缺少'学相伴'的单一纠错,其促学效果势必要打折扣。

最好的纠错方式是防患于未然,不要等到学生犯错之后才去纠正。要采用积极主动的措施,包括摆脱纠错情结、改变教学思路、把教学重心放在语言习得的源头、创造促进语言习得的互动活动、让学生接触大量的正确语言输入、产出与理解紧密结合、与正确的语言输入协同以此来挤压犯错的空间(王初明 2010,2011b)。按此思路教学,语误必会下降,纠错自然减免。在王初明看来,"错误不是要不要纠正的问题,而是怎样纠正的问题,是怎样提高纠错效率的问题,更是革新教学思路的问题"(王初明 2011b:545)。

基于前期理论研究的成果,王初明(2012,2013)首次提出"读后续写"是一种高效的外语练习和纠错方法。此法挑选一篇外语文章,抹去结尾,截留前面部分,从几百个词到上千词不等,要求学生用外语接着原文续写,补全内容,意思连贯,写得越长越好。读后续写的促学优势在于:理解与产出结合,创造与模仿结合,学习与应用结合;能够释放学生的想象力,培养创新思维;激发表达愿望和交际意愿;有语境配合,在语篇层面上补全或扩展内容;创造性地使用语言来表述新内容。总之,语言模仿、内容创新是读后续写促学的根本。相反,写概要(即要求学生按规定的词数将一篇文章浓缩,但须保留原文的主要内容)虽然可以实现产出与理解的结合紧密,但由于缺乏内容创新,无法激发学生的想象力和表达意愿;内容不变,语言也难改动;受限于外语水平,可选的表达法不多,学生通常照抄原文(王初明 2013)。此外,命题作文虽然有内容创新,可以激发学生的想象力与表达意愿,但由于缺少可供语言模仿的输入样板,因而无法促进协同,学习效果势必会受到影响。

此外,读后续写还是有效的纠错方法。当学习者语言表达能力不济时,可借用读物中的词语,对一些外语用法无把握时,可从原文使用的表达式中得以确认;与读物的内容及语言协同,能够有效提高语言运用的准确性。然而在外语教学中,读后续写应用较少,而且对其促学效果的实证考察,国内外鲜有研究见诸报道。

Wang & Wang(in press)探讨了读后续写是否产生协同(alignment)效应 2 以及该效应如何影响写作。实验材料是一篇结尾不全的故事,有英、汉两个版本。48 名大二学生被分成两组错开读英语和汉语故事,然后用英语续写结尾。实验结果显示:英语故事组的续写语言准确性明显高于汉语故事组,例如,由于英语故事使用过去时态,因而英语故事组在续写时也多半使用过去时态,但汉语故事组在续写时却多用现在时态,时态出现错误;此外,英语故事组在续写时使用了不少阅读材料中的英语表达法,这种协同情况在汉语故事组续写时未曾发生。肖婷(2013)考察了回读阅读材料对续写的影响。实验中,一组受试读完材料后留下原文供续写时参考,另一组读完后收走原文。实验结果显示,在有原文可以回读和没有原文可以回读两种情况下,前者续写语言的错误率明显降低,而续写长度却明显提高,平均每篇多写 171 个英语单词。薛慧航(2013)探讨了阅读材料的趣味性对续写的影响,结果发现,续写有趣故事所产生的协同效应明显高于续写乏味的故事,而且前者续写时出现的错误也明显少于后者。

虽然这些研究取得了初步成果,确定了读后续写的部分功效,但仍存在一些不足有待改进。第一,他们关注的均为学习者续写时的即时反应,而即便学习者在续写时错误率明显降低,也不能充分说明读后续写对二语习得有促进作用。事实上,考察语言知识是否被习得,关键要看学习者能否将在当前学习任务中所掌握的语言知识有效应用于新任务(如 Luria 1961),因此对学习者的语言发展做长期跟踪,同时采用新的写作任务来测量他们的语言水平,是评估读后续写促学效果的可靠途径。第二,现有研究主要关注读后续写对语言准确性的影响,然而准确性只是语言产出表现的一个方面,此外还包括复杂性和流利性,三者相互依存、相互交叉,共同构成了语言使用的动态系统(如 Skehan 1998;Larsen-Freeman 2006),因此将这三个方面同时纳入考察范围,有利于揭示读后续写对外语水平发展的整体作用。

2.9 小结

本章介绍了二语习得七大理论流派的主要内容,尤其关注他们对于错误/纠错的认识,表 2.4 对相关内容作了总结。我们以 Krashen 80 年代的二语习得理论作为分水岭,将之前的理论看作早期理论,其后为近期理论。由于受到 Chomsky 先天论的影响,Krashen 认为纠错的作用是表面性的,它对于改善学习者的二语能力没有实质性的帮助。而在此之前的早期理论则受行为主义的影响,强调要及时纠错以免妨碍语言发展。近期二语习得理论受认知心理学和社会文化理论的交叉影响,对纠错有了更为理性的认识,即在肯定纠错作用的同时,更加关注纠错的效率问题。

虽然不同理论对于语言纠错的认识不同,但还是可以从中找出几点"共识"。首先,目前尚无理论认为语言纠错对于外语学习有害。除生成语言学派外,其他二语习得理论都不同程度地肯定了语言纠错的促学作用。即便生成语言学派否认了负面反馈(如纠错)的有效性,但理论本身并不认为语言纠错会对外语学习产生不利影响。

另外,纠错要发挥作用,其形式必须要适合学习者的发展阶段。根据二语学习加工理论,当反馈形式符合学习者的发展阶段时,它可以加快语言学习的进程,促使语言技能由受控加工向自动加工转化。根据基于使用的二语习得理论,学习者的水平决定了他们能否注意到反馈,并最终决定他们从反馈中的获益程度。此外,社会文化理论也强调,只有当反馈处于学习者的最近发展区,才会对语言发展起到支架作用。

表 2.4 二语习得七大理论流派对错误和纠错的认识

理论流派	代表性理论	对于错误和纠错的认识
行为主义学习理论	对比分析 错误分析	错误是不可容忍的，一旦发展成为一种习惯性行为，会阻碍学习者对于新目标知识的掌握，因此要及时、坚决地纠错，以免妨得语言学习。
基于生成语言学的二语习得理论	监控模型	纠错只能帮助学习者学得语言知识，而对外语实际运用能力的发展没有实质作用。
二语习得加工理论	信息加工模型 思维适应性控制模型 可加工性理论 技能习得理论	纠错不能改变语言习得路径，但可以加快语言习得进程。当反馈形式符合学习者的发展阶段，可促进学习者的语言技能由受控加工向自动加工转化。
基于使用的二语习得理论	构式语法 浮现论	纠错可引起学习者注意形式，从而激发显性学习，产生显性知识，显性知识的积累与巩固是隐性知识发展的前提。
二语习得社会文化理论	调整理论 最近发展区理论 活动理论	当纠错处于学习者最近发展区，可对学习者的语言发展起支架作用，推动"它物/他人调整"向"自我调整"转化。
二语习得互动假说	互动假说补缺假说	负面反馈可引起学习者对语言形式的注意，他们通过分析比较，意识到自己的中介语与目标语之间的差距，从而有意识地在接下来的语言输出中修正自己的语言错误。修正语言形式可以巩固学习者已有的知识表征，还可以加强语言形式提取的过程不仅可以巩固第二语言的发展。
二语学习动态系统理论	学伴用随原则	在互动中提供正确用法，结合上下文或丰富的语境进行纠错，使得正确用法与语境融合，加深对正确用法的理解和协同，纠错可能更易奏效。

第三章 写作理论对于错误及纠错的认识

3.1 引言

一语写作研究与教学对早期二语写作研究与教学的发展产生了重要的影响,二者之间的关系被认为是先后顺序的(chronological)单向(unidirectional)关系:一语写作发展在前,二语写作紧跟其后十余年。但近些年来,学界在对二语写作研究史进行深入考察后指出,一语写作与二语写作之间,以及写作研究与应用语言学研究之间的关系并非想象中那么简单:虽然在理论层面上,一语写作与二语写作对于纠错的认识存在着巨大分歧,但在实际教学中,二者的做法却惊人地相似;而且,二语写作研究理论与实践的结合程度要明显好于一语写作。

本章共分五节,首先介绍一语写作理论对于错误及纠错的看法,随后概述二语写作理论的纠错观,重点分析著名的二语写作理论家和研究者 John Truscott 的纠错论,最后一节归纳本章的主要内容。

3.2 一语写作理论对于错误及纠错的认识

3.2.1 错误反映性格缺陷

19 世纪 70 年代,哈佛大学开设了一门名为"新生写作"(Freshman Composition)的课程(现已改名"一年级写作"(First-Year Composition))。开课的初衷是由于在美国内战结束时,各种不同背景的人进入了大学学习,因为这些人不具备英语写作的基本能力,所以学校开设了这门课程来帮助他们提升写作水平。由于这些学生的作文存在了太多的错误,教师不得不花费大量的时间来纠错,同时还要教授他们如何正确使用自己的母语(Brereton 1995)。在当时,语言纠错

第三章 写作理论对于错误及纠错的认识

被认为是写作教学的首要任务,教师必须认真、耐心地纠正学生作文中的错误(Connors 2003;Santa 2006)。

为了能够写出没有语言瑕疵的优秀作文,学生每天都要进行写作训练,教师则要对他们的作文进行全面批改(Santa 2006)。据统计,在当时,一名顶尖的哈佛大学教授一学年要批改近 20000 份作文[①]。由于批改任务繁重,教师已经没有多余的时间和精力再去思考学生犯错的原因,更不用说去探索语言发展的本质了。此外,教师不能按时完成批改任务在当时也是一个非常普遍的现象(Connors 1997)。

早期的一语写作教学之所以要对错误进行如此彻底的纠正,主要是因为错误在当时被认为是反映了学习者性格上的缺陷。直到 20 世纪 60 年代,这一观点还在影响着一语写作教学,如 Baldwin(1960)在其文章中就将犯错的学生描述为邋遢的(slovenly)、粗心的(careless)。

> Technically he is slovenly and careless. More than three spelling errors to the standard page will occur; he may have more than five major errors in grammar in six-hundred-word essay; he omits apostrophes, ignores the imp-personal pronoun, and uses contractions and colloquialisms. The form of his essay will often stop just short of being insulting.
>
> (*Baldwin 1960*:111)

然而,随着描述性语法(descriptive grammar)逐渐取代规定性语法(prescriptive grammar)[②],人们开始意识到,语法规则不是评判语言使用正确与否的绝对标准,它会因地域的不同、时间的发展而发生变化(Dykema 1940;Gilbert 1922;Leonard & Moffett 1927;McCrimmon 1939;Wykoff 1939)。例如,之前一些不被接受的中式英语表达,如 *long time no see*(好久不见)、*people mountain people sea*(人山人海)、*good good study, day day up*(好好学习,天天向上)等,随着时间的发展及使用范围的扩大,已逐渐被英语国家所接受,并成为日常用语。有鉴于此,早期对于语言错误的过度关注和极端作法不

[①] 在 19 世纪,一篇作文的长度在 50—100 字,这种作文在当时被称为 theme。

[②] 规定性语法是指明确规定出正确的语法规则,而描述性语法侧重于描述和分析人们对于语言的实际应用,力图避免作判断,也就是说,它关注于描述语言是如何被人们使用,而不是规定语言应当如何使用。

仅不合理,也不现实,因为语言使用的标准不是永恒不变的。

3.2.2 错误代表发展

Shaughnessy(1977)出版了《错误与期望》(*Errors and Expectations*)一书,标志着写作领域正在经历着一次范式转变,即之前所采取的严厉的、规定性语法式的错误观逐渐淡出视野,取而代之的是错误发展观。

20 世纪 60 年代初,美国高校采取了"门户开放"(open admission)的招生原则。由于不受学历限制,不同背景的人有了进入高校学习的机会,而且此时又恰逢是人口激增的一代,所以在校学生的人数不仅创了历史新高,而且背景也非常复杂,涉及了不同的种族、社会经济地位和文化背景。其中,有很多人完全不像美国高校之前所招收的学生,他们在当时被称为是"学术界的陌生人"(Shaughnessy 1977)。

They were... strangers in academia, unacquainted with the rules and rituals of college life, unprepared for the sorts of tasks their teachers were about to assign them. Most of them had grown up in one of New York's ethnic or racial enclaves. Many had spoken other languages or dialects at home...

(*Shaughnessy 1977*:2)

这些人进入高校后会参加分班考试,然后进修基础写作课程。然而,他们的写作能力让老师感到头痛,有时甚至会认为他们是一群不可救药的文盲。就在此时,Shaughnessy 作为纽约城市大学基础英语写作课程的主讲教师,正在撰写一本题为《错误与期望》的书,她希望通过这本书,可以帮助那些从事基础写作教学的老师学会诊断并纠正学生的语言错误。

该书所包含的分析、例子和教学材料是 Shaughnessy 通过对 1970—1974 年间在纽约城市大学学习的 4000 名新生的作文进行详细分析后归纳出来的。事实上,对学生的作文进行分析、归类并统计错误的作法并非源自 Shaughnessy。根据 Connors & Lunsford(1988)的调查结果,在 1915—1935 年间出现了很多类似的统计研究,如 Harap(1930)就对 33 项研究进行了综述。但是,Shaughnessy(1977)与前人研究的不同之处在于:她不仅考察错误的类型与频率,还分析了错误的根源。

第三章
写作理论对于错误及纠错的认识

在 20 世纪 60 年代以前,错误意味着"难堪(embarrassment)、无知(illiteracy)、懒惰(sloth)、无礼(disrespect),是社会底层的标志"(Santa 2006:60)。然而,Shaughnessy 在综合了一语、二语习得的社会语言学(如 Cazden, John & Hymes 1972;Davis 1972;Labov 1972;Williams 1970;Wolfram & Fasold 1974)及心理语言学研究后指出,学习者的写作错误并不代表着粗心、无能或者智力缺陷,相反,这些错误是遵循一定规则的方言变异(dialect variations),标志着这些经验不足的写作者和语言学习者,在习得学术英语的过程中所经历的必然发展阶段。此外,Shaughnessy 认为,错误一方面干扰了读者的注意力,同时也伤害到了作者,她将这一现象称为"错误严重"(error gravity)。因此,她建议写作教师在纠错时,一定要深思熟虑,尽可能地帮助这些尚未做好准备的学习者提升学术语言水平和文化技能。为了实现这一目标,Shaughnessy 还在书中详细定义了各种写作错误,给出对应的例子,并对错误的性质进行了解释。

Shaughnessy 的研究在写作界迅速掀起了一场革命,她呼吁人们要以更加宽泛的视野来分析犯错的原因,采用更加有效的策略来帮助学生摆脱错误,从而提升他们的语言水平和写作技能。Shaughnessy 的研究方法对之后的写作研究产生了深远的影响。例如,Bartholomae(1980)在 Shaughnessy 研究的启发下,根据应用语言学的最新成果,提倡在写作研究和教学中系统性地使用错误分析法。Bartholomae 认为,错误分析作为一种教学干预手段,可帮助教师准确地判断出学生已经掌握和没有掌握的语言知识,区分出能力错误(errors of competence)和表现错误(errors of performance)。此外,Kroll & Schafer(1978)也建议在二语写作研究中广泛采用错误分析技术。总之,Shaughnessy 的研究在写作发展史上具有里程碑式的意义,它激发写作研究者和写作教师去深入探索错误根源、找出合理解释,致力于培养学习者的语言水平和写作技能。

3.2.3 错误是一种社会构念

尽管 Shaughnessy 的研究在写作界产出了巨大的影响,但对她的批评同样存在。批评不是源于她对错误所采取的宽容态度,而是源于她的保守,尤其是对于错误的定义及作用的认识,她并没有打破现状,取得突破性的进展。虽然 Shaughnessy 的研究对于错误的根源提出了更敏感、更细致入微的解释,但是其根本目的是要训练学生遵守语法规则,符合社会期望,而至于所谓的语法规则是否永恒不变,所谓的社会期望是否公平合理,则不在她研究所关心的范围之内。事实上,早在20世纪20年代初期,在描述性语法的启发下,写作研究者就曾提出,过度关注学生的错误不仅会导致一种失衡的局面,而且缺乏现实性,因为语言的使用标准会因环境的不同、使用群体的不同而发生变化,况且语言自身也会随着时间的发展而不断演变。但是,这一观点直至《错误与期望》一书的出版才被学界广泛接受,人们从此意识到,错误并非代表着一个人性格上的瑕疵,而且错误也不是一种绝对的事物。

就在《错误与期望》一书出版四年后,Williams(1981)创新性地提出,错误不代表作者能力的缺失,而是存在于读者的大脑中。Williams认为,读者在期望错误、寻找错误的过程中创造出错误。例如,教师在批改学生作文时,总是认为自己有责任纠错,因而会努力找出错误并将其改正。为了使这一观点更具说服力,Williams在论文的结尾部分承认,他在这篇论文中故意犯下了100个常见的语言错误。有趣的是,读者几乎都没有发现这些错误,而是直至看到Williams的提醒才恍然大悟,他们无论如何也不会想到,在这样一个著名的国际学术期刊上发表的文章会出现如此多的语言错误。

Williams的观点迅速得到了一些研究的支持(Anson 2000;Hartwell 1985;Horner 1992,1994;Santa 2006)。这些研究认为,错误是一种构建的人造品(constructed artifact),是一种社会观念,所谓的错误实际上是一种"读者反应"(reader response)。根据上述观点,批判理论学家进一步指出:既然学生的错误只是存在于教师大脑中的一种构念,而非学习者的学术能力问题,那么教师完全没有必要再去关注错误、纠正错误;对于错误问题,无论是教师还是学生,都应该采取一种忽视的态度,即所谓的抵制教学法(pedagogy of resistance)(Santa 2006)。抵制教学法的提出是对Shaughnessy的适应教学法(pedagogy of accommodation)的冲击、挑战与否定。

与此同时,写作领域对于"错误严重"(Shaughnessy 1977)现象的考察仍在继续。Beason(2001:48)在对商务写作的调查后指出,错误确实伤害到了作者的形象。该研究连同早期的几个研究(如Hairston 1981;Wall & Hull 1989)为Shaughnessy的写作教学理念提供了支持。他们认为,抵制教学法使得学生无法接触并掌握学术写作的规范和要求,而对于这些知识,学生具有知情权。抵制教学法剥夺了学生的作文可在社会大环境下接受人们评判的机会,这不论是对于学生个人的发展,还是整个写作教学的发展,都极为不利(Santa 2006)。

3.2.4 纠错:理论与实践的分离

Santa(2006)通过梳理写作领域所开展的"错误"研究后指出,写作理论家的错误观与写作教师的错误观并不一致。同样,Anson(2000)也注意到:一方面,教师根据相关的写作理论不得不强迫自己忽视学生的错误;另一方面,他们在阅读学生作文时,又要反复面临着这样那样的语言问题,这使得他们对于是否纠错感到十分的困惑与矛盾。

纵观一语写作理论的发展,学者们普遍反对纠错,具体观点如下。首先,过度关注错误会产生适得其反的作用(Connors 1985)。Knoblauch & Brannon(1981)指出,目前没有研究可以证明学生能够充分理解教师的反馈,并将反馈信息有效运用于新的写作任务。Sommers(1982:149)曾评价写作教师的反馈是"主观的、怪异的、怀有敌意的、卑鄙的"。她认为,在写作教学中过早地纠正学生的错误,会传递给学生一种负面信息,降低他们的写作热情。Brannon & Knoblauch(1982)指出,反馈会打击学生的自信心,削弱学习动机。

其次,反馈只会促使学生去产出符合教师要求的文章,而非自己真实写作意愿的体现。在纠错过程中,教师成了权威,成了唯一的评判员,他们侵占了本应属于学生自己的权利,其结果势必会影响到对学生归属权(ownership)意识的培养,同时也会大大减弱他们的写作热情(Brannon & Knoblauch 1982;Williams 1981)。

最后,错误是一种构建的社会观念,它存在于读者的大脑。在某一篇文章中出现的错误,会随着时间、空间的转换而被接受为是正确的(Williams 1981)。所以,适应教学法(Shaughnessy 1977)提倡学生遵守语法规则、避免犯错的做法是错误的、不可取的。教师和学生要敢于挑战错误,而不是一味地强迫自己去适应所谓的语法规则以避免犯错。

然而,理论归理论,在现实教学中,写作教师仍将大部分的注意力投在了学生作文语言的准确性上,纠错现象随处可见(Ferris, Liu & Rabie 2011;Lunsford & Lunsford 2008)。Searle & Dillon(1980)在分析了12个小学(4—6年级)教师的作文反馈情况后指出,这些教师作文反馈中的69%是针对语言使用方面的问题。在 Ferris et al. (2011)的调查中,129个受访的大学写作教师均表示在批阅学生作文时,会留意学生的语言错误,其中有23个教师还承认自己对于作文语言的关注程度超过了作文的其他方面。

造成上述理论与实践分离的原因主要有两点。第一,各种课外写作辅助活动,包括写作网站、在线写作实验室、写作手册、写作评分量表等,都将语言使用及语法准确性放在了绝对重要的位置,这势必会引导教师和学生去关注写作语言的准确性。第二,虽然有些教师培训、教师手册建议教师不要过度关注学生的语言错误(如 Bean 1996; Glenn & Goldthwaite 2008; Haswell 1983),但并没有告诫他们要彻底摒弃纠错。总之,写作理论一直在倡导要忽视学生的语言错误,但摆在我们眼前的现实却是,大部分的写作教师仍旧经常性地、大规模地纠错,他们笃信纠错,认为只有将错误灭掉,学生的语言水平才会提高。

3.3　二语写作理论对于错误及纠错的认识

3.3.1　错误:被教学遗忘的角落

不论是在研究还是教学中,一语写作都对二语写作产生了重要的影响。在1992年国际著名二语写作杂志 *Journal of Second Language Writing* 创刊之前,二语写作研究论文的参考文献大部分来自于一语写作,二语写作在当时被认为与一语写作相通(张莹 2006)。Zamel(1982)首次分析了二者的相似之处:(1)二语写作者通过写作来表达思想,所使用的策略与一语写作者相似;(2)学习者的一语写作技能对其二语写作有帮助作用,一语写作技能的缺失在二语写作过程中会有所体现;(3)不熟练的二语写作者与不熟练的一语写作者有类似的表现。此外,一语写作和二语写作相似,还有证据支持。例如,Edelsky(1982)证实,学习者能够将一语写作技巧运用到二语写作中;Gaskill(1986)发现,二语写作与一语写作在修改过程方面有共同之处。

鉴于一语写作和二语写作的诸多相似,二语写作教学在早期主要采用一语写作教学的过程写作法③(Process Approach to Writing)(如 Raimes 1985;Zamel 1976,1982,1983)。根据该方法,写作教学要重点关注学生在写作过程中所经历的学习和创作过程,而非最终成稿。"随着过程写作法的推广,二语写作教学的侧重点由传统的篇章结构、语法、词汇,转向了对写作内容及写作过程的关注。不言而喻,在这场教学范式转变的潮流中,传统的语法纠错受到了极大的冲击"(姜琳 2012b:60)。

过程写作法反对过早地纠正学生的语言错误,理由如下:(1)过程法要求学生对一篇作文作几轮修改,因此教师提供反馈的部分很有可能在下一稿的修改中就直接被删除掉了,在这种情况下,反馈没有发挥应有的作用,相反还浪费了教师的时间和精力;(2)过早纠错会使学生特别关注语法、词汇等语言方面的问题,从而占用了他们的认知资源,无法再对作文的内容、结构和论据充分性等问题作深入的思考;(3)过早纠错会对学生产生误导作用,学生会以为写作教学只关注最终成稿,而非创作过程。

以上三点在一语和二语写作教学中被反复强调,其目的就是要灌输给写作教师"纠错无益"的理念(如 Hairston 1986;Krashen 1984;Sommers 1980,1982;Zamel 1982,1985)。而且,此时又恰逢 Krashen 二语习得理论的强盛之时,该理论极力否认纠错对于二语学习的作用。在教学与理论的双重影响下,语法纠错彻底摆在了被遗忘的角落。所以,在上世纪 80 年代,二语写作教师只对学生前几稿作文的内容和结构提供反馈,直到最后才对语言错误提供反馈,可以说,语言在二语写作教学中是最后一个被想到的问题。Ferris 在其专著《二语学生写作中的纠错》(*Treatment of Error in Second Language Student Writing*)中就对这一现象有过相应的描述:

> ESL writing teachers in the 1980s had been trained to be "process-approach" writing teachers... with attention to

---

③ 过程写作法的创始者是美国西北大学的 Wallace Douglas 教授。该方法视写作为一个有交际目的、复杂、非线性的交互过程,强调学生在预写、起草、修改、重写和编辑等过程中反复、多层次的交互活动。该方法主张将学生带入写作过程,学生不仅仅是通过最后的成稿来了解和改进自己的写作,而是能够进入到写作的各个步骤之中,逐一地了解和学习写作,解决写作中出现的问题,从根本上提高写作水平。将过程写作法应用于英语二语写作教学实践的两位倡导者是美国的 Raimes 和 Zamel。到了 80 年代中期,过程写作法已为二语写作教学全面采用(Ferris & Hedgcock 2005;Johns 1990;Matsuda 2003;Silva 1990)。

language issues... being intentionally postponed to the very end of the composing process. What this often meant, in practice, was that grammar and editing issues were almost never addressed by teachers or their students in the ESL writing classroom.

(Ferris 2002: xi)

事实上,过程写作法反对语法纠错的根本原因在于:二语学习者的注意能力和认知资源有限,无法同时兼顾写作内容和写作语言方面的反馈,因此当两种反馈同时存在时,他们只能选择处理相对简单的语言反馈,而舍弃内容反馈。然而有研究发现,当二语学习者同时接收语言和内容反馈时,他们完全有能力对作文的语言和内容同时进行有效的修改(Ashwell 2000;Fathman & Whalley 1990;Ferris 1997)。这样看来,过程写作法的上述顾虑似乎有些多余。此外,有调查显示,学生期望并重视教师对其作文各方面问题给予反馈(Ferris 1995b;Hedgcock & Lefkowitz 1994,1996;Montgomery & Baker 2007);倘若没有教师的反馈,学生会感到非常的失意和焦虑(Ferris 2002,2003;Ferris & Roberts 2001;Leki 1991;Truscott 1996,1999)。综上可见,过程写作法反对纠错的理由是不成立的;而且,他们只对终稿语言提供反馈的做法,对于二语发展也极为不利,Ferris(2002)对此给出了自己的分析:

One argument for providing at least some grammar feedback on all marked student drafts is that not doing so misses the opportunity to provide feedback at a teachable moment. Since many L2 student writers have significant accuracy problems, they arguably need all the input they can get from their teachers. By refusing to provide such feedback until the very last draft, teachers can severely limit these opportunities for needed input.

(Ferris 2002: 62)

3.3.2 写作教学:平衡好写作技能与语言水平之间的关系

二语写作教学是否可以生吞活剥地搬用一语写作教学法,该问题在二语写作内部一直存在争议,争议的焦点包括:(1)具有非干涉性、表现主义(expressivist)特征的过程写作法是否适合二语写作教学(如 Eskey 1983;Horowitz 1986;Johns 1995;Reid 1994);(2)二语写作者是否同一语写作者相似(Leki 1990a,1990b;Silva 1988,1993,1997;Zamel 1987);(3)同伴反馈、师生面谈(teacher-student conferences)等一语写作活动是否适用于二语写作教学(Ferris 2003;Jacobs, Curtis, Braine & Huang 1998;Patthey-Chavez & Ferris 1997;Zhang 1995,1999)。

事实上,大量研究显示,一语写作和二语写作存在诸多不同(如 Ferris 1994;Hinkel 2002;Hyland 2002;Silva 1993,1997)。Raimes(1983)发现,二语写作者似乎更关注如何把自己的想法写在纸上,而在修改及校订过程中的表现却不尽如人意。Arndt(1987)注意到,一语写作者与二语写作者在词汇运用上存在差异,而且二语写作者无论水平高低,都希望在谋篇布局方面得到反馈。Campbell(1990)指出,二语写作者用在写作准备阶段的时间较少,而对于阅读的依赖程度要远远超过一语写作者。

总之,二语写作者毕竟在思维模式、所处环境以及语言实践等方面都有其独到之处,这就要求二语写作教师对此要有清楚的认识,不应把一语写作教学的方法及策略全盘应用于二语写作教学。此外,二语写作者尚处于第二语言习得的过程中,故需要教师对其语言错误给予适当的关注。二语写作教学应该平衡好培养写作技能与语言水平之间的关系,而不能完全置写作语言准确性于不顾(Eskey 1983;Leki 1990a;Raimes 1987;Taylor 1981;Zamel 1982)。

> It should not be concluded... that engaging students in the process of composing elementates our obligation to upgrade their linguistic competencies. Raimes (1979) talks bout the numerous language skills that ESL composition teachers need to attend to. But what needs to be emphasized is that this obligation should not form the basis of our writing instruction.
>
> (Zamel 1982:207)

目前,尽管二语写作教学赞同纠错,但也承认教师没有必要去纠正一些不重要的语言错误,因为错误是语言学习的必然产物。至于"学生作文中的错误是由读者构建"的这一观点(Williams 1981),二语写作研究者并不认同,例如,无论谁读到 *Yesterday I go to the cinema* 这样的句子,都不会将其看做成正确的句子。由于二语写作错误在性质和根源上要比一语写作错误复杂,这就决定了二语写作研究对于错误的关注程度要高于一语写作。当前,二语写作反馈研究主要围绕以下四个方面展开:(1)反馈对于提高写作语言准确性的短期及长期效果(如 Chandler 2003;Ferris 1995a,1997,2006;Polio,Eleck & Leder 1998);(2)不同反馈形式对于学习者修改原稿作文的影响(Ashwell 2000;Fathman & Whalley 1990;Ferris & Roberts 2001;Sheppard 1992);(3)教师如何纠正学生的错误(Ferris 2006;Ferris et al. 2011;Lee 2008,2009;Montgomery & Baker 2007);(4)学生对于教师反馈的看法(Ferris & Roberts 2001;Leki 1991;Montgomery & Baker 2007)。本书的第五、六章会对这些研究做详细的介绍。

3.4 Truscott 的纠错论

Truscott 是"台湾国立清华大学"的教授,他在认知心理学、二语习得及理论语言学等领域有着深入的研究。然而,真正使其扬名国际学术领域是他对于语法纠错的独到认识。在此之前,虽然有理论学家对纠错持否定的态度,但并未引起人们太多的关注,而学界对纠错问题进行大规模探讨则始于 Truscott 1996 年在 Language Learning 上发表的一篇文章。该文从理论、研究、教学三个层面,论述了二语写作中的语法纠错对于二语写作能力的发展不仅无益,反而有害,建议彻底摒弃。此后十余年,他又陆续发表数篇文章来捍卫自己的观点(如 Truscott 1999,2001,2004,2007,2009,2010),其言论在学界引起了广泛争鸣,并激发了大量的实证研究(如 Bitchener & Knock 2008;Chandler 2003;Ferris 2010;Sheen 2007)。下面,我们具体介绍一下 Truscott 的纠错论。

3.4.1 理论层面

首先,纠错促学的理念违反了二语习得的规律。教师在纠错时,总是以为一条简单的反馈信息就可以帮助学生改正错误,并避免再次犯错。但事实上,语言发展是一个多层次、多变量融合渗透的认知过程,它具有复杂性、动态性、开放性、适应性、自组织性和非线性的特点(Larsen-Freeman 1997)。学习者甚至对于单个语言结构的学习都是"一个循序渐进的过程(gradual process),而非一个偶然的发现(a sudden discovery)"(Truscott 1996:342)。

其次,句法、形态及词汇知识分别以不同方式被习得(Schwartz 1993),因此单一形式的纠错(single form of correction)不可能对上述三个层面都奏效。以句法习得为例,句法知识不是一个个独立知识点的集合体,因此无法通过反馈这种分散提供信息的方式来获得。另外,习得不仅仅只是语言形式的习得,还涉及意义以及与其他语言形式在一起配合使用的问题,甚至还会涉及一些非语言学方面的认知系统。因此,单一形式的纠错无法促进语言知识的综合发展。

再次,根据 Krashen 的监控模型,二语习得遵循自然顺序(如 Krashen 1985),它不由语言结构的难易程度来决定,也不依赖于课堂教学中所授语言内容的次序。这就意味着,当学习者没有做好充分准备时,纠错的促学价值就会大打折扣。因此,教师需要根据学习者当前的发展阶段有选择性地纠错,而这势必会增加教师的工作负担。

最后,纠错不会促进语言习得,而仅仅是产生了一种表面的、暂时性的、不具有语言实际运用价值的知识,Lightbown(1985)将这种表面成功(apparent success)称为"假习得"(pseudoacquisition),Truscott (1996)称之为"假学习"(pseudolearning)。基于一些二语习得理论,Truscott 指出不是所有的学习都是等值的,例如,Ellis(1988)区分了模板学习(modelled learning)和交际学习(communicative learning),Ellis(1993,1994)区分了显性学习和隐性学习,Krashen(1987)区分了习得和学得。除了理论支持外,Truscott 还提供了实验证据来说明假学习的存在,例如,虽然二语学习者对于某些语法规则熟背于心,但在实际运用时,表现却不尽如人意(如 Kadia 1988;Schumann 1978a,1978b;Terrell,Baycroft & Perrone 1987),并且这些语法规则会随着时间的发展而被逐渐遗忘。

3.4.2 研究层面

Truscott 在总结了相关的一语和二语实证研究后指出,对于不同的学习环境(包括一语环境、英语二语环境、英语外语环境、德语外语环境和西班牙语外语环境),针对不同母语背景和不同外语水平的学习者,提供不同形式的纠错反馈(包括直接/间接纠错,全面/选择性纠错),通过不同时间间隔(包括一个季度、一个学期或一年)及不同形式的后测(包括写作、完形填空等)评估,语法纠错均被证实不能促进一语和二语写作能力的发展,具体表现如下。

众多一语写作研究发现,语法纠错不能促进写作能力的发展。Knoblauch & Brannon(1981)及 Hillocks(1986)在对相关实证研究进行综述后指出,不论学习者的类型,不论多少错误被纠正、哪些错误被纠正以及如何纠正,语法纠错总体上不能促进学习者写作能力的发展。

二语写作研究结果与一语写作基本一致。Hendrickson(1978)认为二语写作者的语言错误应该被纠正,但在对相关实证研究进行综合分析后,却没有找到有力的支撑证据。同时,Hendrickson通过实验还发现,全面纠错与选择性纠错的效果没有明显差异,都不能促进二语写作能力的发展。Cohen & Robbins(1976)考察了三名就读于英语高级班的学习者接收书面反馈的情况,结果发现,反馈没有帮助他们提高英语使用的正确率,而导致这一结果的根本原因在于反馈方式不科学。

Semke(1984)的实验包含了四组学生:第一组接收作文内容方面的直接反馈,第二组接收作文语言方面的直接反馈,第三组同时接收作文内容和语言的直接反馈,第四组仅指出语言错误但不提供正确形式,需由学生自行改正。实验结果显示,四组学生在接收了相应的反馈干预后,他们的写作语言准确性并未出现显著差异,但第一组在写作语言流利性以及完形填空后测中的表现比其他三组都要好。Truscott(1996)认为,该结果说明语法纠错对于二语发展不仅无益,反而有害。

Robb,Ross & Shortreed(1986)考察了四种反馈形式的效果:(1)显性纠错,即指出错误并提供正确形式;(2)代码纠错,即使用代码来说明错误的类型与位置;(3)间接纠错,即指出错误的位置,但不提供任何解释;(4)最小批改,即在作文每一行的页边空白处给出对应行的错误数量,但不说明错误的类型及位置。实验结果显示,四组受试在接收了相应的反馈干预后,他们的写作能力并没有出现明显的差异,说明反馈无效。Truscott(1996)指出,如果该实验能包含一个没有接收过任何反馈的对照组,那么结论会更具说服力,尽管如此,当前结论依然有效,理由如下。第一,四种反馈形式不同,理应产生不同的促学效果,而目前这种"无差异"的结果说明反馈不具有促学价值。第二,Frantzen & Rissel(1987)发现,即便告知学习者错误出现的位置,他们还是经常找不出错误,根据这一发现,接收第四种反馈的实验组在一定程度上就可以被看作对照组,由于其他反馈组与第四组在写作能力上不存在显著差异,由此可以说明语法纠错对于外语写作能力的发展没有任何帮助。

Kepner(1991)比较了西班牙语课堂中的两种反馈效果。其中一半学生接收针对语法错误的全面反馈,另一半学生接收有关作文内容的反馈,反馈持续了12周。随后,Kepner对学生作文语言的准确性及内容质量进行了评估,结果发现,在两种反馈下,学生的语法准确性没有明显差异,但接收内容反馈的学生在写作内容方面的表现要明显好于接收语法反馈的学生,这说明语法纠错没有效果。

Sheppard(1992)对比了写作课堂中的两种反馈效果。一组学生接收有关作文语言的代码反馈,然后再与教师面谈;另一组学生接收有关作文内容的代码反馈和面谈。实验结果显示:在语言准确性方面,语言反馈组并没有展示出应有的优势,相反,内容反馈组的表现更胜一筹;在语言复杂性方面,内容反馈组的前后表现没有太大变化,而语言反馈组则表现出倒退的迹象。Sheppard认为,语言反馈组对于教师的反复纠错已经产生了恐惧感,为了避免再次犯错,他们不得不采用比较简单的词汇和结构,这势必会降低写作语言的复杂性。

除了从上述正面角度提供"语法纠错无效"的证据外,Truscott还对现有的一些支持"语法纠错有效"的研究进行了抨击,指出这些所谓的促学证据存在着严重的逻辑问题。第一,这些研究所引用的促学证据不相关。例如,Higgs(1979)只是描述了有效的纠错形式,并未通过实验加以验证。Gaudiani(1981)也只是提供了写作课程的设计模式,并未给出任何有关纠错可以促学的证据。此外,有一些口头纠错研究(如 Chaudron 1977;Herron 1981;Herron & Tomasello 1988;Ramirez & Stromquist 1979;Tomasello & Herron 1988,1989)常常被用来作为纠错有效的证据,但事实上,口头纠错与书面纠错存在很大区别(详见4.2节论述),而且这些口头纠错研究结论的可信度还存在争议(Felix 1981;Holley & King 1971;Lightbown 1983;Plann 1977)。

第二,所引用的证据不可信。Fathman & Whalley(1990)发现,受试在接收反馈后,其修改稿质量要明显好于没有接收反馈的受试。但Truscott(1996)认为,该结果不能作为纠错有效的证据,因为即便受试修改了原文错误也不能说明其外语学习发生了质的变化,相对保险的做法是通过写新作文来检测其语言的发展情况,从而判定反馈的作用。Lalande(1982)比较了写作课堂中的新纠错方式与传统纠错方式的效果,结果发现前者的效果要明显好于后者。但Truscott经过分析后指出,这种差异不是因为新纠错方式降低了错误率,而是由于传统纠错方式提高了错误率而造成的,这也进一步说明了纠错有害。

第三,所采用的测量方法存在问题。Cardelle & Corno(1981)发现,接收反馈的学习者在作业中的表现要明显好于只接收表扬或者没有接收到任何反馈的学习者。但Truscott(1996)发现,学习者的作业主要是语法题,与写作没有直接关系。因此,如果说该研究证明了纠错存在任何促学价值的话,那只能是纠错可以帮助学习者提高做语法题的准确性,而不能说明纠错可以促进写作能力的发展。

3.4.3 教学层面

Truscott(1996)指出,纠错在写作教学中会遇到一些不可避免的现实问题,而且纠错对于发展学生的语言能力和写作课程的质量都具有危害性。

首先,教师是否有能力并愿意纠错,以及学生是否有能力并愿意接受纠错是一个普遍存在的问题。Cohen & Cavalcanti(1990)发现,在很多情况下,外语写作教师并不能发现学生的错误,尤其是对于非本族语者教师,这一现象尤为明显;即便教师发现了错误,也可能无法提供正确的语法解释;再或许,教师提供了正确的语法解释,但学生却不一定能理解。Knoblauch & Brannon(1981)等研究证实,即便是母语学习者也常常不能理解教师的反馈,就算理解了这些反馈,但如果反馈内容过于复杂或者反馈量过大,学生很快就会忘记。

其次,即便学生能够理解教师的反馈,但他们还需要学习动机来进一步消化和吸收这些反馈信息。Cohen(1987)发现,母语学习者根本不会关注教师的反馈,也不会在新的写作任务中运用这些反馈。Radecki & Swales(1988)等研究发现,二语学习者同样不认真对待教师的反馈,相反,更多地将反馈看做成一种惩罚;即便学习者能够将这些反馈应用于新任务,也不会坚持太久,因为当写作教师发生变换后,写作方式和重点也会随之发生改变,在这种情况下,学生很容易就会摒弃前任教师的反馈建议。

再次,虽然针对性纠错一方面降低了教师的批改负担,同时还能通过强化学习者的注意力来达到促学的目的,但现有的一语和二语习得研究(如 Hendrickson 1981；Hillocks 1986；Knoblauch & Brannon 1981)并未发现全面纠错与针对性纠错的促学效果存在显著差异。Truscott 认为导致这一结果的原因主要有两点：(1) 针对性纠错必须符合学习者的发展阶段才能发挥促学作用，然而，教师由于缺少相关二语习得专业方面的知识，在纠错时就会常常忽视这一点，因此纠错效果不明显；(2) 针对性纠错必须保证前后一致(consistent)才能发挥效用，这就需要教师首先找出全部语言错误，然后再辨别出哪些错误需要纠正，避免过度纠错，可想而知，这项工作对于教师的能力、时间和精力都是一个不小的挑战，所以他们常常难以保证纠错的一致性，因而纠错效果不理想。

最后，语法纠错的危害性主要体现在以下三个方面。(1) 纠错会提升学习者的焦虑感，打击自信心，削弱学习动机，从而降低学习效率。这种危害在母语习得研究中已经被多次印证，即没有接收反馈的学习者比接收反馈的学习者具有更加正面的学习态度(Hillocks 1986；Knoblauch & Brannon 1981)。(2) 语法纠错会降低写作语言的复杂性。学习者为了避免再次犯错，会在新的写作任务中使用相对简单的词汇和结构，从而降低了写作语言的复杂性(Kepner 1991；Sheppard 1992)。(3) 纠错占用了教师和学生大量的时间与精力，从而使得他们忽略了写作教学更有意义、更富有创造性的一面(Krashen 1984)。Cohen(1987)发现，由于写作教师将大部分的注意力放在语法错误上，因而不得不减少对于文章结构和内容的关注。王初明(2000)也指出，有的外语写作课几乎成了改错课，为了便于批改，限制作文字数，或让学生在课堂上写，隔周一次，觉得只有帮助学生改正错误，才显示教师的水平，才尽到了教师的责任。可见，这样的写作课已经完全失去了它的意义。

3.4.4 对 Truscott 纠错论的反驳

Truscott 的上述观点迅速得到了回应。其中，Ferris(1999)(The case of grammar correction in L2 writing classes：A response to Truscott(1996)，*Journal of Second Language Writing*)是第一篇抨击 Truscott"纠错论"的文章。该文指出，Truscott 的结论是建立在有限的、自相矛盾的证据之上，因此其结论必然是草率的；在对"纠错是否有效"这一问题作出任何定论之前，需要先进行大量的研究。此后，以 Ferris 为代表的一派学者通过一系列实证研究证明,有效的反馈对于提高某些学习者作文语言的准确性大有裨益(如 Bitchener & Knock 2008;Chandler 2003;Ellis et al. 2008;Ferris 1999,2004;Sheen 2007,2010)。除了实证方面的反驳外,学者们还陆续找出了 Truscott"纠错论"中的一些漏洞,具体如下。

第一,Truscott 认为,教师在纠错时往往会忽视学习者的发展阶段,而在学习者没有做好准备的情况下,纠错不具有促学价值。然而,Bitchener & Ferris(2012)对此观点进行了反驳。他们认为,学习者在很多情况下都已准备就绪,完全能够学习相关的目标结构,而这一结果的实现不依赖于教师是否懂得中介语发展机制,也不依赖于教师是否理解、同意或者反对加工理论中有关"陈述性知识在经过练习(包括纠错)后可转化为自动化知识"的观点。此外,外语教师根据其教学经验很容易就会辨认出自己学生的外语水平,识别出他们的问题之处以及最常犯的语言错误。即便是教学经验不足的教师,也可以通过查阅市面上专门为不同外语水平学习者设计的各种参考书,找出哪些语言形式和结构适合自己学生当前的外语发展阶段。

第二,Truscott 认为,单一的纠错形式不可能对句法、形态及词汇三个层面的习得都奏效。该观点虽有一定的道理,但我们不能因为教师没有对不同类型的错误提供适合的反馈形式,就完全否定纠错的价值。事实上,大量研究已经证实,反馈可以成功地纠正某些类型的语言错误,而且学习者语言准确性的提高,不因反馈形式的不同而产生明显差异。

第三,Truscott 否认全面纠错的有效性,这不无合理之处,因为全面纠错的方法确实存在弊端。例如,实验人员无法保证对每一处语言错误都提供反馈,而这种非系统性的纠错极大地削弱了实验结果的可信度;另外,学习者的注意资源和加工能力有限,很难消化和吸收全部反馈,因而容易造成反馈研究的"高耗低效"现象。与之相比,针对性纠错更符合外语学习和认知发展的规律,它通过强化学习者的注意力,进而推动语言知识的吸收与内化。然而,Truscott 同样否认针对性纠错的效果,并声称有 Hendrickson(1981)的研究为证。事实上,已有大量的口头和书面反馈研究证实了针对性纠错的效果,本书在第四、六章对此有相关的介绍。

在过去的 20 年间,Truscott 始终坚持"纠错无用"的观点,尽管他也曾在文章中多次暗示过,纠错可能会在少数几种情况下奏效,但不管他是否会将这些少数情况看做"反馈促学"的重要证据,对于大部分的二语习得、二语写作理论学家和实证研究人员来说,他们更关心的是为纠错搭建一个站得住脚的理论平台,同时深入探讨纠错在实际教学中的效果问题(Bitchener & Knock 2010a,2010b;Ferris 2010;Hartshorn et al. 2010),这也正如王初明(2011b:545)所言,"错误不是要不要纠正的问题,而是怎样纠正的问题,是怎样提高纠错效率的问题,更是革新教学思路的问题"。

3.5 小结

本章介绍了一语、二语写作理论对于语法纠错的认识,并重点分析了 Truscott 的纠错论。一语写作对于二语写作理论、研究及教学的发展产生了重要的影响。一语写作理论对于错误的认识经历了几次范式的转变,由最初的"错误反映了性格缺陷,应全面纠正"到"错误反映了学习者处于发展之中,要帮助他们避免犯错",再到"错误是一种社会观念,存在于读者的大脑,应抵制纠错",这一系列理念上的变化与应用语言学科的发展密不可分。然而,理论上的变化似乎对于写作教学没有产生丝毫的影响,一语写作教师始终秉持着"有错必究"的信念,坚信语法错误是写作教学的重要组成部分。

在过去 20 年间,二语写作对于纠错的研究取得了一定的进展,这要归功于 Truscott(1996)文章的发表。在此之前,学者们从未质疑过纠错的促学价值,他们将"纠错可以促学"看做天经地义的事情,因此相关研究的数量非常有限。然而,Truscott(1996)从理论、研究和教学三个层面,论述了二语写作中的语法纠错不仅无益,反而有害,建议彻底摒弃。自此,理论学家、实证研究者、教师们才恍然意识到,自己长期以来所信奉的真理(即纠错可以促学)并非可靠,他们需要开展研究来证实纠错的作用。Truscott(1996)本想唤起二语写作教师摒弃纠错,然而却引发了学界对于纠错问题的大讨论,并催生了众多支持"反馈促学"的研究,这着实是一件很讽刺的事(Ferris 2010)。目前,二语写作教学与二语写作理论遥相呼应,对纠错采取了理性的态度,即二语写作者的知识结构和经验基础与一语写作者不同,他们除了会犯和一语写作者类似的错误之外,还会犯下更多由于母语负迁移和二语知识缺失所造成的错误。因此,恰当的干预(即纠错)可帮助他们摆脱错误,促进二语写作水平的发展。

纵观整个写作领域,每一次具有里程碑意义的发展似乎都与高校学生结构的变化有着直接关系。例如,哈佛大学《一年级写作》课程的开设与美国内战后高校学生背景的复杂化密不可分,Shaughnessy(1977)专著的出版与20世纪60年代美国高校采取开放式招生原则有关。如今,具有多种语言背景的学习者成为了二语写作课堂的主体,这一变化也必将会引起写作界的又一次革命。

第四章 反馈研究综述

4.1 引言

书面反馈研究发展至今取得了一定的成果,已有百余篇(部)论文(专著)发表(出版)。然而,与口头反馈研究相比,书面反馈研究的发展还相对滞后,原因主要包括以下三个方面:(1)外语学习的目的是实现语言使用自动化,即表现为流利、正确的口语交际,因此外语教学长期以来存在重口语、轻书面的现象,在这种情况下,口头反馈自然比书面反馈更易引起人们的关注;(2)在书面反馈研究之初,学者们从未质疑过它的促学价值,他们坚信反馈可以促学,因而将注意力投向了反馈在实际教学中的效率问题,这一状况一直持续到Truscott(1996)文章的发表,该文掀起了一场有关书面纠错问题的革命,在学界引发了巨大反响;(3)书面反馈的内容比口头反馈复杂,涉及了写作的方方面面,如内容、结构、语法、词汇等等,而口头反馈内容集中,主要针对语言问题而提出,这势必决定了书面反馈研究在二语习得领域的边缘地位(Leki 2000)。

口头反馈研究在研究理念、数据收集等方面都相对规范和完善,为书面反馈研究提供了不少借鉴。例如,早期书面反馈研究主要采用全面纠错的范式,即对学习者作文中的每一处语言错误都提供反馈,然后通过让学习者写修改稿和新作文来观察其语言发展,继而判定反馈的作用(如Chandler 2003;Ferris 2006)。但事实上,实验人员无法保证对每一处语言错误都提供反馈,而这种非系统性的纠错极大地削弱了实验结果的可信度。此外,学习者的注意资源和加工能力有限,很难消化和吸收全部反馈,故容易造成"高耗低效"的研究局面。此时,在口头反馈研究成果的启发下,书面反馈研究转而开始关注针对性纠错对于消除语言错误、促进外语发展的作用,具体做法是,针对学习者作文中的一两类语言错误(如冠词、介词、一般过去式等错误)提供系统性的反馈,然后通过后测、延迟后测对他们的外语发展做长期跟踪。在这一思路的引导下,书面反馈的促学效应在很多实证研究中都得到了证实(如 Bitchener & Knoch 2008;Sheen 2007,2010)。

鉴于口头反馈研究对书面反馈研究的重要影响,我们有必要先了解一下口头反馈研究的情况,包括取得的成果及存在的问题,然后再回顾书面反馈研究的发展历史,而在此之前,我们先对口头反馈与书面反馈的区别作简要分析。

4.2 口头反馈与书面反馈的区别

根据 Sheen(2010)的研究成果,本节对口头与书面反馈的区别作简要的归纳和分析:(1)口头反馈的纠错意图不一定会被感知(如重铸),而书面反馈的纠错意图一定会被意识到;(2)口头反馈是及时提供,而书面反馈通常是延迟提供;(3)口头反馈大多针对个体学习者提出,但其他听者也可以获取相关信息;相反,书面反馈的信息不易为其他学习者获取,除非进行作文传阅;(4)口头反馈需要学习者做出即时的认知加工和比较,而书面反馈不会给学习者造成太多的认知和记忆上的负担;(5)口头反馈可以促成学习者与教师间的交互协商,而书面反馈是单向的,难以实现双方的互动协商;(6)书面反馈的内容比口头反馈复杂,书面反馈可针对写作的不同方面提出,如整体质量、语法准确性、句法复杂性、词汇、写作内容、标点拼写、语篇连贯和语言流利程度等,而口头反馈主要是在互动协商中,针对说话人的语言问题而提出。

基于上述分析,反馈的效果可能会受到所处媒介(口头 VS 书面)的影响,然而,目前有关口头和书面反馈的对比研究屈指可数。Doughty & Varela(1998)在实验中同时提供了口头和书面反馈,但是没有区分二者的效果,所以学习者所取得的进步很难说是受益于口头反馈、书面反馈,还是二者的共同作用。Bitchener et al.(2005)发现,当书面反馈附加上五分钟的一对一面谈后,其效果明显好于单纯的书面反馈。这说明,将口头反馈与书面反馈结合可优化学习者对反馈的加工过程,强化反馈的促学效应。但是,该结果无法区分书面反馈与口头反馈各自的效果。Sheen(2010)比较了口头反馈与书面反馈对于冠词习得的作用,共涉及了四种反馈形式:口头重铸、口头元语言反馈、书面直接反馈和书面元语言反馈。实验结果显示,除口头重铸无效外,其他反馈均能帮助学习者提高冠词使用的正确率,这说明反馈自身的显性程度而非所处媒介决定了他们的促学效果。

4.3 口头反馈研究综述

口头反馈研究的发展主要受到了注意假说和互动假说的影响。根据注意假说,二语学习进步的充要条件是学习者有意识地注意到语言形式及其意义,而反馈恰好激发了学习者的注意。根据互动假说,在意义协商的过程中,反馈可以将输入、学习者的选择性注意及输出有机地结合在一起。综上可见,口头反馈促学外语有着坚实的理论基础。

在实证研究方面,近年来涌现出大量在课堂或实验室环境下,通过面对面或计算机媒介的交互方式,针对不同教学背景、不同年龄阶段学习者所开展的口头反馈实验,主要研究内容包括:(1)不同形式反馈的出现情况(Lyster 1998,2001;Lyster & Ranta 1997);(2)学习者对于反馈的感知程度(Carpenter, Jeon, MacGregor & Mackey 2006;Mackey, Gass & McDonough 2000);(3)反馈的整体效果(Mackey, Oliver & Leeman 2003;McDonough 2005;Oliver & Mackey 2003);(4)重铸的效果(Loewen & Philp 2006;Nabei & Swain 2002;Nicholas, Lightbown & Spada 2001;Philp 2003);(5)学习者对反馈的反应(uptake)情况(Loewen 2004;Panova & Lyster 2002);(6)不同反馈形式的效果对比(Ammar & Spada 2006;Carroll & Swain 1993;Ellis, Loewen & Erlam 2006;Lyster 2004)。

这些口头反馈研究的结果可以归纳为以下四点:(1)重铸是课堂教学中最常见的反馈形式(Lyster & Ranta 1997;Sheen 2004);(2)重铸有利于二语发展(Han 2002;Mackey & Philp 1998);(3)反馈形式不同,作用亦不同;总体上,显性反馈比隐性反馈更有效(Ellis et al. 2006),提示反馈(prompts)比重铸更有效(Ammar & Spada 2006;Lyster 2004);(4)学习者对反馈的反应会受到反馈形式(Loewen & Philp 2006)和环境因素(Lyster & Mori 2006)的影响。

如今,"口头反馈能否促进二语发展"已不再是互动研究的核心问题,他们更关注的是哪些因素会影响到反馈的效果,例如:(1)学习者的内在认知和情感因素(如 Iwashita 2003; Mackey & Philp 1998; Philp 2003; Sheen 2007);(2)外部环境因素,如互动活动的性质和教学环境等(如 Lyster & Mori 2006; Oliver & Mackey 2003; Révész 2009; Révész & Han 2006; Sheen 2004);(3)反馈提供者的个体因素(如 Gurzynski-Weiss 2010)。

口头反馈的具体形式包括理解校验、确定核准、澄清请求、元语言反馈、重述和重铸等(详见表2.3)。其中,重铸,如句(1)所示,在过去的十多年间受到了最为广泛的关注,出现了不少相关的实证研究(如 Lyster & Ranta 1997; Mito 1993; Ortega & Long 1997)、综述研究(Ellis & Sheen 2006; Long 2007; Nicholas et al. 2001)和元分析研究(Keck et al. 2006; Li 2010; Lyster & Saito 2010; Mackey & Goo 2007; Russell & Spada 2006)。重铸之所以会引起学界如此浓厚的兴趣,一方面是因为它在现实教学中最为常见,另一方面在于它的促学潜质。

(1) NNS: *Where do he work?
　　 NS: Where does he work? ←
　　 NNS: Yeah.
　　 NS: A local hospital.

从认知心理角度看,重铸具有以下三个特点:首先,重铸是基于学习者的语言输出而形成的,因此学习者可以部分或全部地理解重铸的内容,这样他们就可以将额外的注意资源转向重铸中新的语言信息,从而促进形式-功能的映射;其次,重铸总是发生在错误的语言输出之后,这势必增加了重铸中正面证据的突显度,故容易引起学习者的注意,而这种注意可以激发认知比较,学习者通过分析、比较自己的语言输出与对方的语言输出,从而注意到中介语与目标语之间的差距,一旦注意到差距,他们便会有意识地学习目标语言形式;最后,重铸的纠错意图相对隐性,它可以在不打断对话,保证学习者始终关注交际意义的同时,注意到语言形式问题(Long 1996, 2007),为实现"注意形式"(focus-on-form)构建了有利的条件。

从社会文化角度看,人本质上是社会的,个体认知能力的发展是通过社会互动来实现的(Vygotsky 1962,1978)。在最近发展区内,人各种能力的发展需要从他人那里得到支架式的帮助才能得以实现,而重铸恰好能提供外语学习者这种帮助。通过与本族语者互动协商,学习者可以利用重铸中的语言形式来表述自己现有二语水平还无法表述的概念。由于学习者在互动中不是被动的接收者,而是主动的参与者,因此重铸可以促进其二语能力的发展。

以上,我们从认知心理和社会文化的角度分析了重铸促学的理论基础,但理论的说服力需要有实证研究来支撑。下面,我们具体介绍三类重铸研究:(1)重铸作为语言输入的促学效果;(2)学习者对重铸的注意情况;(3)重铸所引发的语言输出情况。

4.3.1 语言输入研究

在过去的 20 年间,互动研究把重铸作为考察重点,将其促学效果与其他形式的输入作了系统比较。例如,Mito(1993)、Ortega & Long(1997)、Inagaki & Long(1999)、Iwashita(2003)比较了重铸和正面证据对于习得若干个语言特征的短时效应,实验结果总体表明,虽然重铸比正面证据的促学效果显著,但至少总会有一个语言特征,不论是在重铸还是在正面证据的刺激下都不能被成功习得。例如,Ortega & Long(1997)比较了重铸和正面证据对习得两个西班牙语结构—宾语话题化和副词位置—的影响。30 个学习西班牙语的成人二语学习者被分成两个实验组和一个对照组,实验采用前测—干预—后测的设计模式。前测结果表明,30 个受试完全不了解这两个西班牙语结构。随后,两个实验组在互动中分别接收了重铸或正面证据,而对照组则不予任何输入。后测结果表明,对照组没有习得这两个结构,两个实验组都没有习得"宾语话题化"这一结构,但重铸组对于"副词位置"的习得情况要明显好于正面证据组。根据上述实验结果,Long et al.(1998)建议未来研究可以将后测时间再延迟一些,或者采用纵向研究。

Carroll & Swain(1993)、Carroll(2001)、Ellis et al.(2006)比较了重铸和元语言反馈的促学效果。元语言反馈是一种显性负面反馈,是对学习者语言输出中的错误进行评论,如 *You need past tense*。实验结果总体表明,元语言反馈比重铸更能促进语言特征的习得。例如,

Ellis et al.(2006)比较了元语言反馈和重铸对于习得英语一般过去式的作用。34个在新西兰学习的东亚裔学生被分成两个实验组和一个对照组,实验采用前测—干预—后测的设计模式。前测结果表明,34个受试对英语一般过去式已有一定的掌握。随后,对于互动中出现的目标错误,一个实验组接收重铸,另一个接收元语言反馈,而对照组不予反馈。后测包括口试和语法测试,前者考察隐性知识,后者考察显性知识。后测结果表明,元语言反馈组对英语一般过去式隐性及显性知识的掌握情况要明显好于重铸组。Ellis等人由此认为,对于实验前受试就已经有所掌握的语言结构,如一般去式,显性负面反馈(即元语言反馈)比隐性负面反馈(即重铸)更能促进相关隐性及显性知识的发展,但同时他们也承认,该结论不一定适合于新的语言结构,即受试在实验前完全没有接触过的结构。

Pica(1988)、Pica et al.(1989)、Linnell(1995)、Lyster & Ranta(1997)、Anton(1999)比较了重铸和澄清请求对二语习得的影响。澄清请求需要学习者对其语言输出中的问题给予澄清,如 Can you repeat。实验结果总体表明,澄清请求能够促使学习者修正错误的语言输出,而重铸却不能,故质疑重铸的促学效果。然而,有研究对这一结论的有效性提出了反驳意见,具体可归纳为以下两点。

第一,Gass & Varonis(1994)认为,立即修正错误并不意味着语法重建已经开始,由此推理,没有做出立即修正也不等于语法重建还没有发生。不少研究发现,重铸对二语发展的促进作用是独立于学习者的即时反应而存在的。例如,Mackey & Philp(1998)考察了互动对于习得英语问句形式的影响,结果发现,虽然受试没有在重铸之后修正错误的问句形式,但他们对于目标结构的掌握有了明显的提升。因此,仅仅由于学习者没有在重铸之后修正错误,就否定重铸的效果是不成立的。Long(2007)认为,重铸对二语发展的促进作用不是即时的,而是延迟的,不应该仅凭学习者没有做出即时的口头修改,就对重铸的功效大打折扣。

第二,Oliver(1995)指出,在两种情况下,学习者没有真正的机会在重铸之后修正错误的语言输出。一种情况,本族语者提供重铸以后,通过停顿留给学习者修正错误的机会,但学习者会以为对方只是需要自己做出简单的 Yes 或 No 的意思确认即可,如句(2)所示。另一种情况,本族语者为学习者提供重铸以后,并没有通过停顿留给对方修正错误的机会,而是继续自己的话题,如句(3)所示。

(2) NNS: what we do with it?
　　 NS: what do we do with it? ←
　　 NNS: yeah.

(3) NNS: what we do with it?
　　 NS: what do we do with it? ←
　　 Uh let's see well we could talk about the purpose if you want.

综合以上论述,重铸促学之谜仍未彻底揭开,还需进一步的探索。此外,虽然重铸为学习者提供了正面和负面的语言输入,但这些输入能否为学习者所注意,直接关系到重铸的效果。那么如何测量学习者的注意情况呢？接下来,我们介绍相关的研究方法和结果。

4.3.2 "注意"研究

根据互动假说,学习者对语言形式的注意程度,决定了语言输入能在多大程度上转化为摄入,这与 Krashen 的输入假说不同。Krashen 认为,只要学习者注意到可理解性输入的意义,就可以保证习得的发生。而互动假说则强调只有注意到形式,习得才会发生(Schmidt 1990,1994;Sharwood Smith 1981,1993),其证据来自于加拿大法语浸入式教学。在这种教学环境中,虽然学习者使用法语的流利性、自信心和能力都有了很大提高,但他们对于某些语言结构的掌握情况仍不理想,原因就在于他们缺少对相关形式的注意。

众所周知,学习者加工处理语言输入的能力有限,很难同时兼顾意义和形式。VanPatten(1990)发现,学习者尤其是初学者,在关注意义的同时,很难再关注形式;同样,当他们关注形式时就很难获取意义。在这种情况下,以意义协商为基础的互动活动,为学习者加工语言信息提供了所需的时间,保证了他们能在处理信息内容的同时关注语言形式。随后,学习者通过认知比较,意识到自己当前对于目标结构的掌握情况与目标语之间还存在差距,一旦注意到这种差距,他们便会有意识地学习目标结构,从而增强对它的掌握。

Long(1996)明确指出,"注意"是"人际互动促进二语习得"的媒介。当前对"注意"的测量方法有内省法(introspective methodology)、出声思考(think-aloud)、自我话语(private speech)、学习日记(learning journal)等。其中,内省法最为常用,包括受激回忆(stimulated recall)和即时回忆(immediate recall);前者是离线(offline)测量,后者是在线(online)测量。

Mackey et al.(2000)第一次使用受激回忆的方式考察了学习者对于互动中重铸的注意程度,实验设计如下:首先,对学习者和本族语者的互动过程进行录像;然后,让学习者立即观看该录像,当录像播放至本族语者就学习者的错误语言输出提供重铸的时候,实验人员会立即暂停播放,并要求学习者回忆出当时对该重铸的理解;最后,通过考察学习者的口述,推断其对于重铸的注意程度,具体说来,如果学习者正确说出了一个重铸的焦点(focus),表明他/她注意到了该重铸,反之则没有注意到。

Mackey等人的研究将互动中的重铸分为四类:语音重铸、形态-句法重铸、词汇重铸、语义重铸。由于语义重铸的数量较少,所以暂且不考虑学习者对语义重铸的注意程度。对于语音重铸、形态-句法重铸和词汇重铸,学习者的平均注意率分别为39%、18.5%和74.5%。该结果表明,学习者对词汇和语音重铸的注意程度,要明显高于形态-句法重铸。导致这一结果的原因主要有两个:(1)与形态-句法类型的错误相比,词汇、语音类型的错误更会影响意思的表达,所以相关的重铸更容易引起学习者的注意;(2)与形态-句法重铸相比,语音、词汇重铸更简短,所以更容易被注意到,例如,Carpenter et al.(2006)发现,语音重铸的平均长度为3个单词,词汇重铸的平均长度为6个单词,形态-句法重铸的平均长度为10个单词。

使用受激回忆来考察学习者的"注意"情况,需要明确以下两点:首先,学习者的口述过程涉及了察觉(detection)和信息的再加工,因此受激回忆所考察的是比"注意"高一等级的认知加工过程;此外,由于受到工作记忆的限制,学习者不能完全复述出所注意到的事物,因此口述失败并不等于注意的失败。

Philp(2003)使用即时回忆考察了学习者对重铸的注意程度,实验设计如下:在实验人员与学习者的互动中,实验人员就学习者语言输出中的错误提供重铸,在重铸之后,实验人员立即通过声音提示(如拍击两下桌子)中断对话,学习者听到提示声音后,要马上重复发生在提示声音前的一句话。该方法在保证互动正常进行的同时,考察了学习者对重铸的注意。同样,由于受到工作记忆的限制,学习者也不能完全复述出所注意到的事物。Philp 还发现,过长或过于复杂的重铸都会增加学习者注意资源的负荷,从而提升了即时回忆的难度。

总之,内省法是测量"注意"的一种保守方法,它不可能捕捉到所有被学习者注意到的事物,但是这种方法适合检测互动中的注意情况。Swain(2005)指出,内省法不仅是一种收集数据的方法,同时也是一种学习方法,因为学习者的口述过程涉及了对语言输入的理解和再塑(reshaping),可见,输出为语言学习提供了条件。接下来,我们介绍重铸所引发的语言输出情况。

4.3.3 语言输出研究

输出对语言习得的作用不容忽视。Swain(1985)对加拿大法语浸入式教学的研究发现,仅有可理解性输入和交际互动仍不能帮助学习者习得目标语形式,学习者需要语言输出的机会,因为输出能迫使他们在句法层面加工语言,进而注意到形式与意义的关联。基于上述分析,Swain 提出了输出假说,总结了输出的重要功能(Swain 1995,2005)。早期的输出假说从信息加工的视角分析了输出中形式注意与形式加工的过程(Swain & Lapkin 2002);后期的输出假说借鉴社会文化理论的中介思想(mediation)和支架概念,强调合作中的对话可以创造反馈和互助机会,使学习者在合力解决问题的协商过程中内化、习得语言知识(Swain 2005;Swain & Lapkin 2007)。

根据互动假说,反馈不仅能激发学习者关注形式,还可提供语言输出的机会,尤其是修正语言输出的机会,如句(4)所示。倘若学习者在修正语言输出的过程中产出了一个高级、准确的语法结构,根据结构启动(structural priming)效应(如姜琳 2009,2012a),他们就很可能会在接下来的语言输出中,重复使用这一高级结构,从而促进外语学习的进步。修正语言输出的过程不仅可以巩固学习者已有的知识表征(Nobuyoshi & Ellis 1993),还可以加强语言形式提取的自动化(de Bot 1996),促进二语习得。

(4) NNS: * What the boy doing?
　　　NS: What?

NNS: What is the boy doing? ←

McDonough 等一批学者首先将结构启动引入互动研究,并且发现,结构启动在人际互动促进二语发展的过程中起到了重要的作用。McDonough & Mackey(2006)将发生在重铸之后的修正的语言输出分成两类:一类是学习者对重铸的立即重复,我们称其为"重复的语言输出",如句(5)所示;另一类是由重铸所启动的、新的、符合目标语结构的语言输出,我们称其为"启动的语言输出",如句(6)所示。

(5) NNS: when it happen?
　　NS: When did it happen?
　　NNS: When did it happen? ←
(6) NNS: why he hit the deer?
　　NS: Why did he hit the deer? He was driving home and the deer ran out in front of his car.
　　NNS: What did he do after that? ←

McDonough & Mackey(2006)比较了重铸、重复的语言输出和启动的语言输出,对泰国学生习得英语问句形式的影响。58 个英语专业的泰国大学生被分成实验组和对照组,实验采用前测—干预—后测的模式。对于互动中出现的问句形式错误,实验组接收了重铸干预,对照组则不予任何反馈。后测结果显示,受试对英语问句形式的习得情况,分别与重铸、启动的语言输出之间有着显著的相关性,而与重复的语言输出之间没有显著相关性。该结果表明,虽然启动的语言输出和重复的语言输出,都是发生在重铸之后的修正的语言输出,但二者对受试习得英语问句形式的作用却完全不同,只有被启动的语言输出才能促进外语学习。

McDonough(2006)使用同盟者脚本技术,考察了互动中的结构启动现象,涉及的目标结构是英语介宾和双宾结构。实验中一名是真受试,即母语为汉语或韩国语的高水平英语学习者;另一名是假受试,即实验人员,但真受试对此并不知情。实验规定两名受试轮流描述图片,当一方描述时,另一方要根据其描述找出相应的图片。假受试表面上是在描述图片,实际上是朗读事先写好的脚本,这一过程相当于呈现启动句,而接下来真受试向对方描述图片的过程相当于产生目标句。实验结果显示,当启动句是介宾结构时,存在结构启动效应,当启动句是双宾结构时,则不存在启动效应。McDonough 认为,造成双宾结构启动失败的根本原因在于受试还没有完全建立起该结构的句法表征,他们对双宾结构的掌握还只是局限于特定语境中的特定动词。此外,姜琳(2012a)指出,实验任务的性质是造成双宾结构启动失败的另一个重要原因。该实验任务是对话双方轮流描述图片,这种互动是机械的、缺少协商的,并非真正意义上的人际互动。互动强则协同强,互动弱则协同弱(王初明 2010),因此这样的实验任务自然会削弱结构启动效应。

4.3.4 研究不足及未来展望

虽然重铸研究取得了长足的发展,但仍存在一些问题有待解决。Long(2007)对负面反馈尤其是重铸研究,提出了 11 个需要改进的方向(参阅戴曼纯、魏淑兰(2007)):(1)定义要清晰、一致、可操作;(2)要区分语言习得和语言运用;(3)要注意提供反馈的时机;(4)事后要询问受试是否注意到重铸的纠错目的;(5)书面反馈的效果还需进一步研究;(6)重铸促学效果的持久性和稳定性还需进一步验证;(7)针对不同年龄学习者的重铸研究,其结论是否可靠,还需要确定;(8)重铸的可靠性和有效性还没有得到充分重视;(9)负面反馈效果的概括性还有待检验;(10)正面输入和负面反馈的相对有效性还有待研究;(11)有研究发现负面反馈(尤其是重铸)比正面输入更有效,导致这一效果差异的原因还有待探讨。

4.4 书面反馈研究综述

据统计,书面反馈研究目前已有百余个,包括观察性研究、调查性研究、准实验性研究、综述/元分析研究,每个类型下面又包含了一些具体的研究题目,如表 4.1 所示。其中,前三种类型属于原创性研究,第四种属于整合性研究。本书第五章将对观察性、调查性研究的发展情况作具体介绍,第六章将探讨准实验性研究所取得的成果及存在的问题。

表 4.1　书面反馈研究分类

研究类型	研究题目
1. 观察性研究	(1) 语言反馈在教师作文反馈中的比例 (2) 学生写作语言的错误类型 (3) 教师纠正的语言错误类型
2. 调查性研究	(1) 学生对反馈的态度 (2) 教师对反馈的态度
3. 准实验性研究	(1) 控制型研究（二语习得派） (2) 纵向课堂研究（二语写作派）
4. 综述/元分析研究	(1) 综述研究 (2) 元分析研究

在这100多项书面反馈研究中，有三项研究具有里程碑式的意义，对于整个书面反馈领域的发展起到了极大的推动作用。首先是Harap(1930)。Harap在综合了前人研究成果的基础上，详细分析了学生常犯的106种语言错误，并将这些错误归纳成八类。可以说，该研究掀开了书面反馈研究的第一页。其次是Cohen & Robbins(1976)。它是第一个书面反馈实验性研究，对于反馈实验的发展起到了奠基石的作用。最后是Truscott(1996)。它虽为综述研究，却在书面反馈领域掀起了一场革命，改变了人们最初对于反馈作用的理想化认识。在此之前，学者们从未质疑过书面反馈的促学价值，他们将"纠错利于学习"看做为天经地义的事情。然而，Truscott(1996)从理论、研究和教学三个层面，论述了二语写作中的语法纠错不仅无益，反而有害，建议彻底摒弃，该言论在学界引起了广泛争鸣，并激发了大量的实证研究，促成了书面反馈领域长达15年的黄金发展期。

书面反馈是一个充满活力、生机勃勃的研究领域，引发了外语教师和研究人员的浓厚兴趣，相关文章在国际著名二语写作期刊*Journal of Second Language Writing*上的下载和引用率均居榜首。近年来出现的一些理论和实证研究，对于改进实验方法、创新研究问题、提高教学质量、完善教师培训等都大有裨益。为了继续保持良性发展、持续繁荣的态势，实现书面反馈研究的更大突破，各研究间的交流与借鉴实属必要。在这种情况下，本节在Ferris(2012)研究成果的基础上，选取了80个代表性研究，制成了书面反馈研究年表（见表4.2)，并简要概述每个研究的主要发现。通篇阅读该年表不仅可以增强对于书面反馈研究领域的宏观把控能力，同时还可以加深认识各研究间的联系、交叠、差异、甚或冲突。

表 4.2 书面反馈研究年表

年代	文献	主要内容
1930	Harap, H. 1930. The most common grammatical errors. *English Journal* 19: 440-446.	This brief paper provides a composite profile of students' written and oral errors and is based upon 33 earlier studies dating from 1908—1927. 106 error types were described under eight major sub-categories.
1967	Corder, S. P. 1967. The significance of learners' errors. *International Review of Applied Linguistics* 5: 161-170.	Corder's paper was significant because it challenged prevalent views about learner errors (that they were distracting and needed to be eradicated), arguing, rather, that errors provide important clues about SLA. This thesis influenced SLA-focused studies of error, especially in the 1970s and 80s.
1976	Cohen, A. D. & Robbins, M. 1976. Toward assessing interlanguage performance: The relationship between selected errors, learners' characteristics, and learners' expectations. *Language Learning* 26: 45-66.	In this early, often-cited study, three students (L1 Mandarin) in a university ESL class were studied over a ten-week quarter to assess the effects of error correction on their use of verb forms in written English. The authors noted that inadequate correction techniques, not correction itself, may provide an explanation for lack of student progress.
1977	Shaughnessy, M. P. 1977. *Errors and expectations*. New York: Oxford University Press.	In this important book, Shaughnessy analyzes over 4000 texts written by college students (including L2) in New York, identifying error patterns and suggesting pedagogical strategies for teachers of at-risk (developmental) student writers.

85

续表

年代	文献	主要内容
1978	Kroll, B. M. & Schafer, J. C. 1978. Error-analysis and the teaching of composition. *College Composition and Communication* 29: 242-248.	Citing CORDER (1967) and SHAUGHNESSY (1977), the authors argue that composition instructors should use error-analysis techniques informed by applied linguistics to study errors made by student writers.
1980	Bartholomae, D. G. 1980. The study of error. *College Composition and Communication* 31: 253-269.	Like KROLL & SCHAFER (1978) and SHAUGHNESSY (1977), Bartholomae argues for a situated analysis of student errors, including sample transcripts from his interactions with his own students.
1980	Hendrickson, J. M. 1980. The treatment of error in written work. *The Modern Language Journal* 64: 216-221.	In this influential paper, Hendrickson discusses approaches to error correction in L2 writing. Most notably, the terms 'direct' and 'indirect' correction, found in later papers, derive from this piece.
1981	Williams, J. M. 1981. The phenomenology of error. *College Composition and Communication* 32: 152-168.	In an extremely influential paper, Williams counters SHAUGHNESSY (1977) and BARTHOLOMAE (1980) to some extent by arguing that much student 'error' is created or 'read' by teachers who are looking for problems.
1982	Sommers, N. 1982. Responding to student writing. *College Composition and Communication* 33: 148-156.	Sommers examined comments given by 35 university writing teachers to three sample student papers, criticizing, like WILLIAMS (1981), teachers who 'read...expecting to find errors' (p. 154), who give error feedback too early in the writing process, and who give students contradictory messages about error and revision.

续表

年代	文献	主要内容
1982	Brannon, L. & Knoblauch, C. H. 1982. On students' rights to their own texts: A model of teacher response. *College Composition and Communication* 33: 157-166.	Using the same teacher commentary sample as SOMMERS (1982), the authors argue that teachers use feedback to create an 'Ideal Text' and, in so doing, usurp student authorship: 'By focusing on error, the teacher is…the judge of the writing' (p. 162).
1982	Lalande, J. F. II 1982. Reducing composition errors: An experiment. *The Modern Language Journal* 66: 140-149.	In this experimental study, 60 college-level students of German received either direct or indirect error feedback. Posttest results indicated that students receiving indirect feedback to engage them in 'guided learning and problem-solving' (p. 143) were more successful in reducing written errors over time.
1983	Haswell, R. H. 1983. Minimal marking. *College English* 45: 600-604.	Haswell assessed the effectiveness of his 'minimal marking' error correction technique (checkmarks in margins indicating presence of error) with his 24 first-year composition students, finding them able to quickly self-edit 61% of the errors noted. Like LALANDE (1982), Haswell argues for less explicit correction that places more responsibility with the student.
1984	Semke, H. 1984. The effects of the red pen. *Foreign Language Annals* 17: 195-202.	Semke looked at the effects of four different feedback treatments (direct error feedback, indirect error feedback, direct error correction + content comments, content comments only) on the journal writing of college-level German foreign language students, finding no posttest differences across groups in error ratios.
1985	Zamel, V. 1985. Responding to student writing. *TESOL Quarterly* 19: 79-102.	As in the L1 composition studies by SOMMERS (1982) and BRANNON & KNOBLAUCH (1982), Zamel examined comments written by teachers on ESL students' compositions, concluding that teachers focused heavily on surface errors and seemed to view themselves primarily as language teachers rather than writing instructors.

续表

年代	文献	主要内容
1986	Robb, T., Ross, S., & Shortreed, I. 1986. Salience of feedback on error and its effect on EFL writing quality. *TESOL Quarterly* 20: 83-93.	mLike LALANDE (1982) and SEMKE (1984), Robb et al. investigated the effects of four different error feedback treatments on 134 Japanese EFL learners over one school year. The treatments ranged from very explicit (direct feedback) to inexplicit (error totals in the margins, similar to HASWELL (1983)). Though all four groups made progress, there were no significant differences across treatment groups, leading the authors to conclude that less time-consuming approaches could be equally effective.
1987	Cohen, A. 1987. Student processing of feedback on their compositions. In A. L. Wenden & J. Rubin (eds.), *Learner strategies in language learning* (pp. 57-69). Englewood Cliffs, NJ: Prentice-Hall.	Cohen questioned 217 college student writers (including ESL and native English speakers) about their perceptions of teacher feedback. Students claimed that most of their teachers' feedback was about grammar and that they read and attended to teacher commentary.
1988	Connors, R. & Lunsford, A. A. 1988. Frequency of formal errors in current college writing, or Ma and Pa Kettle do research. *College Composition and Communication* 39: 395-409.	Building on the early twentieth-century work summarized in HARAP (1930), Connors & Lunsford analyzed 3000 student papers marked by teachers from around the US, classifying 28,571 errors into 20 different categories. Of the errors marked by independent raters, 41% had been marked by the original teachers, and various error types were marked more/less frequently by teachers.
1988	Radecki, P. & Swales, J. 1988. ESL student reaction to written comments on their written work. *System* 16: 355-365.	In a study similar to that of COHEN (1987), the authors surveyed 59 university ESL students about their reactions to teacher commentary on their writing. Student said their teachers gave them a combination of error correction and feedback on content and that they preferred direct teacher correction of all their errors.

续表

年代	文献	主要内容
1990	Cohen, A. & Cavalcanti, M. 1990. Feedback on written compositions: Teacher and student verbal reports. In B. Kroll (ed.), *Second language writing: Research insights for the classroom* (pp. 155-177). Cambridge: Cambridge University Press.	Following the study by COHEN (1987), the authors surveyed nine Brazilian EFL student writers about their perceptions of teacher feedback, triangulating the data collection by also talking with the three teachers and examining samples of their commentary. Again, students reported that most teacher feedback focused on grammar and mechanics, but the authors note 'a poor fit' (p. 169) between student views and actual teacher feedback.
1990	Fathman, A. & Whalley, E. 1990. Teacher response to student writing: Focus on form versus content. In B. Kroll (ed.), *Second language writing: Research insights for the classroom* (pp. 178-190). Cambridge: Cambridge University Press.	Seventy-two ESL students at two US colleges were divided into four feedback treatment groups: content only, error only, content plus error, and no feedback. Students in the two groups that received grammar feedback significantly reduced their errors in a revision; those in the other two groups did not.
1991	Kepner, C. G. 1991. An experiment in the relationship of types of written feedback to the development of second-language writing skills. *The Modern Language Journal* 75: 305-313.	Like FATHMAN & WHALLEY (1990), the author looked at the effects of content vs. form-based feedback on student writing. Sixty college-level FL students of Spanish were divided into two groups: one received only meaning-focused feedback on their journal entries, and the other group received only grammar-focused feedback. Both groups showed improvement over time in the realm in which they had received feedback.
1991	Leki, I. 1991. The preferences of ESL students for error correction in college-level writing classes. *Foreign Language Annals* 24: 203-218.	One hundred college-level ESL writers in composition classes were questioned about error correction preferences. Most preferred comprehensive teacher correction with correction clues over direct feedback (contrary to RADECKI & SWALES (1988)).

续表

年代	文献	主要内容
1992	Sheppard, K. 1992. Two feedback types: Do they make a difference? *RELC Journal* 23: 103-110.	As in KEPNER (1991) and FATHMAN & WHALLEY (1990), the primary contrast was between students receiving feedback on content and those receiving feedback on form. Twenty-six upper-intermediate ESL learners were divided into two groups for a ten-week period: one received written CF on content and the other received written CF on form. The two groups showed no differences with respect to gains in accuracy.
1993	Enginarlar, H. 1993. Student response to teacher feedback in EFL writing. *System* 21: 193-204.	Following RADECKI & SWALES (1988), 47 EFL students in Turkey were surveyed about their teacher feedback preferences. As to grammar correction, students preferred a problem-solving collaborative approach (similar to LEKI (1991)).
1994	Hedgcock, J. & Lefkowitz, N. 1994. Feedback on feedback: Assessing learner receptivity in second language writing. *Journal of Second Language Writing* 3: 141-163.	The authors surveyed 247 university students-both ESL and FL-about teacher feedback, finding that FL students said their teachers primarily provided error correction while ESL students received feedback on a broader range of writing issues. Some students expressed confusion over teacher correction techniques.
1994	Saito, H. 1994. Teachers' practices and students' preferences for feedback on second language writing: A case study of adult ESL learners. *TESL Canada Journal* 11: 46-70.	Saito surveyed 39 college-level ESL writers taught by three different teachers, also examining student texts and teacher feedback, as in COHEN & CAVALCANTI (1990). She found that the three teachers had different approaches to feedback and that the students were equally favorable toward indirect and direct teacher error correction. Students also preferred feedback that asked them to articulate a rule for self-correcting errors.

年代	文献	主要内容
1995	Ferris, D. R. 1995a. Can advanced ESL students be taught to correct their most serious and frequent errors? *CATESOL Journal* 8: 41-62.	A group of 30 university-level ESL writers was followed during a semester-long composition class. They received error feedback tailored for their individual needs on three out-of-class and two in-class essays. They also had in-class mini-lessons on common grammar problems and maintained error logs (similar to LALANDE (1982)). All students made some progress over time in reducing specific error types, but there were differences across students and across in-class vs. out-of-class tasks.
1995	Ferris, D. R. 1995b. Student reactions to teacher response in multiple-draft composition classrooms. *TESOL Quarterly* 29: 33-53.	In this study, 155 students in two levels of a university ESL composition program responded to a survey very similar to the ones utilized by COHEN (1987) in single-draft settings. The results of the survey indicated that (1) students pay more attention to teacher feedback provided on preliminary drafts (vs. final drafts) of their essays; (2) they utilize a variety of strategies to respond to their teachers' comments; (3) they appreciate receiving comments of encouragement; (4) overall, they find their teachers' feedback useful in helping them to improve their writing; (5) students had a variety of problems in understanding their teachers' comments, suggesting that teachers should be more intentional in explaining their responding behaviors to their students.
1996	Truscott, J. 1996. The case against grammar correction in L2 writing classes. *Language Learning* 46: 327-369.	Truscott argues that 'grammar correction' is not effective and may even be harmful and that teachers should 'abandon' it. Reviewing several earlier studies such as KEPNER (1991), FATHMAN & WHALLEY (1990), SEMKE (1984), and LALANDE (1982), Truscott claims that (1) the evidence suggests that grammar correction is futile; (2) teachers' correction practices ignore findings from SLA; and (3) the practical problems faced by teachers and students militate against correction being useful. He further argues that correction takes teacher/student time and energy away from more important writing issues.

续表

年代	文献	主要内容
1997	Ferris, D. R. 1997. The influence of teacher comentary on student revision. *TESOL Quarterly* 31: 315-339.	47 advanced university ESL students had 110 first drafts of their papers marked and revised drafts of each paper were examined to observe the influence of the first-draft commentary on the students' revisions and assess whether the changes made in response to the teacher's feedback actually improved the papers. A significant proportion of the comments appeared to lead to substantive student revision, and particular types and forms of commentary appeared to be more helpful than others.
1997	Ferris, D. R., Pezone, S., Tade, C., & Tinti, S. 1997. Teacher commentary on student writing: Descriptions and implications. *Journal of Second Language Writing* 6: 155-182.	In a longitudinal study of how one writing teacher provided feedback to 47 university ESL writers in three composition courses, over 1500 comments were classified. The researcher found that the teacher made comments on a wide range of issues, with about 15% focused on grammar or mechanics. Feedback varied also according to the point in the semester, task type, and student ability level.
1999	Ferris, D. R. 1999. The case for grammar correction in L2 writing classes: A response to Truscott (1996). *Journal of Second Language Writing* 8: 1-11.	This article evaluates TRUSCOTT's (1996) arguments by discussing points of agreement and disagreement with his claims and by examining the research evidence he uses to support his conclusions. Ferris concludes that Truscott's thesis that "grammar correction has no place in writing courses and should be abandoned" (1996, p. 328) is premature and overly strong.
1999	Truscott, J. 1999. The Case for "The case against grammar correction in L2 writing classes": A response to Ferris. *Journal of Second Language Writing* 8: 111-122.	Truscott responds to FERRIS (1999) criticisms by arguing that these criticisms are both unfounded and highly selective, leaving large portions of his case unchallenged and, in some cases, even strengthening them. If the case for correction has any appeal, it rests on a strong bias-that critics must prove beyond any doubt that correction is never a good idea, while supporters need only show that uncertainty remains.

续表

年代	文献	主要内容
2000	Ashwell, T. 2000. Patterns of teacher response to student writing in a multiple-draft composition classroom: Is content feedback followed by form feedback the best method? *Journal of Second Language Writing* 9: 227-258.	In an approach similar to that of ROBB ET AL. (1986), Ashwell divided 50 Japanese EFL university students into four feedback groups, with three of the four receiving form-based feedback at different stages of the writing process. He found that the groups receiving written corrective feedback (CF) wrote significantly more accurate revisions than the control group that received no correction, and that there was no need to separate content-and form-based feedback on the same draft of student papers.
2001	Ferris, D. R. & Roberts, B. J. 2001. Error feedback in L2 writing classes: How explicit does it need to be? *Journal of Second Language Writing* 10: 161-184.	A group of 72 ESL university students wrote short essays and were divided into three treatment groups: (1) indirect error feedback with correction codes; (2) indirect error feedback with no codes (errors underlined); and (3) no feedback. As found by ASHWELL (2000), the two treatment groups significantly outperformed the control group in editing their texts successfully. The authors argue (as do ROBB ET AL. (1986)) that for some contexts, less explicit error feedback may be adequate.
2001	Hyland, F. & Hyland, F. 2001. Sugaring the pill: Praise and criticism in written feedback. *Journal of Second Language Writing* 10: 185-212.	The authors surveyed 500 feedback acts given to 17 texts of six students by two teachers over a 15-week semester in an ESL program in New Zealand, finding that 19 percent of the feedback points focused on form.
2002	Ferris, D. R. 2002. *Treatment of error in second language student writing*. Ann Arbor, MI: University of Michigan Press.	Ferris offers a realistic, well-reasoned account of what L2 writing teachers–or teachers with L2 students in their classes–need to know about error and how to put what they know to use. She persuasively addresses the fundamental error treatment questions that plague novice and expert writing specialists alike: What types of errors should teachers respond to? When should we respond to them? What are the most efficacious ways of responding to them? And ultimately, what role should error treatment play in the teaching of the process of writing?

续表

年代	文献	主要内容
2003	Chandler, J. 2003. The efficacy of various kinds of error feedback for improvement in the accuracy and fluency of L2 student writing. *Journal of Second Language Writing* 12: 267-296.	In an approach similar to that of LALANDE (1982), ROBB ET AL. (1986), ASHWELL (2000), and FERRIS & ROBERTS (2001), Chandler compared the effects of differing error correction treatments on 31 university ESL students divided into two groups. The treatment group was required to rewrite compositions to correct errors after every first draft, while the control group was not asked to do so until weeks later. The treatment group significantly decreased its error ratios over time and outperformed the control group.
2003	Ferris, D. R. 2003. *Response to student writing: Research implications for second language students*. Mahwah, NJ: Lawrence Erlbaum.	This volume synthesizes and critically analyzes the literature on response to the writing of L2 students, and discusses the implications of the research for teaching practice in the areas of written and oral teacher commentary on student writing, error correction, and facilitation of peer response.
2004	Ferris, D. R. 2004. The 'grammar correction' debate in L2 writing: Where are we, and where do we go from here? (and what do we do in the meantime...?) *Journal of Second Language Writing* 13: 49-62.	Following TRUSCOTT (1996) and FERRIS (1999), this essay outlines problems with the current research on written CF, some possible research questions for the future, and some suggestions for teachers based on existing knowledge.
2004	Lee, I. 2004. Error correction in L2 secondary writing classrooms: the case of Hong Kong. *Journal of Second Language Writing* 13: 285-312.	The present investigation seeks to explore the existing error correction practices in the Hong Kong secondary writing classroom from both the teacher and student perspectives. Data were gathered from three main sources: (1) a teacher survey comprising a questionnaire and follow-up interviews, (2) a teacher error correction task, and (3) a student survey made up of a questionnaire and follow-up interviews. The results revealed (1) both teachers and students preferred comprehensive error feedback, (2) the teachers used a limited range of error feedback strategies, (3) only about half of the teacher corrections of student errors were accurate, (4) the students were reliant on teachers in error correction, and (5) the teachers were not much aware of the long-term significance of error feedback.

续表

年代	文献	主要内容
2004	Truscott, J. 2004. Evidence and conjecture on the effects of correction: A response to Chandler. *Journal of Second Language Writing* 13: 337-343.	In the first section, Truscott argues that CHANDLER's (2003) claims are conjectures, not research findings, leading to the conclusion that correction in the studies was ineffective or harmful. He then discusses the literature review, arguing that previous research also points to negative conclusions.
2005	Bitchener, J., Young, S., & Cameron, D. 2005. The effectiveness of different types of corrective feedback on ESL student writing. *Journal of Second Language Writing* 14: 191-205.	Fifty-three university ESL students were divided into three treatment groups, receiving (1) direct correction of three specific error types; (2) direct correction with added oral metalinguistic explanation; or (3) control (no correction). The researchers found that group (2) outperformed the other groups on written posttests on two error categories (verb tense and articles) but found no difference in the third (prepositions).
2006	Ferris, D. R. 2006. Does error feedback help student writers? New evidence on the short-and long-term effects of written error correction. In K. Hyland & F. Hyland (eds.), *Feedback in second language writing: Contexts and issues* (pp. 81-104). Cambridge: Cambridge University Press.	The essays written by 92 ESL university students in six sections of a course taught by three different teachers were marked in 16 error categories over a semester. The students successfully revised over 81% of the errors marked by their teachers, with success rates varying across error type and teacher correction approach.
2006	Hyland, K. & Hyland, F. 2006. Feedback on second language students' writing. *Language Teaching* 39: 83-101.	The Hylands' state-of-the-art article covers several subtopics regarding feedback, including error correction. They review research on several written CF issues, including explicitness of feedback and its short-and long-term effects on writing improvement and SLA.

续表

年代	文献	主要内容
2007	Guénette, D. 2007. Is feedback pedagogically correct? Research design issues in studies of feedback in writing. *Journal of Second Language Writing* 16: 40-53.	Like FERRIS (2004), Guénette argues that flaws and inconsistencies in research designs account for the lack of consistent or conclusive findings across the research on written CF. After reviewing previous studies across several design variables, she concludes that for such research to be useful for teachers and students, these variables must be more carefully controlled, and other external variables need to be accounted for.
2007	Montgomery, J. L. & Baker, W. 2007. Teacher-written feedback: Student perceptions, teacher self-assessment, and actual teacher performance. *Journal of Second Language Writing* 16: 82-99.	Following the smaller study by COHEN & CAVALCANTI (1990), the researchers surveyed 15 writing teachers and 98 ESL students in an intensive ESL program about the teachers' priorities and strategies in providing written feedback. Teachers' commentary was also examined. The authors noted discrepancies between teachers' self-perceptions and their actual commenting behavior. Specifically, they were likely to give more local/grammar-oriented feedback, especially on early drafts, than they believed they did (or should).
2007	Sheen, Y. 2007. The effect of focused written corrective feedback and language aptitude on ESL learners' acquisition of articles. *TESOL Quarterly* 41: 255-283.	Sheen divided 91 intermediate-level ESL writers into three treatment groups. Group 1 received direct correction on their errors with direct and indirect article use. Group 2 received direct correction plus written metalinguistic explanations for the article rules. Group 3 was the control (no feedback) group. Groups 1 and 2 outperformed Group 3 on posttests, and Group 2 outperformed Group 1.
2007	Truscott, J. 2007. The effect of error correction on learners' ability to write accurately. *Journal of Second Language Writing* 16: 255-272.	With the goal of updating his 1996 argument against error correction, Truscott combines 'qualitative analysis of the relevant studies with quantitative meta-analysis of their findings' (p. 255), concluding that error correction has very little potential benefit for student writers. His quantitative sample was quite small, as he excluded many studies (for a variety of reasons that he explains in the paper).

续表

年代	文献	主要内容
2008	Bitchener, J. 2008. Evidence in support of written corrective feedback. *Journal of Second Language Writing* 17: 102-118.	In an approach similar to that of SHEEN (2007), Bitchener examined the effects of written CF on article errors with 75 low-intermediate ESL learners. To Sheen's three groups, Bitchener added a fourth: direct correction with written and oral metalinguistic explanation. All three treatment groups outperformed controls on immediate and delayed posttests, and the group receiving additional oral explanation outperformed the group receiving only written explanations.
2008	Bitchener, J. & Knock, U. 2008. The value of written corrective feedback for migrant and international students. *Language Teaching Research* 12: 409-431.	The article reports on a two-month study (with 144 international and migrant ESL students in Auckland, New Zealand) that investigated the extent to which different written CF options (direct CF, written and oral metalinguistic explanation; direct CF and written metalinguistic explanation; direct CF only; no CF) help students improve their accuracy in two functional uses of the English article system (referential indefinite 'a' and referential definite 'the'). The study found (1) the students who received all three written CF options outperformed those who did not receive written CF, (2) their level of accuracy was retained over seven weeks, and (3) there was no difference in the extent to which migrant and international students improved the accuracy of their writing as a result of written CF.
2008	Ellis, R., Sheen, Y., Murakami, M., & Takashima, H. 2008. The effects of focused and unfocused written corrective feedback in an English as a foreign language context. *System* 36: 353-371.	Like SHEEN (2007) and BITCHENER (2008), the researchers looked at the effects of written CF on article acquisition. This study emphasized differences between focused and unfocused correction. Forty-nine intermediate ESL students were divided into three groups: (1) direct focused feedback; (2) direct unfocused feedback; (3) controls. The two treatment groups outperformed the controls in a delayed posttest ten weeks later, but there were no significant differences between the focused and unfocused feedback groups.

续表

年代	文献	主要内容
2008	Lee, I. 2008. Understanding teachers' written feedback practices in Hong Kong secondary classrooms. *Journal of Second Language Writing* 17: 69-85.	Like COHEN & CAVALCANTI (1990), ENGINARLAR (1993), and MONTGOMERY & BAKER (2007), Lee examined written feedback given by 26 secondary EFL teachers in Hong Kong on 174 student papers, also interviewing six teachers. She found that the teachers focused primarily on grammar in their feedback and that their feedback philosophies and practices were constrained by contextual factors (culture and institution) and by a lack of adequate teacher training.
2008	Lunsford, A. A. & Lunsford, K. J. 2008. 'Mistakes are a fact of life': A national comparative study. *College Composition and Communication* 59: 781-806.	In this replication of CONNORS & LUNSFORD (1988), the researchers examined a corpus of 877 teacher-marked student texts to see if student errors and/or teacher correction approaches had changed over the 20 years since the previous study. They found differences in student error patterns that they argued were partially attributable to changing assignment types (lengthier and more complex) and to the increased use of computers.
2008	Truscott, J. & Hsu, A. Y.-P. 2008. Error correction, revision, and learning. *Journal of Second Language Writing* 17: 292-305.	Forty-seven EFL graduate students were divided into two treatment groups. One received underlined, indirect written CF on errors (similar to the design in FATHMAN & WHALLEY (1990)) and one of the groups in FERRIS & ROBERTS (2001)) and the control group received no feedback. The treatment group outperformed the control group in self-editing revisions of the same text, but there were no differences between the groups on a posttest one week later. The authors argue that this finding demonstrates that gains seen in revision tasks do not transfer to learning.
2009	Bitchener, J. & Knoch, U. 2009a. The relative effectiveness of different types of direct written corrective feedback. *System* 37: 322-329.	Building on BITCHENER & KNOCK (2008), the authors investigated the relative effectiveness of error correction of thirty-nine low intermediate ESL learners in Auckland, New Zealand, with three different direct written CF options (direct CF, written and oral metalinguistic explanation; direct CF and written metalinguistic explanation; direct CF only). Two functional uses of the English article system (referential indefinite 'a' and referential definite 'the') were targeted in the feedback. No difference in effect upon accuracy was found between the three treatment options, suggesting that the provision of error correction alone may be sufficient for learners at a low intermediate proficiency level.

续表

年代	文献	主要内容
2009	Bitchener, J. & Knoch, U. 2009b. The value of a focused approach to written corrective feedback. *ELT Journal* 63: 204-211.	This article examined the effectiveness of targeting only two functional uses of the English article system (referential indefinite 'a' and referential definite 'the') with written CF in order to see if such an approach was also helpful for ESL writers. The study found that those who received written CF on the two functions outperformed the control group on all four posttests.
2009	Bruton, A. 2009. Improving accuracy is not the only reason for writing, and even if it were… *System* 37: 600-613.	Bruton reviews some of TRUSCOTT'S later papers as well as several of the latest studies on written CF. He reminds readers that decisions about written CF must be carefully considered within the larger context of the goals of writing instruction.
2009	Ellis, R. 2009. A typology of written corrective feedback types. *ELT Journal* 63: 97-107.	The author presents a typology of the different types written CF available to teachers and researchers. The typology distinguishes two sets of options relating to (1) strategies for providing feedback (for example, direct, indirect, or metalinguistic feedback) and (2) the students' response to the feedback (for example, revision required, attention to correction only required).
2009	Sheen, Y., Wright, D., & Moldawa, A. 2009. Differential effects of focused and unfocused written correction on the accurate use of grammatical forms by adult ESL learners. *System* 37: 556-569.	Building on SHEEN (2007), this article investigated whether direct focused CF, direct unfocused CF and writing practice alone produced differential effects on the accurate use of English articles by adult ESL learners. Four groups were formed: focused written CF group, unfocused written CF group, writing practice group, and control group. It is indicated that all three experimental groups gained in grammatical accuracy over time in all the posttests. This suggested that doing writing tasks is of value by itself. Overall, these results suggested that unfocused CF is of limited pedagogical value whereas focused CF can contribute to grammatical accuracy in L2 writing.

续表

年代	文献	主要内容
2009	Xu, C.-Q. 2009. Overgeneralization from a narrow focus: A response to Ellis et al. (2008) and Bitchener (2008). *Journal of Second Language Writing* 18: 270-275.	This article presents a critical analysis of two recent studies on error correction, ELLIS ET AL. (2008) and BITCHENER (2008) and argues that neither study constitutes evidence for error correction based on discussion of the comparability of participants, design issues, and analysis flaws in both studies. The author further suggests that research into the efficacy of error correction should focus on linguistic features that are more treatable but less teachable if this practice is to hold out any pedagogical promise.
2009	Yeh, S.-W. & Lo, J.-J. 2009. Using on-line annotations to support error correction and corrective feedback. *Computers & Education* 52: 882-892.	The authors developed an online CF and error analysis system called Online Annotator for EFL Writing. The system consisted of five facilities: Document Maker, Annotation Editor, Composer, Error Analyzer, and Viewer. An experiment conducted to evaluate the effectiveness of this system shows that the experimental group receiving CF with the developed system has significantly better performance on recognizing writing errors than the control group who used the paper-based error correction method.
2010	Bitchener, J. & Knoch, U. 2010a. The contribution of written corrective feedback to language development: A ten month investigation. *Applied Linguistics* 31: 193-214.	This study was similar in design to BITCHENER (2008), except that the delayed posttest here was ten months later (compared with two months for the earlier study). Again, all treatment groups outperformed the control group.
2010	Bitchener, J. & Knoch, U. 2010b. Raising the linguistic accuracy level of advanced L2 writers with written corrective feedback. *Journal of Second Language Writing* 19: 207-217.	In this study, 63 advanced ESL learners were divided into four treatment groups: (1) direct written CF with written metalinguistic input; (2) indirect focused circling; (3) direct written CF with written and oral metalinguistic input; (4) control (no feedback). The two direct focused groups outperformed the indirect group, and all three treatment groups outperformed controls on a ten-week delayed posttest.

续表

年代	文献	主要内容
2010	Bruton, A. 2010. Another reply to Truscott on error correction: Improved situated designs over statistics. *System* 38: 491-498.	Bruton argues that research design questions are much more important than statistical analyses, very often used to hide defects in the research. Since error correction in L2 writing has a fundamental pedagogical purpose, it is necessary to situate research into L2 error correction in writing not only contextually, but also within a decision-making framework.
2010	Evans, N., Hartshorn, J., McCollum, R., & Wolfersberger, M. 2010. Contextualizing corrective feedback in second language writing pedagogy. *Language Teaching Research* 14: 445-463.	The authors emphasize three contextual variables that must be considered if we are to understand the current research of written CF and maximize the utility of future research. These include the learner, the situation, and the instructional methodology. As an examination of how one of these contextual variables might affect L2 writing accuracy, this article presents an innovative instructional methodology specifically designed to improve L2 writing accuracy. The authors refer to the central component of this methodology as dynamic written CF.
2010	Ferris, D. R. 2010. Second language writing research and written corrective feedback in SLA: Intersections and practical applications. *Studies in Second Language Acquisition* 32: 181-201	This article briefly traces the history of second language acquisition and second language writing research on written CF and notes both contrasts and convergences. It then moves to a focused discussion of the possible implications and applications of this body of work for the L2 language and writing classroom and for future research efforts.
2010	Hartshorn, J. K., Evans, N. W., Merrill, P. F., Sudweeks, R. R., Strong-Krause, D., & Anderson, N. J. 2010. The effects of dynamic corrective feedback on ESL writing accuracy. *TESOL Quarterly* 44: 84-109.	This article describes an instructional strategy called dynamic written CF, in which students write short, frequent texts, receive immediate, comprehensive correction, and revise their corrected texts (an approach somewhat similar to that of HASWELL (1983)). This study aims to test the methodology's efficacy by comparing the performance of two groups of students, one using a conventional process approach to writing instruction and the other using the dynamic written CF approach. Test results demonstrated that although rhetorical competence, writing fluency, and writing complexity were largely unaffected by the dynamic written CF pedagogy, significant improvement was observed for writing accuracy.

续表

年代	文献	主要内容
2010	Sheen, Y. 2010. Differential effects of oral and written corrective feedback in the ESL classroom. *Studies in Second Language Acquisition* 32: 201-234.	Building on SHEEN (2007), this article examines whether there is any difference between the effect of oral and written CF on learners' accurate use of English articles. Five groups were formed: oral recasts, oral metalinguistic, written direct correction, written direct metalinguistic, and control. The results indicated that all CF groups, except for oral recasts, significantly outperformed the control group in the immediate and delayed posttests. Overall, these results suggest that the degree of explicitness of both oral and written CF-rather than the medium in which the CF is provided-is the key factor that influences CF effectiveness.
2010	Storch, N. 2010. Critical feedback on written corrective feedback research. *International Journal of English Studies* 10: 29-46.	Storch argues that, in the desire to conduct more robust research, the pendulum has swung too far towards experimental studies. Such studies tend to employ 'one off' treatments, often provided on a very restricted range of errors, and ignore the learners' goals and attitudes to the feedback provided and to improvement in accuracy.
2010	Storch, N. & Wigglesworth, G. 2010. Learners' processing, uptake, and retention of corrective feedback on writing: Case studies. *Studies in Second Language Acquisition* 32: 303-334.	The investigation focused on the nature of the learners' engagement with the feedback received to gain a better understanding of why some feedback is taken up and retained and some is not. The results show that uptake and retention may be affected by a host of linguistic and affective factors, including the type of errors the learners make in their writing and, more importantly, learners' attitudes, beliefs, and goals. The findings suggest that, although often ignored in research on CF, these affective factors play an important role in uptake and retention of feedback.
2011	Evans, N. W., Hartshorn, K. J., & Strong-Krause, D. 2011. The efficacy of dynamic written corrective feedback for university matriculated ESL learners. *System* 39: 229-239.	Building on previous studies of dynamic written CF, which targets all linguistic errors simultaneously, a comparative study was conducted measuring ESL learners who were taught using dynamic written CF against students who received traditional process writing instruction. Results indicated that students who received traditional process writing instruction experienced some declines in linguistic accuracy while those who received dynamic written showed significant improvement in the linguistic accuracy of their L2 writing.

续表

年代	文献	主要内容
2011	Sheen, Y. 2011. *Corrective feedback, individual differences and second language learning*. Springer Publishing.	This book offers a new perspective by reviewing a wide body of research on both oral and written CF and its contribution to second language acquisition. It also reports the results of the author's own study, pointing to the need to examine how individual factors such as anxiety and language aptitude mediate learners' ability to benefit from the oral and written feedback they receive.
2012	van Beuningen, C., de Jong, N. H., & Kuiken, F. 2012. Evidence on the effectiveness of comprehensive error correction in second language writing. *Language Learning* 62: 1-41.	Working with 268 secondary learners of Dutch as a foreign language, the researchers examined the effects of written CF in both short-term revisions and on new texts over time. They examined a broader range of error types than in the 'article studies' (BITCHENER ET AL. 2005; SHEEN 2007; BITCHENER 2008; ELLIS ET AL. 2008; BITCHENER & KNOCH 2010a, 2010b) and further examined TRUSCOTT'S (2007) claim that error reduction might simply stem from learners' avoidance of problematic structures. They found that all learners who received written CF outperformed controls over time, that different types of feedback seemed beneficial for different linguistic domains (direct for grammar errors; indirect for lexical errors), and that learners did not simplify their texts to avoid errors.
2012	Bitchener, J. 2012. A reflection on 'the language learning potential' of written CF. *Journal of Second Language Writing* 21: 348-363.	This article takes stock of what we know, both theoretically and empirically, and what we do not know about the language learning potential of written CF. It looks therefore at what the theoretical literature has to say about such a role and assesses what empirical studies have found about the effectiveness of written CF for L2 learning and acquisition. To move the field forward, a range of recommendations for further research are discussed.
2012	Bitchener, J. & Ferris, D. R. 2012. *Written corrective feedback in second language acquisition and writing*. New York: Routledge.	This book provides a scholarly synthesis and analysis of theory, research, and practice on written CF to date, examining it from the dual perspective of applied linguists studying second language acquisition and composition scholars studying second language writing.

续表

年代	文献	主要内容
2012	Polio, C. 2012. The relevance of second language acquisition theory to the written error correction debate. *Journal of Second Language Writing* 21: 375-389.	This article discusses written error correction from the perspective of various approaches to SLA and what they might have to say about written error correction. In addition, studies that are conducted within the various approaches are described. The author argues that despite differences in the various approaches, some conclusions can be drawn, most notably, that written error correction could be effective in certain conditions.
2012	Riazantseva, A. 2012. Outcome measure of L2 writing as a mediator of the effects of corrective feedback on students' ability to write accurately. *System* 40: 421-430.	This study examines the effect of the outcome measure of L2 writing on the accuracy rates. In this study, three outcome measures (in-class essays, in-class summaries and at-home summaries) of writing performance produce different estimates of L2 writers' accuracy. This study also found differences in the longitudinal changes in accuracy of L2 writing depending on the types of errors that are included in the operational definition of accuracy. These findings provide evidence for opening a discussion about the nature and technical characteristics of the outcome measures to be used as indicators of a learner's ability to produce accurate L2 texts in real-life contexts.
2013	Lee, I. 2013. Research into practice: Written corrective feedback. *Language Teaching* 46: 108-119.	Lee discusses what current written CF research has succeeded in getting through to classroom teaching, and what has not succeeded, and why. The author examines three kinds of relationship between research and practice with regard to written CF: areas in which research findings have not been well applied, areas in which research findings are reasonably well applied, and areas in which research findings are over-applied.
2013	Guénette, D. & Lyster, R. 2013. Written corrective feedback and its challenges for pre-service ESL teachers. *The Canadian Modern Language Review* 69: 129-153.	This study explored the emerging CF practices of a group of 18 pre-service ESL teachers. Serving as tutors to a group of 61 high school ESL learners during a school semester, the pre-service teachers provided CF on texts written by the learners and exchanged via e-mail. The authors analyzed the types of CF they used and the types of errors they chose to focus on, along with the factors that explained their choices. Quantitative analyses of the frequency distribution of CF types relative to error types and qualitative analyses of data collected through journals and interviews confirmed that, similar to their in-service colleagues, pre-service teachers overused direct corrections at the expense of more indirect CF strategies.

4.5 小结

本章首先归纳了口头与书面反馈的六点主要区别。这些差异能否影响到反馈的效果,目前只有 Sheen(2010)开展了较为系统的实证研究,结果发现:反馈自身的显性程度而非反馈所处的媒介(口头 VS 书面),对反馈的效果起到了决定性的作用。随后,本章介绍了口头反馈研究所取得的成果及存在的问题,讨论主要集中于重铸。重铸是课堂环境和自然环境中出现频率最高的反馈形式,它能确保学习者在始终关注意义的同时,注意到形式问题,并为学习者提供了认知比较的机会,即学习者可以将自己偏离标准的语言产出与正确的语言输入进行比较,从而加速语言体系重构。然而在实证研究中,重铸的促学效果并未得到普遍证实,还需进一步的探索。

书面反馈部分以年表的形式介绍了 80 个代表性的反馈研究,这些研究发现深化了我们对于书面反馈促学机制和效果的认识,并在一定程度上推动了反馈领域的发展。纵观整个领域,我们可以将它的发展历史划分成两段。第一段为早期阶段(1976—1996),该阶段反馈研究数量不多,且主要为观察性、调查/访谈性研究。20 世纪 80 年代,二语写作教学主要采用过程写作法,关注写作内容和过程,反对传统的语法纠错。同时,在二语习得领域,Krashen 的监控模型影响广泛,该模型否认纠错对二语发展的作用。因此在早期阶段,纠错无论是在教学还是理论研究中都不被看好,而且相关的实证研究也非常有限。

第二段为近期阶段(1996 至今),该阶段的反馈研究数量明显增多,其中一个重要原因是由于受到了 Truscott 系列论文(Truscott 1996,1999,2001,2004,2007,2009,2010;Truscott & Hsu 2008)的影响。Truscott 的观点不仅没有促使人们放弃纠错,相反激发起了浓厚的研究兴趣。该阶段的研究多为实验性研究,重点探讨反馈的促学效果和促学机制问题,而且已经基本证实,有效的书面反馈对于提高某些学习者作文语言的准确性大有裨益(如 Chandler 2003;Ferris 1999,2004)。

第五章　观察性和调查性书面反馈研究

5.1　引言

本章将介绍和评价观察性与调查性反馈研究。这两类研究均为非实验性研究，前者是在自然状态下对研究对象的特征进行观察、记录，并对结果进行描述和对比分析，后者是通过谈话、问卷、测验等科学方法，对研究对象进行有计划、周密的、系统的了解，并对搜集的数据进行分析和比较。本章首先介绍现有的观察性反馈研究，然后对调查性反馈研究进行概述，最后归纳本章的主要内容。

5.2　观察性反馈研究

观察性反馈研究主要考察以下三方面内容：（1）语言反馈在教师作文反馈中的比例情况；（2）学生写作语言的错误类型；（3）教师纠正的语言错误类型。接下来，我们具体介绍每一类研究的主要发现。

5.2.1　语言反馈在教师作文反馈中的比例

很多一语和二语写作研究描述了教师对学生作文的反馈情况，其发现大致可归为两类（见表5.1）：第一类，教师反馈的重点在作文的内容、观点和结构，语言反馈大概只占反馈总数的20%，该比例不会随着教学环境及实验方法的不同而发生明显变化；第二类，语言反馈是教师作文反馈的主体，超过内容反馈。

有些一语写作研究(Connors & Lunsford 1993; Straub 2000; Straub & Lunsford 1995)发现,语言反馈不是教师作文反馈的主体,大概只占反馈总数的20%,该比例数与二语写作研究结果很相似。例如,Ferris(1997)和Ferris et al.(1997)分析了一位教师对47名大学英语二语学习者的111篇作文所给出的1526条反馈,结果表明,只有15%的反馈是针对学习者的语言问题。Hyland & Hyland(2001)调查了在新西兰的一个英语教学课堂中,两位教师对于六名学生的17篇作文所给出的500条反馈,结果同样显示,针对语言问题的反馈只占19%。造成上述结果的一个重要原因在于,这些研究所分析的文本多来自经验丰富的教师,他们能够对学生作文的各方面问题给予高质量的反馈,而非仅仅拘泥于语言问题。但不可否认的是,在现实教学中,大部分写作教师对于语言问题的关注要超过作文的其他方面。

相反,还有一部分研究发现,语言反馈是作文反馈的主体。例如,Searle & Dillon(1980)分析了九位教师对135篇作文所给出的1146条反馈,结果发现,语言反馈占了69%。造成该结果的主要原因是当时的二语写作教学关注写作结果,忽视写作过程。Zamel(1985)调查了写作教师对英语二语学习者作文的反馈情况,结果表明,教师反馈主要聚焦于表面的语法错误,他们更多地将自己看做语法教师而非写作教师。Montgomery & Baker(2007)考察了美国个性化教学(Individualized Education Program)中的13位小学教师对78名学生作文的反馈情况,结果显示,语言反馈多于内容反馈,该结果与这些受访教师原本的反馈理念相矛盾。Lee(2008)考察了26位香港初中英语教师对174篇学生作文的反馈情况,结果发现,语言反馈是绝对的主体。Lee认为,教师一方面受到文化和制度的影响,另一方面缺少必要的教师培训是造成该结果的主要原因。

表 5.1 语言反馈在教师作文反馈中的比例

	研究	类型	教师	调查对象及材料 学生	作文	反馈	结果
第一类：语言反馈不是作文反馈的主体	Connors & Lunsford(1993)	一语写作	全美各地教师	大学生	3000 份		语言反馈占 22%
	Straub & Lunsford(1995)	一语写作	12 名写作专家		12 份		语言反馈占 21%
	Straub(2000)	一语写作	6 名教师	6 个班级的学生			虽然新手教师比有经验的教师提供更多的语言反馈，但总体而言，语言反馈占 25%。
	Ferris(1997);Ferris et al.(1997)	二语写作	1 名教师	47 名大学英语学习者	111 份	1526 条	语言反馈占 15%
	Hyland & Hyland(2001)	二语写作	2 名教师	6 名学生	17 份	500 条	语言反馈占 15%
	Searle & Dillon(1980)	二语写作	9 名美国小学教师		135 份	1146 条	语言反馈占 69%
第二类：语言反馈是作文反馈的主体	Montgomery & Baker(2007)	一语写作	13 名教师	78 名学生			语言反馈的比例高于内容反馈
	Cohen(1987)	一语/二语写作		217 名大学生（包括英语学习者和英语本族语者）			语言反馈占主体
	Cohen & Cavalcanti(1990)	二语写作	3 名教师	9 名巴西英语学习者			语言反馈占主体
	Lee(2008)	二语写作	26 名香港初中英语教师		174 份		语言反馈占主体

5.2.2 学生写作语言的错误类型

Connors & Lunsford(1988)通过分析全美各地高校教师所批改的 3000 份学生作文,归纳出学生作文最常犯的 20 类语言错误(见表 5.2)。Lunsford & Lunsford (2008)复制了这个研究,对 877 份学生作文进行了批改,重新归纳出了学生最常犯的 20 类语言错误(见表 5.2)。两份错误列表前后相隔 10 年,通过对比可以看出二者的差异,这说明错误是动态发展的,会随着学生个体因素及时间的发展而发生变化。

然而,上述两个研究在调查方法上受到了一些质疑。首先,调查对象和材料存在混杂因素。调查对象是来自全美各地高校的学生和教师,其语言背景、英语水平及学习/工作态度都存在较大差异;调查材料是几千份学生作文,其写作内容、题材与类型都不相同。另外,没有对实验材料进行彻底分析。两个研究都承认,他们只是对其中的一部分作文进行了评改,从而归纳出 20 类最常见的语言错误。综上可见,两份错误列表的可靠性确实值得推敲,对其内容信息的利用需要谨慎解读。

Ferris(2006)通过分析 92 名在美国加利福尼亚高校读书的外国学生的 146 份作文,归纳出了 15 类最常见的语言错误(见表 5.2)。调查中的学生来自同一课程的六个平行班级,作文批改者是该校三位英语教师。此研究的目的是考察反馈对于英语二语写作能力发展的短期和长期效果,而所归纳出的 15 类语言错误只是用来辅助作文批改。

尽管上述三个研究在调查对象和材料等方面存在这样或那样的差异,但他们所提供的学习者每 100 字的犯错数非常相似。而且,Lunsford & Lunsford(2008)发现,这个错误率不会随时间的发展而变化,即便是二语写作者,也不会发生明显改变。

5.2.3 教师纠正的语言错误类型

在 Connors & Lunsford(1988)和 Lunsford & Lunsford(2008)的研究中,教师只对学生作文语言错误的 40% 提供了反馈,而在 Ferris (2006)的研究中,教师批改了 83% 的语言错误,造成该差异的主要原因是不同的实验环境所致。Ferris(2006)要求三位教师全面纠正学生作文中的错误,并事先提供了一个错误列表供批改用,而且这些教师批改的是学生的二稿作文,其一稿主要接收内容方面的反馈。但是,Connors & Lunsford(1988)和 Lunsford & Lunsford(2008)这两个研究没有说明采用的是全面纠错还是针对性纠错,而且也不清楚教师批改的是学生的第几稿作文。这里需要指出的是,Ferris(2006)要求教师根据事先提供的错误列表来批改学生的作文,但如果不提供错误列表,结果又会如何呢?

此外,Connors & Lunsford(1988)和 Lunsford & Lunsford(2008)的研究还发现,学生最常犯的语言错误与教师最常批改的语言错误并不一致。例如,在 Connors & Lunsford(1988)的研究中,教师最常批改的语言错误是"wrong word",但是它在学生的错误列表中只排在第四位,而且教师只对这类错误的 50% 做了批改。事实上,还有一些例子可以说明教师与学生之间的不一致,但由于这些研究都没有对教师当时的批改策略作进一步的调查分析,因此导致这一矛盾的真正原因还不得而知,不过我们可以推测出两个可能的原因:(1)教师存在一个内在的错误过滤系统,这使得他们更容易注意到某些错误,而忽视其他错误(Williams 1981);(2)教师比较反感某些类型的错误,他们希望通过反馈可以引起学生的注意。

最后,英语二语学习者的写作语言错误主要集中在词汇、形态和句法结构方面(见 Ferris(2006)的错误列表);而英语本族语者更多犯一些机械性(mechanical)错误,如标点符号和文献引用的错误等(见 Connors & Lunsford(1988)和 Lunsford & Lunsford(2008)的错误列表)。如果上述错误列表能在一定程度上反映出学习者的语言状况,那么一语写作教师和二语写作教师在批改作文时,就需要分别有所侧重。

5.3 调查性反馈研究

与观察性研究不同,调查性研究通过访谈、问卷等方式来收集数据,研究目标更加明确。通过这一方法所开展的书面反馈研究主要探讨学生、教师对反馈的态度。接下来,我们具体介绍此类研究的主要发现。

表5.2 语言错误列表

错误排序	Connors & Lunsford (1988: 403, Figure 1) 调查对象：美国高校学生 每100字的错误数量：2.26	Lunsford & Lunsford (2008: 795, Figure 7) 调查对象：美国高校学生 每100字的错误数量：2.38	Ferris (2006: 103, Appendix) 调查对象：美国高校的外国留学生 每100字的错误数量：2.45
1	No comma after an introductory element	Wrong word	Sentence structure
2	Vague pronoun reference	Missing comma after an introductory element	Word choice
3	No comma in compound sentence	Incomplete or missing documentation	Verb tense
4	Wrong word	Vague pronoun reference	Noun endings (singular/plural)
5	No comma in non-restrictive element	Spelling error (including homonyms)	Verb form
6	Wrong/missing inflected endings	Mechanical error with a quotation	Punctuation
7	Wrong or missing preposition	Unnecessary comma	Articles/determiners
8	Comma splice	Unnecessary or missing capitalization	Word form
9	Possessive apostrophe error	Missing word	Spelling
10	Tense shift	Faulty sentence structure	Run-ons
11	Unnecessary shift in person	Missing comma with a non-restrictive element	Pronouns
12	Sentence fragment	Unnecessary shift in verb tense	Subject-verb agreement
13	Wrong tense or verb form	Missing comma in a compound sentence	Fragments
14	Subject-verb agreement	Unnecessary or missing apostrophe (including its/it's error)	Idiom
15	Lack of comma in series	Fused (run-on) sentence	informal
16	Pronoun agreement error	Comma splice	
17	Unnecessary comma with restrictive element	Lack of pronoun-antecedent agreement	
18	Run-on or fused sentence	Poorly integrated quotation	
19	Dangling or misplaced modifier	Unnecessary or missing hyphen	
20	Its/it's error	Sentence fragment	

5.3.1 学生对反馈的态度

早期研究发现,教师主要对学生作文的语法和机械性错误提供反馈(如 Cohen 1987)。随着过程写作法在二语写作教学中的推广,教师的反馈范围从原来的语法和词汇扩展到了作文的内容与结构(如 Hedgcock & Lefkowitz 1994),而且学生对于教师的多方面反馈表现出了积极正面的态度。目前,尚无研究发现学生不希望教师对其作文语言给予反馈,或者是提供非常少量的反馈。换句话说,学生希望得到多方面的作文反馈,尤其是针对语言问题的反馈,如果缺少这类反馈,他们会感到非常失望。

此外,有些研究会询问学生非常具体的问题,以了解他们所喜欢的反馈形式,例如,是否希望教师全面纠正作文中的语言错误,还是只纠正一些比较重要的语言错误?是否希望教师直接将错误改正过来,还是仅仅指出错误而留给学生自己去修改?针对这些问题,不同背景的学生给出了一致的答案:(1)学生普遍倾向于全面纠错而非选择性纠错,因为他们担心,那些没有被纠正的错误会对随后的学习产生负面影响(如 Leki 1991);(2)学生希望教师能够直接纠错,因为这会节省他们的时间和精力,但同时也承认,间接纠错可能更利于外语发展(如 Radecki & Swales 1988)。

总之,虽然一些理论学家反对纠错,并宣称纠错有害(如 Krashen 1982;Truscott 1996),但对于学生而言,他们非常希望教师可以直接、全面地纠正他们的语言错误。

5.3.2 教师对反馈的态度

Truscott(1996)指出,虽然学生以积极正面的态度看待反馈,但这并不代表写作教师就要按照学生的想法去纠错,理由如下:

Abundant evidence shows that students believe in correction... but this does not mean that teachers should give it to them. The obligation teachers have to students is not to use whatever form of instruction the students think is best, but rather to help them learn... When students hold a demonstrably false belief about learning, the proper response is not to encourage that belief, but rather to show them that it is false.

Truscott(1996:359)

Truscott 指出,教师的理念与实践会影响到学生对于纠错的态度,从而进入一个恶性循环,即"通过纠错,教师鼓励学生相信纠错有用,因为学生相信,教师不得不继续纠错"(Truscott 1999:116)。Truscott 承认,改变学生对于纠错的态度并非易事,但教师有责任去改变现状,他还进一步引用自己班上的例子来说明学生完全可以适应没有纠错的教学方式,而且他们的学习动机不会受到任何影响。

对于 Truscott 的上述观点,Bitchener & Ferris(2012)提出了异议:如果教师认为一种教学方式(如纠错)不仅无益,反而有害,他们肯定会尽快将其摒弃,不论学生对它有多么喜欢。此外,Truscott 有关"教师应该对学生崇尚纠错的态度负有不可推卸的责任"的观点,很容易让人联系到 Williams(1981)的错误观,即错误不是由作者能力缺失造成的,错误存在于读者的大脑,读者在期望错误、寻找错误的过程中创造出错误。这也就是说,教师在批改学生作文时,总是认为自己有责任纠错,因此寻找错误、发现错误并将其改正。事实上,Truscott 和 Williams 的观点都过于片面和绝对,我们不排除有些学生已经习惯性地期望教师改错,并产生了极强的依赖性,但大部分学生对纠错还是持理性的态度:根据反馈,他们认识到了自己的外语水平与目标语之间的差距,并通过进一步分析错误原因,避免在接下来的语言产出中再次犯错。

综合以上分析,教师与学生应该通力合作,构建出高效的反馈形式,而不是由教师一人来决定哪种反馈形式好,哪种不好。这种合作性的教学理念有利于建立以人为本、行之有效、过程性而非总结性的反馈机制,切实提高学习效率。

5.4 小结

本章概述了观察性和调查性反馈研究的主要发现。观察性反馈研究主要涉及三个方面:(1)语言反馈在教师作文反馈中的比例;(2)学生写作语言的错误类型;(3)教师纠正的语言错误类型。研究发现,语言反馈是教师作文反馈的主体,教师更多地将自己看做语言教师而非写作教师。然而,随着外语水平的发展和教学经验的丰富,教师在批改作文时,不会再拘泥于语言问题,而会对作文的各方面问题给予反馈。

Connors & Lunsford(1988)、Lunsford & Lunsford(2008)和Ferris(2006)通过分析大量的作文材料,分别归纳出了学生常犯的20类语言错误。虽然错误类型会因时间的发展及学生个体差异而发生变化,但错误率非常相似。由于调查对象、材料及方法存在缺陷,因此对这些结果需谨慎解读。

此外,学生最常犯的语言错误与教师最常批改的语言错误并不一致。例如,Connors & Lunsford(1988)发现,教师最常批改的语言错误是"wrong word",而它只排在学生常犯错误的第四位。造成这一结果的原因包括:(1)教师可能存在一个内在的过滤系统,从而使得他们更容易注意到某些错误(Williams 1981);(2)教师可能比较反感某些类型的错误,希望通过反馈以引起学生的注意。

调查性反馈研究主要探讨学生和教师对反馈的态度。从学生的角度看,他们普遍希望教师改错,而且改得越细致越好。从教师的角度看,Truscott(1996)认为,虽然学生对于纠错持积极正面的态度,但教师不能完全按照学生的想法去做,否则便会进入一个恶性循环,即通过纠错,教师鼓励学生相信纠错有用,因为学生相信,教师不得不继续纠错。Truscott 的观点遭到了不少反对(如 Bitchener & Ferris 2012)。事实上,教师与学生应该通力合作,建立高效的反馈模式,切实提高学生的外语运用能力。

第六章 准实验性书面反馈研究

6.1 引言

实验性研究是按照随机分配的原则,将研究人群分为具有可比性的实验组和对照组,对实验组人为地给予某种干预因素,对照组则不予任何处理,然后通过随访观察和分析,来判定干预因素效应的研究方法。与实验性研究紧密相关的另一种研究方法是准实验性研究(Quasi-experimental research),它是指在无法保证随机安排受试的情况下,运用原始群体,在较为自然的条件下进行实验处理的研究方法。由于反馈实验采用的都是原始班级(intact classes),因此其实质是准实验性研究,本章将对此类研究做系统的归纳与分析。

本书的第二、三章分别介绍了各种二语习得理论、写作理论对于错误及纠错的认识。理论上的差异和冲突需要实证研究来解决,但这并不是说,实证研究的发现与启示就不具有任何争议了。事实上,通过本章的介绍,我们会发现,反馈研究在实验方法上还存在缺陷,因此对其结果需谨慎解读。

准实验性反馈研究主要围绕六个方面展开:(1)反馈对于习得二语语法结构的作用;(2)反馈对于学生修改原稿作文的短期影响;(3)反馈对于学生写作语言发展的长期影响;(4)对比不同反馈形式的效果;(5)错误类型、纠错数量与反馈效果之间的关系;(6)个体因素、环境因素对反馈效果的影响。下面,我们具体介绍每个方面的研究。

6.2 反馈对于习得二语语法结构的作用

在 Truscott(1996)文章发表前,书面反馈并未引起人们的关注。一方面可能是因为二语习得领域更关注口头反馈研究;另一方面,早期研究将"书面反馈可以促学"看做理所当然的事情。直到 Truscott

(1996)对二语写作中的语法纠错进行了猛烈抨击后,学者们才意识到考察反馈对二语习得作用的重要性,并开展了大量的准实验性研究。其中,反馈能否促进二语语法结构的习得,是一个基础性问题,如果它的答案是否定的,那么反馈研究的其他问题就失去了考察的意义。

近五年来,二语习得领域集中出现了一批研究专门考察反馈对于习得特定语法结构(如冠词、一般过去式、虚拟语气等)的作用(见表6.2)。这些研究只针对学生作文中的一类或有限的几类语法错误提供反馈,然后通过后测、延迟后测评估学生对于目标结构的掌握情况,研究结果普遍证实,反馈有帮于学习者减少目标错误。

6.2.1　反馈对于冠词习得的作用

冠词作为一项重要的语法结构,在反馈领域吸引了广泛的关注(如 Bitchener et al. 2005;Bitchener & Knock 2008,2009a,2009b,2010a,2010b;Sheen 2007),究其原因主要有三点:(1)冠词具有复杂的形式—意义映射关系,是英语学习中公认的难点,而学习者对于冠词的掌握程度无疑是衡量其英语能力的重要标尺,如果反馈能帮助学习者提高冠词使用的正确率,那么足以说明反馈的促学价值;(2)冠词复杂的用法功能仅仅依靠自然输入(naturalistic input)是难以习得的(Ellis 2006),这便为考察显性干预(explicit intervention)的效果提供了条件,而反馈恰好是一种典型的显性干预手段;(3)反复检验反馈对于同一语言结构习得的效果,可避免其他变量因素对实验结果的干扰,从而为反馈的促学价值提供强有力的证据。

目前,反馈研究已经证实:对于不同学习环境(包括英语二语学习环境、外语学习环境)中的不同水平(包括初、中、高级)的学习者,在对他们作文中的冠词错误提供系统性的反馈后,这些受试在后测中的冠词使用情况要明显好于没有接收到反馈的受试,而且反馈的效果可以长达10个月。然而,Truscott(2007)认为,上述研究结果不能说明反馈可以帮助学习者提高冠词使用的正确率,理由如下:学习者为避免在新的写作任务中再次犯错,会倾向于简化他们的写作语言,并有意识地避免使用曾经出错的结构,这会造成"冠词错误减少"的假象。但是,Bitchener & Ferris(2012)对此进行了反驳:(1)这些研究所采用的评估标准是冠词使用正确率而非正确使用冠词的数量;(2)这些研究在设计写作任务时会尽可能地引导受试使用冠词,例如,在看图写作中给出提示名词以引导受试产出目标冠词,当然不排除在有些情况下,受试会采用回避策略,但这只是个别现象,不能以偏概全。

然而值得注意的是,这些反馈研究只关注冠词的两种特指用法,即不定冠词 a/an 作为第一次指代,定冠词 the 作为照应指代,如 He bought *a* bicycle two months ago, but *the* bicycle was stolen yesterday。事实上,英语冠词有特指与类指两大功能,八种主要用法(Quirk et al. 1985)(见表 6.1),而只有将这些典型用法同时纳入考察范围,才能充分探讨反馈对于冠词习得的作用。

表 6.1　英语冠词的特指和类指用法

	定冠词	不定冠词
特指	(1) 在特定语境中使用,意思为这、那 *The* roses are very beautiful.[said in a garden]	(5) 相当于数词 one *A* mile or two
	(2) 与专有名词连用 *The* United States	(6) 作泛指,指代某一个 Leonard wants to marry *a* princess who speaks five languages.
	(3) 做照应指代,指代前文出现的事物 John bought a TV and a video recorder, but he returned *the* video recorder.	(7) 作为第一次指代 *An* intruder has stolen *a* vase. The intruder stole the vase from *a* locked case. The case was smashed open.
	(4) 做照应指代,指代后文出现的事物 *The* girls sitting over there are my cousins.	
类指	(8) 类指用法有三种,如 a, b, c 中的斜体部分所示,三种形式均指代 lion 这个种类的集合 　a. *The lion* is fierce[①]. (定冠词+单数名词) 　b. *A lion* is fierce. (不定冠词+单数名词) 　c. *Lions* are fierce. (零冠词+复数名词)	

尽管学习者对冠词的掌握程度是衡量其英语能力的重要标尺,尽管聚焦于冠词可以从研究的深度上为反馈促学提供有效的证据,但冠词毕竟不是外语学习的全部,反馈研究有必要针对多种语法结构进行实验(如 Xu 2009;姜琳、陈锦 2013),同时从研究的深度和广度上求证反馈的效果。目前,仅少数几个研究考察了反馈对于习得其他语法结构的作用(Bitchener et al. 2005;Sheen et al. 2009;陈晓湘等 2013;姜

---

① 在特定的语境下,(8)a 可表达特指意义或类指意义,此处只关注它的类指意义。

琳、陈锦 2013),接下来,我们简要介绍这些研究的主要发现。

6.2.2 反馈对于其他语法结构习得的作用

姜琳、陈锦(2013)考察了反馈对于中国学生习得英语类指名词短语的影响。英语有三种类指名词短语(如 Quirk et al. 1985;Lyons 1977),如表 6.1 的句(8)所示。其中,the lion、a lion 及 lions 均指代 lion 这个集合,而不是某一只或者某一群 lion。汉语没有冠词,因此类指名词短语主要以光杆名词的形式出现,如"狮子很凶猛"。

该研究将纠错目标锁定于英语类指名词短语主要是基于以下两点考虑:(1)在与实验所涉及班级的英语任课教师讨论后,研究人员确信,英语类指名词短语用法被明示教学(explicitly taught)的几率近乎为零,这样就可以排除明示语法教学对实验结果可能造成的影响;(2)正确掌握英语类指名词短语用法,要求中国学生摆脱来自母语的负迁移影响,同时还要做到句法和语用层面认知的自然整合。然而在中国的英语教学环境中,学生常常是脱离了语境去学习抽象的语法规则,故容易造成两个认知层面接口的割裂,难以保证语言形式学以致用。事实上,该实验结果也恰好证实了这一点,受试者虽为接受过 8 年英语教育的大学生,但在前测中的类指名词短语使用正确率仅为 57%。

该研究采用"前测-干预-后测-延迟后测"的设计模式,通过汉译英和写作两种测试方法来考察反馈的作用,实验结果显示:元语言反馈可有效促进英语类指名词短语的习得,而间接反馈则不能。研究认为,元语言反馈不仅提供了充分的可理解性输入,还凸显了语境的效用,有助于学习者在语篇层面上学用语言,学习者通过重复、模仿正确的语言输入,推动语言输出向语言输入看齐,从而促进类指名词短语的习得;间接反馈没有提供充分的语言输入,故需要学习者通过形成假设、验证假设的过程中来增强对于目标结构的掌握,尽管这种认知投入可以提高所习得知识的稳定性与持久性,但对于受试者的外语能力、语言分析能力以及学习自觉性要求较高。因此,就受试者当前的外语发展阶段而言,间接反馈的促学效果并不理想。

陈晓湘等(2013)考察了聚焦与非聚焦反馈对英语非真实条件虚拟语气习得的影响。96 名受试者被分成五组:直接聚焦组、间接聚焦组、直接非聚焦组、间接非聚焦组和对照组。实验结果显示,从短期看,聚焦和非聚焦反馈的效果无明显差异,但直接反馈优于间接反馈;从长期看,聚焦反馈优于非聚焦反馈,间接反馈优于直接反馈;此外,受试者的外语水平会影响反馈的效果。总之,所有实验组在两次后测中的成绩都显著高于对照组,驳斥了Truscott纠错无效反而有害的观点,为反馈有效提供了正面证据。

Bitchener et al.(2005)同时考察了纠错对于冠词、一般过去式和介词习得的影响,实验结果表明,纠错对于前两种语法错误(即冠词和一般过去式)的效果比较明显,而对于后一种词汇错误(即介词)的作用却并不理想。对此,Bitchener等人认为,介词用法常常约定俗成,与具体的语境有关,属于特质型(idiosyncratic)知识,故对于纠错不敏感。Sheen et al.(2009)发现,反馈能促进学习者对冠词、系动词be、规则与不规则动词过去式以及介词的掌握。总之,反馈研究有必要针对不同语言结构进行考察,从多方面求证反馈的促学效果。

6.3 反馈对学生修改作文的短期影响

6.3.1 主要研究发现

早期研究多关注反馈对于学习者修改作文的影响,如果修改稿的语言准确性有了提升,至少可以说明反馈在短期内具有促学作用,这类研究被称为修改型研究(revision studies)。基于Bitchener & Ferris(2012:83,Figure 4.3)的研究,表6.3总结了现有的十个修改型研究,尽管这些研究在反馈形式(包括页边反馈、间接反馈、直接反馈等)、错误类型、写作/修改条件、学生背景(包括美国大学一年级新生、英语二语学习者、台湾地区英语研究生等)等方面存在差异,但研究结果非常一致,即反馈可以显著提升学习者修改稿语言的准确性。除了Haswell(1983)和Ferris(2006),其他修改型研究都包含了对照组(即没有接收任何反馈),学生根据反馈修改原稿作文,其修改稿的语言错误明显减少,而对照组则没有显著变化。事实上,Truscott在其研究中也承认了这一发现:

> Our findings confirm once again that correction does help students reduce their errors on the writing on which they receive the corrections, and that the effect is substantial.
>
> (*Truscott & Hsu 2008:299*)

表 6.2 反馈对习得二语语法结构的影响

Studies	*Participants*	*Treatments*	*Error types receiving treatments*	*Findings*
Bitchener et al. (2005)	53 Post-intermediate ESL learners	1) Direct, explicit written feedback and student-researcher 5 minute individual conferences 2) Direct, explicit written feedback only 3) Control	Prepositions, the past simple tense and the definite article	A significant effect was found for the combination of written and conference feedback on accuracy levels in the use of the past simple tense and the definite article in new pieces of writing but no overall effect on accuracy improvement for feedback types when the three error categories were considered as a single group
Sheen (2007)	91 Intermediate ESL learners	1) Direct focused correction 2) Direct focused correction and written meta linguistic input 3) Control	The use of the indefinite article for first mention and of the definite article for subsequent mention	Both treatment groups outperformed control group on immediate and delayed posttest, but the direct metalinguistic group performed better than the direct-only correction group in the delayed post-test

续表

Studies	Participants	Treatments	Error types receiving treatments	Findings
Bitchener (2008)	75 Low-intermediate ESL learners	1) Direct focused correction, written and oral metalinguistic input 2) Direct focused correction and written metalinguistic input 3) Direct error correction 4) Control	The use of the indefinite article for first mention and of the definite article for subsequent mention	All three focused written CF groups outperformed control group in immediate and two months delayed posttest
Bitchener & Knoch (2008)	144 Low-intermediate ESL learners	1) Direct focused correction, written and oral metalinguistic input 2) Direct focused correction and written metalinguistic input 3) Direct focused correction 4) Control	The use of the indefinite article for first mention and of the definite article for subsequent mention	All three focused written CF groups outperformed control group in immediate and two months delayed post-test
Ellis et al. (2008)	49 Intermediate EFL learners	1) Direct focused correction 2) Direct unfocused feedback 3) Control	The use of the indefinite article for first mention and of the definite article for subsequent mention	All 3 groups performed with greater accuracy in immediate posttest; focused and unfocused groups outperformed control group in 10 week delayed posttest

121

续表

Studies	Participants	Treatments	Error types receiving treatments	Findings
Bitchener & Knoch (2009a)	39 Low-intermediate ESL learners	1) Direct focused correction, written and oral metalinguistic input 2) Direct focused correction and written metalinguistic input 3) Direct focused correction 4) Control	The use of the indefinite article for first mention and of the definite article for subsequent mention	No difference in effect upon accuracy was found between the three treatment options
Bitchener & Knoch (2009b)	52 Low-intermediate ESL learners	1) Direct focused correction, written and oral metalinguistic input 2) Direct focused correction and written metalinguistic input 3) Direct focused correction 4) Control	The use of the indefinite article for first mention and of the definite article for subsequent mention	Those who received written CF on two functional uses of the English article system outperformed the control group on all four posttests
Sheen et al. (2009)	49 Intermediate ESL learners	1) Direct focused correction 2) Unfocused correction 3) Writing practice 4) Control	Articles, copula 'be', regular/irregular past tense, and prepositions	Groups 1-3 outperformed control group in immediate and delayed posttests; Group 1 made greater gains than group 2

续表

Studies	Participants	Treatments	Error types receiving treatments	Findings
Bitchener & Knoch (2010a)	52 Low-intermediate ESL learners	1) Direct focused correction, written and oral metalinguistic input 2) Direct focused correction and written metalinguistic input 3) Direct focused correction 4) Control	The use of the indefinite article for first mention and of the definite article for subsequent mention	All three focused written CF groups outperformed control group in immediate and three delayed posttest over 10 months
Bitchener & Knoch (2010b)	63 Advanced ESL learners	1) Written metalinguistic input 2) Indirect focused circling 3) Written and oral metalinguistic input 4) Control	The use of the indefinite article for first mention and of the definite article for subsequent mention	All three treatment groups outperformed control group in immediate posttest; both direct focused treatment groups outperformed indirect and control groups in 10 week delayed posttest
Sheen (2010)	177 Intermediate ESL learners	1) Recasts 2) Oral metalinguistic correction 3) Written direct correction 4) Written metalinguistic correction 5) Control	The use of the indefinite article for first mention and of the definite article for subsequent mention	The results indicated that all CF groups, except for oral recasts, significantly outperformed the control group in the immediate and delayed post-tests

续表

Studies	Participants	Treatments	Error types receiving treatments	Findings
陈晓湘等(2013)	96名非英语专业大二学生	1) 直接聚焦 2) 间接聚焦 3) 直接非聚焦 4) 间接非聚焦 5) 对照	英语非真实条件虚拟语气	所有实验组在两次后测中的成绩都显著高于对照组;从短期看,聚焦和非聚焦反馈的效果无明显差异,但直接反馈优于间接反馈;从长期看,聚焦反馈优于非聚焦反馈,间接反馈优于直接反馈;此外,受试的外语水平会影响反馈的效果
姜琳、陈锦(2013)	79名中下级英语水平大一学生	1) 间接反馈 2) 元语言反馈 3) 对照	英语类指名词短语	元语言反馈可有效促进英语类指名词短语习得,而间接反馈则不能

尽管上述实验结果清晰且一致,但同样引来了不少质疑,主要集中在:成功的语言修改能否等同于语言能力的长期发展,换句话说,虽然学习者利用反馈提高了修改稿的语言质量,但他们能否在新任务中同样给出令人满意的语言表现呢?该问题不论是对于科研人员还是外语教师都极为重要。

表6.3 反馈对学生修改作文的影响

Study	*Description*	*Findings*
Haswell (1983)	24 students in a freshman composition course self-edited errors marked by checkmarks in the margins	Students were able to quickly correct (in 15 minutes or fewer) over 61 percent of marked errors, regardless of error type; students who corrected their texts after receiving "minimal marking" improved their written accuracy over time
Fathman & Whalley (1990)	72 ESL students at two US colleges were divided into four treatment groups; two of the four received comprehensive, indirect, uncoded grammar feedback (all errors underlined); they had 30 minutes in class to revise their marked errors	Students who received grammar feedback significantly reduced their number of errors; the two groups not receiving grammar feedback did not
Ferris (1997)	47 advanced university ESL students had 110 first drafts of their papers marked; revised drafts of each paper were examined	A significant proportion of the comments appeared to lead to substantive student revision, and particular types and forms of commentary appeared to be more helpful than others
Ashwell (2000)	50 Japanese university students (EFL context) in four treatment groups; three of the four received form-based feedback before revising their texts	Students who received form-based feedback wrote significantly more accurate revised drafts than a control group receiving no feedback
Ferris & Roberts (2001)	72 ESL students were divided into three treatment groups; two of the three received error feedback on five major error types; they had 30 minutes in class to revise their marked errors	Students who received error feedback successfully revised 60—64 percent of their total errors; their correction ratio was significantly higher than a control group's ratio

Study	Description	Findings
Chandler (2003)	31 university ESL students were divided into two groups; the treatment group was required to rewrite compositions to correct errors after every first draft, while the control group was not asked to do so until weeks later	Direct correction is best for producing accurate revisions; students who did immediate rewriting after written CF reduced their error ratios significantly more than those who did not make corrections until weeks later
Ferris (2006)	92 ESL college students had second drafts of their essays marked by their teachers in 16 error categories; their papers were revised at home; 146 pairs of second and third drafts (two different assignments) were analyzed for self-editing success	Students successfully revised over 81 percent of the errors marked by their teachers; success ratios varied across error categories and teacher correction techniques
Truscott & Hsu (2008)	47 EFL graduate students were divided into two treatment groups: one received underlined, indirect written CF on errors and one of the groups in FERRIS & ROBERTS (2001); the control group received no feedback	Students in the experimental group significantly outperformed the control group in self-correcting errors during revision; the accuracy improvement of the experimental group during revision did not lead to improved accuracy in the new text
van Beuningen et al. (2008)	The effectiveness of direct and indirect CF was compared to the effect of two control treatments: a treatment that offered students an extra opportunity to practice their writing skills, and a treatment in which students self-corrected their errors without any available feedback	Both types of CF have short-term effects on students' revisions. Neither of the control treatments had a significant effect on students' accuracy
van Beuningen et al. (2012)	268 secondary learners of Dutch as a foreign language were divided into three groups: direct CF, indirect CF and control. The researchers examined the effects of written CF in both short-term revisions and on new texts over time	All learners who received written CF outperformed controls not only during revision but also in new pieces of writing

6.3.2 修改成功不等于语言能力提升

Manchon(2011,2012)指出,修改型研究实质上是在考察语言准确性而非语言习得。Truscott 也极力反对这类研究,认为它们不仅没有任何意义,而且索然无味,如 Truscott(1996)对 Fathman & Whalley(1990)的研究给予了如下评价:

The result... does not address the question: Does grammar correction make students better writers? Fathman & Whalley have shown that students can produce better compositions when teachers help them with those particular compositions. But will students be better writers in the future because of this help?

Truscott(1996:339)

Truscott(2007)继续对这类研究提出了批评:

A writing task that students do with help from the teacher (the revision) is obviously not comparable to one they do on their own (the original essay), and so a study with this design does not yield any measure of learning, short-term or otherwise.

Truscott(2007:257)

此外,还有研究指出,即便受试修改了原稿中的错误,也不能说明其外语学习发生了质的变化,相对保险的做法是通过写新作文来检测受试语言的发展,从而判定反馈的作用(如 Polio et al. 1998;Truscott 1999;Truscott & Hsu 2008)。Truscott & Hsu(2008)研究发现,反馈只能帮助学习者提升修改稿语言的准确性,而对于新作文则没有帮助,他们由此认为,语言修改成功不等于语言能力提升,短期的变化不代表二语能力的长期发展。针对这一结果,学者们分析了三点可能的原因:(1)受试初稿语言的错误率已经非常低了,其语言水平的提升空间相对有限(Bruton 2009);(2)实验采用全面纠错的方法,但学习者的注意资源和加工能力有限,很难消化和吸收全部反馈(Bitchener & Ferris 2012),从而影响了反馈的效果;(3)受试为英语外语学习者,他们的学习动机比较低,很可能不会充分利用教师的反馈(Bitchener & Ferris 2012)。

6.3.3 修改成功有利于语言能力的长期发展

有研究认为,修改稿语言质量的提升是学习者二语能力发展的重要开端,没有成功的修改,何谈二语能力的提升(如 Ferris 2004,2010;Sachs & Polio 2007)。根据 Sachs & Polio(2007)的观点,"习得"的概念涵盖了各种形式的逐步、非线性的语言学及元语言行为上的变化,它不仅包括正确使用语言形式,还包括诸如浮现、察觉、重建和意识等思维观念上的变化。反馈可以帮助学习者意识到其语言产出中存在错误,从而引发一系列的认知心理变化,这些变化是实现二语能力长期发展的必要前提。通过对当前各种二语习得研究证据的分析,Sachs & Polio(2007)进一步给出了以下两点结论:(1) 不同形式的反馈(包括口头/笔头,显性/隐性)均可促使学习者意识到其语言水平与目标语之间的差距,从而激发他们对错误作进一步分析,并在接下来的语言产出中对相关形式给予关注,避免再次犯错;(2) 当前研究已经证实了口头反馈对于二语习得的作用,因此我们有理由相信书面反馈同样可以促学,因为它不需要学习者做出即时的认知加工和比较,不会给学习者造成过多的记忆负担,所以它的促学效果会更加理想。

Ferris(2004)指出,学习者修改作文时的认知投资(cognitive investment)是实现二语能力长期发展的基础。随后,她从学习策略的角度进一步指出,反馈对于学生修改作文的短期影响可以演变成对其写作水平发展的长期影响,反馈是学习者修改和编辑作文的有效工具,学习者会将学到的修改/编辑策略运用于新的写作任务。但 Ferris(2010)同时也承认,这种随时间发展的策略意识上的变化,难以通过实验测量出来,因此未来研究要大力考察短期修改与二语长期发展之间的关系。

目前,一语和二语研究领域都有证据可以支持"语言成功修改有利于语言能力的长期发展"。Haswell(1983)从一语研究的角度证实,学习者根据反馈修改原文的做法有利于提升他们在新作文中的语言准确性。Chandler(2003)的二语研究也同样发现,根据反馈做及时修改的受试,在日后写作任务中的语言错误率要明显低于那些不做修改的受试。

van Beuningen et al.(2008,2012)考察了短期修改与二语写作语言长期发展之间的关系,实验结果显示,反馈(尤其是直接反馈)有助于提升修改稿和新作文语言的准确性。但 van Beuningen 等人想由此说明修改成功等同于语言能力提升,还需要对以下问题作进一步澄清和完善:(1) 是否确保受试在实验干预之后、后测之前的一周时间里没有接触到相关的语言输入;(2) 对照组虽然没有收到作文反馈,但被要求修改自己的作文,这会促使他们关注语言形式,从而影响其在后测中的表现。

6.4 反馈对学生写作语言发展的长期影响

上一节介绍了修改型研究,探讨了语言成功修改与语言能力长期发展之间的关系。事实上,判定反馈作用相对保险的做法,是通过让学习者写新作文来检测其语言发展,从而判定反馈的作用。因此,本节将重点介绍反馈对于学生新作文语言的影响,我们将这类研究称为纵向研究(longitudinal studies),其目的是探讨反馈对于学习者二语能力发展的长期作用。事实上,相比修改型研究,纵向研究在解读实验结果方面遇到了更多的问题和困难。

基于 Bitchener & Ferris(2012:88, Figure 4.4)的研究,表 6.4 列举了现有的 14 个纵向研究。这些研究不仅关注反馈对于语言准确性的影响,还包括对语言复杂性、流利性的影响。值得注意的是,早期研究(Kepner 1991;Robb et al. 1986;Semke 1984;Sheppard 1992)未发现反馈的效果,而近期研究(除了 Truscott & Hsu(2008))则毫无例外地证实了反馈的作用。接下来,我们分别介绍反馈对于写作语言准确性与复杂性发展的长期效果。

表 6.4 反馈对新作文语言的影响

Study	Description	Findings
Semke (1984)	141 German FL students in a US university were divided into four groups: direct error correction, coded feedback with self-correction by the students, comments-on-content only (interpreted as the control group), and a combination of direct error correction and comments-on-content	There was no significant differences in accuracy between the three written CF groups and the comments-on-content group
Robb et al. (1986)	134 EFL learners in Japan were divided into four groups: direct error correction, coded feedback, highlighted feedback, or marginal feedback in the form of the total number of errors per line (interpreted as the control group)	Even though all groups improved, there was no difference between the groups; a significant positive effect was found for indirect CF on one of their complexity measures

续表

Study	Description	Findings
Kepner (1991)	One group of intermediate Spanish FL learners received direct error correction on their linguistic errors while another group received content comments on their texts (interpreted as the control group)	There was no significant difference in the number of errors between the two groups after a 12-week period
Sheppard (1992)	One group received written CF over a 10-week period while another group received comments relating to content (interpreted as the control group). Both groups had one-on-one conferences with their teacher about their respective theme	No advantage was gained in terms of improved accuracy by the written CF group; there was a negative effect for written CF on structural complexity
Ferris (1995a)	30 ESL freshman composition students at a US university followed over a 15-week semester; each student had individual error pattern identified at the beginning of the course, and written CF throughout the term focused specifically on those patterns; no control group	All but two of the students showed improvement on at least some of the individually targeted error patterns over the semester; results varied as to error type and writing task
Chandler (2003)	31 international students at a US music conservatory wrote five papers; treatment group was required to correct marked errors after every first draft	Experimental group significantly decreased its overall error ratios between Paper1 and Paper5; this was also significantly better than a control group's ratios; written CF did not affect the complexity of L2 learner writing
Ferris (2006)	92 ESL students in six sections of a developmental writing course at a US university; errors made on Paper1 and Paper4 (end of semester) were compared across five error categories after students received systematic written CF all semester	Students significantly reduced their total error ratios and their verb errors; changes in other categories were non-significant; tremendous individual variation as to long-term improvement
Foin & Lange (2007)	58 students in an advanced ESL composition class at a US university; errors made on an early draft and a final draft were compared across eight categories	"Treated" (marked) errors were successfully corrected in 77—81 percent of the cases; unmarked errors were corrected 32 percent of the time

续表

Study	*Description*	*Findings*
Truscott & Hsu (2008)	47 EFL graduate students were divided into two treatment groups: one received underlined, indirect written CF on errors and one of the groups in FERRIS & ROBERTS (2001); the control group received no feedback	The treatment group outperformed the control group in self-editing revisions of the same text, but there were no differences between the groups on a posttest one week later
van Beuningen et al. (2008)	The effectiveness of direct and indirect CF was compared to the effect of two control treatments: a treatment that offered students an extra opportunity to practice their writing skills, and a treatment in which students self-corrected their errors without any available feedback	While both types of CF have short-term effects on students' revisions, only direct CF proved to have a significant long-term effect; neither of the control treatments had a significant effect on students' accuracy
Ferris et al. (2010)	10 ESL students in a developmental writing course at a US University, studied with qualitative case study methodology; students received written CF on up to four error patterns on four texts apiece, were given time to revise those texts, and then were each interviewed three times about their strategies and understanding of the feedback	Students all showed improvement in at least some error categories over time and all felt that the combination of individually targeted written CF and in-person discussion of errors was very helpful on both in-class and especially out-of-class writing
Hartshorn et al. (2010)	47 ESL students were divided into a treatment group and a contrast group; the former using the dynamic written CF approach, while the latter using a conventional process approach to writing instruction	Although rhetorical competence, writing fluency, and writing complexity were largely unaffected by the dynamic written CF pedagogy, significant improvement was observed for writing accuracy.
van Beuningen et al. (2012)	268 secondary Dutch FL learners were divided into three groups: direct CF, indirect CF and control. The researchers examined the effects of written CF in both short-term revisions and on new texts over time	All learners who received written CF outperformed controls not only during revision but also in new pieces of writing; moreover, CF did not result in simplified writing in students' new texts
王颖、刘振前 (2013)	40名高校英语专业二年级学生被分成两组,一组接收反馈并作修改,另一组只接收反馈	反馈修改组的语言准确性比反馈组有明显提高;受试写作语言准确性与流利性的提高不会影响到语言复杂性

6.4.1 反馈对写作语言准确性的影响——早期研究综述

早期研究(Kepner 1991；Robb et al. 1986；Semke 1984；Sheppard 1992)发现，实验组与对照组在新作文语言的准确性方面不存在显著差异，由此判定反馈不能促进外语水平的长期发展。但是，这些研究在实验设计上存在缺陷，研究结论的可靠性因而受到了影响，所以他们不能作为证明"反馈无效"的证据。接下来，我们逐一分析这些研究所存在的问题。

根据 Guénette(2007)的分析，Semke(1984)的实验存在两个问题：(1) 虽然对照组没有接收作文语言的反馈，但接收了作文内容的反馈，而很多内容方面的问题是由语言问题造成的，内容反馈可能会激发学习者去关注语言，所以该实验中的对照组并非真正意义上的对照组；(2) 对照组作文的评分标准是字数，而实验组是语言的准确性，不同的评分标准导致受试对语言准确性持不同态度，从而影响到最终的实验结果。

Robb et al.(1986)的研究结论也具有争议性。该研究将页边反馈作为一种考察的反馈形式，可见它并非想真心考察反馈的作用(Bitchener & Ferris 2012)，因为页边反馈的促学价值可视为零，接收页边反馈的实验组等同于没有接收任何反馈的对照组(Truscott 1996，2007)。

Kepner(1991)的研究存在三点不足：(1) 同 Semke(1984)一样，对照组没有接收作文语言的反馈，但接收了作文内容的反馈；(2) Kepner分析和比较了受试在第六次写作任务中的表现，并以此来评定反馈的作用，但他没有分析和比较第一次作文，因此便无法知晓所有受试在实验之初是否处于同一外语水平(Ferris 2003)；(3) 所有写作任务均在课下完成，没有对受试的写作过程给予必要的监控，这势必会影响到实验结果的可靠性(Ferris 2003)。

Sheppard(1992)的实验包含两个组，一组接收作文语言方面的反馈，一组接收内容方面的反馈，两组都与实验人员就反馈内容作一对一面谈。Bitchener & Ferris(2012)认为该实验有三个地方需要作进一步的澄清和完善：(1) 在整个实验过程中，两组是否接收过语法教学；(2) 实验人员与内容反馈组的面谈是否涉及了由语言问题造成的内容问题；(3) 作文评改缺少评分员信度检验。

此外，上述研究均采用非聚焦反馈，这需要实验人员对受试作文中的每一处语言错误都提供反馈，事实上，实验人员难以保证对每一处语误都提供反馈，而这种非系统性的纠错极大地削弱了实验结果的可信度；另外，学习者的注意资源和加工能力有限，很难消化和吸收全部反馈，这自然会影响到反馈的效果。

6.4.2 反馈对写作语言准确性的影响——近期研究综述

除 Truscott & Hsu(2008)外，近期的纵向研究(自 Ferris(1995a)之后的研究)都证实了反馈可以提升学习者新作文语言的准确性，但想由此说明反馈具有促学作用，还需要在以下三个方面做出改进。

第一，大部分研究都缺少严格意义的对照组。例如，Chandler(2003)的对照组也接收了反馈，只是比实验组晚了几周而已。根据 Truscott(2007)等研究，如果反馈实验缺少对照组，那么它将无法说明反馈能否有效促进学习者语言的发展。针对这一问题，相关研究也试图给予澄清，例如，Chandler(2003)根据调查结果指出，绝大多数学生都希望得到教师全面、认真的反馈，所以教师不得不为对照组提供反馈，但这又在一定程度上影响了实验结果的可信度。Ferris(2004)称上述情形为"方法的左右为难"(Methodological Catch-22)：如果教师不为对照组提供反馈，他们会感到愧疚，但如果提供了反馈，实验的有效性就会受到质疑。此外，在 van Beuningen et al.(2008,2012)的研究中，对照组虽然没有接收任何反馈，但被要求修改自己的作文，这会促使他们关注语言形式，从而影响后测的表现。综上可见，"对照组"是未来反馈研究要解决的首要问题，它会直接影响到研究结论的有效性。

第二，学习者在写作语言准确性方面的发展存在很大的个体差异，Ferris et al.(2010)对此分析了四点原因：(1) 学习者的知识背景，以及对形式教学的认识存在差异；(2) 他们的学习动机不同，对待自己的作文和所上课程的态度亦不同；(3) 课堂之外，他们还会受到诸如作业、兼职和家庭方面的干扰；(4) 上述研究都采用了限时写作，而学习者在限时写作中的表现均不理想。以上四点原因会对学习者产生交叉影响，从而关系到他们从反馈中的获益程度。

第三，反馈对某些错误的效果要好于其他错误，这可能与学习者的早期教育、目标结构的难度，以及写作任务的性质有直接关系。需要说明的是，各种写作任务在类型和题材上的差异，会带给学习者不同的语言产出机会，从而决定了犯错的情况；此外，当写作任务给学习者造成较大的认知负担时，其写作语言的准确性会呈下降趋势。

总之，虽然这些研究存在着一定的问题，还不能充分证实反馈的长期效果，但至少可以肯定的是，目前尚无研究发现学习者在接收反馈后，其写作语言的准确性退步了，或者说没有丝毫的进步。这也正如 Ferris(2004)所言，虽然现有研究不能充分证实"反馈有效"，但也不能证实"反馈有害"。

6.4.3 反馈对写作语言复杂性的影响

Truscott(1996)反对语言纠错，因为它会对外语学习产生诸多不利影响，例如，会降低学习者写作语言的复杂性。Truscott(2004,2007)进一步指出，反馈研究之所以发现受试在接收反馈后，其语言准确性有了明显提升，原因就在于，为了避免再次犯错，他们在新的写作任务中会有意识地采用相对简单的语法结构和单词，从而使得作文语言的准确性有了一定的提升，这造成了"反馈促学"的假象。Truscott的言论与注意能力模型的基本观点不谋而合，即学习者必须在语言准确性与复杂性之间做好权衡（如 Skehan 1998），当学习者愿意去尝试和体验目标语时，其语言的复杂性就会明显提高；但是，当他们的注意力集中在语言的准确性时，就会采取保守主义来选择所要使用的语言形式，即只选取自己有把握的词语和结构，放弃那些复杂、易出错的语言形式(Skehan & Foster 2001)。

目前，只有少数几个研究(Chandler 2003；Hartshorn et al. 2010；Robb et al. 1986；Sheppard 1992；van Beuningen et al. 2012；王颖、刘振前 2013)考察了反馈对写作语言复杂性的影响，且结论不一致。Sheppard(1992)发现，反馈对学习者写作语言的复杂性有负面影响，但影响不具有显著性。Robb et al.(1986)发现，反馈对学习者写作语言的复杂性具有正面影响，但该实验缺少对照组。Chandler(2003)发现，反馈不会影响学习者写作语言的复杂性，但她的实验同样缺少对照组；此外，该研究还误将作文的整体质量作为评判语言复杂性的标准，事实上，作文的整体质量没有发生变化不等于语言复杂性没有发生变化(van Beuningen et al. 2012)。

与早期研究相比，近期研究的结果比较一致。Hartshorn et al. (2010)考察了动态反馈(dynamic written CF)的促学效果。实验人员通过计算终结性单位(T-unit)内的平均字数来判定语言的复杂性，结果发现，反馈不会对学习者作文语言的复杂性产生负面影响。van Beuningen et al. (2012)考察了新作文语言的结构复杂性和词汇多样性，结果显示，反馈不会降低作文语言的复杂性。王颖、刘振前(2013)同样证实，学习者写作语言准确性与流利性的提高不会对语言复杂性产生负面影响，但是，后者的发展速度要比前两者慢。

虽然近期三个研究的发现比较一致，但他们的实验方法存在一个共同缺陷，即缺少对照组。Hartshorn et al. (2010)不仅为对照组提供了写作修辞和语言方面的反馈，而且还额外提供了语言指导。van Beuningen et al. (2012)的对照组虽然没有收到作文反馈，但被要求修改自己的作文，这会促使他们关注语言形式，从而影响其后测表现。王颖、刘振前(2013)的对照组和实验组接收了同样形式的反馈，只不过对照组不需要修改作文而实验组需要修改，事实上，这种实验设计是在考察作文修改(而非反馈)对于写作语言准确性和复杂性的影响。

6.5 反馈形式与效果

本书在第一章对书面反馈的形式做了具体的介绍，而对比不同形式反馈的效果，一直是反馈研究的核心问题，相关研究大致可分为四类：(1)对比直接与间接反馈的效果；(2)对比不同形式直接反馈的效果；(3)对比不同形式间接反馈的效果；(4)对比聚焦与非聚焦反馈的效果。接下来，我们分别概述每类研究的主要发现。

6.5.1 对比直接反馈与间接反馈的效果

直接反馈指出错误并提供正确形式，而间接反馈仅指出错误，不提供正确形式。从理论上看，直接反馈与间接反馈各具促学优势。间接反馈可以鼓励学习者去发现学习，并通过形成假设、验证假设的过程进入到深层次的内部加工，从而增强对于目标结构的掌握，这种认知投入可以提高所学知识的稳定性和持久性(如 Ferris 2010；Lalande

1982)。与之相比,直接反馈有如下优点:(1)学生在分析间接反馈时会遇到困难或产生误解,直接反馈可避免这一情况发生;(2)有利于学生解决比较复杂的语言问题,如句法结构、习语等方面的错误;(3)所提供的信息有利于学生在第一时间对假设进行验证(如Chandler 2003)。

虽然直接反馈与间接反馈各有所长,但它们能在多大程度上发挥促学作用,还取决于教学目的和学生水平。首先,如果教学目的是促进学习者习得具体的语言结构,那么直接反馈可以帮助他们更富有成效地内化目标知识;但如果教学目的是帮助学习者发展有效的元认知技能(metacognitive skills),以及修订、编辑作文的能力,那么具有隐性学习特征的间接反馈会更有效(Ferris 2010)。此外,学生的外语水平也会影响反馈的效果:对于高水平学习者,直接反馈和间接反馈可能同样奏效;但对于低水平学习者,直接反馈的效果可能会更明显。

关于直接反馈与间接反馈的争议,不仅理论上各说各的理,且实证研究的结果也并不一致(见表6.5)。Lalande(1982)通过考察德语学习情况,指出间接反馈的效果好于直接反馈,但事实上,二者的差异并未达到显著程度,而且间接反馈组比直接反馈组还多参加了语言形式方面的练习活动(van Beuningen et al. 2012)。Robb et al.(1986)通过考察134名日本学生的英语学习情况,指出两种反馈的效果不存在差异。同样,Semke(1984)在考察德语学习时也未发现两种反馈的效果存在差异,但Guénette(2007)指出,Semke的两个组不仅接收的反馈形式不同,而且写作量也存在差别,这可能会对实验结果造成影响。

近些年来,又出现了一批研究(Bitchener & Knock 2010b;Chandler 2003;Ferris 2006;van Beuningen et al. 2008,2012;姜琳、陈锦2013)专门探讨直接反馈与间接反馈的效果,他们逐步克服了早期研究的弊端,给出了相对统一的结论,即从长期看,直接反馈比间接反馈更利于学习者语言的发展。但Ferris(2006)作为这些研究中的特例,发现间接反馈的长期效果比直接反馈显著。事实上,这一结果只是该研究的一个意外发现,Ferris原本只是考察间接反馈的效果,但由于其中一名实验人员提供给受试的反馈不是实验所要求的间接反馈,而是直接反馈,所以才得到了上述发现。

姜琳、陈锦(2013)对比了间接反馈和元语言反馈(即附加了元语言信息的直接反馈)对于中国学生习得英语类指名词短语的影响,实验结果显示,元语言反馈可有效促进英语类指名词短语习得,而间接反馈则不能。该研究认为,元语言反馈作为语言形式、语境和情感的交融体,为语言学习提供了良好的条件。第一,元语言反馈提供了正确的类指名词短语形式,受试可据此验证自己之前有关类指名词短语用法的假设是否正确,从而反思自己存在的问题,并在接下来的语言输出中对相关用法形式给予重视,这有利于英语类指名词短语使用自动化。

第二,元语言反馈凸显了语境的效用。元语言反馈所提供的类指名词短语形式不是孤立存在的,其背后有着丰富的语境(即作文语篇语境)支撑,而且这种语境完全是受试自己构建出来的,他们必然会格外关注。根据"学伴用随原则"(王初明 2009),如果语言形式是伴随着丰富的语境变量而习得时,那么这些变量能在日后相似的语境中激活该语言形式,确保其用得出、用得对。由此可见,元语言反馈作为语境效用的放大镜,能帮助受试在语篇层面上学用语言,类指名词短语形式与类指语境相伴而学,驱动了句法和语用层面认知的自然整合,这不仅能提高语言学习的效率,还能保证受试日后可以流利、正确地使用英语类指名词短语。

第三,元语言反馈满足了受试的情感诉求。王初明(2011b)曾指出,在我国外语教学中,纠错已经成为师生间的共同默契,学生普遍期望教师改错,而且改得越细致越好。从这个意义上讲,元语言反馈可以满足受试的这一情感诉求,并能进一步激发他们的学习热情。如此一来,他们便会有意识地与元语言反馈中的类指名词短语形式协同,并逐渐将其内化为自己的二语知识,实现对其自由运用。

相比元语言反馈,间接反馈的促学劣势可能源于其形式上的局限。间接反馈仅指出错误而不提供正确形式,所以受试只能藉由"形成假设、验证假设"的过程来认清错误并找到正确答案,从而增强对于英语类指名词短语用法的掌握。这种认知投入虽可以提高所学知识的稳定性和持久性,但对于受试的外语能力、语言分析能力以及学习自觉性要求较高,因此间接反馈的促学效果不理想。

表 6.5 对比直接反馈与间接反馈的效果

Studies	Participants	Feedback types	Effectiveness
Lalande (1982)	60 intermediate German FL learners	1) Direct feedback 2) Indirect coding	Advantage reported for indirect coding but not statistically significant
Semke (1984)	141 German FL learners	1) Direct error correction 2) Content comments 3) Direct error correction & content comments 4) Indirect coding	No difference
Robb et al. (1986)	134 Japanese EFL learners	1) Direct feedback 2) Indirect coding 3) Indirect highlighting 4) Indirect marginal error totals	No difference
Chandler (2003)	31 Hong Kong ESL learners	1) Direct feedback 2) Underline & error description 3) Marginal error description 4) Underline	Direct feedback more effective for both revisions & new papers
Ferris (2006)	55 SL learners	1) Direct feedback 2) Indirect feedback using 15 standard error codes 3) Indirect feedback with nonstandard codes 4) Indirect feedback with no codes 5) Unnecessary correction	Both direct & indirect feedback effective during revisions; indirect feedback more effective long-term

续表

Studies	*Participants*	*Feedback types*	*Effectiveness*
van Beuningen et al. (2008)	62 secondary Dutch FL learners	1) Direct feedback 2) Indirect feedback 3) Writing practice 4) Self-correction revision	Both direct & indirect feedback effective short-term; direct feedback more effective long-term
Bitchener & Knock (2010b)	63 advanced ESL learners	1) Direct metalinguistic explanation 2) Indirect circling 3) Direct metalinguistic explanation & oral explanation 4) Control	All feedback options equally effective short-term; direct feedback more effective long-term
van Beuningen et al. (2012)	268 secondary Dutch FL learners	1) Direct feedback 2) Indirect feedback 3) Writing practice 4) Self-correction revision	Both direct & indirect feedback effective short-term; direct feedback more effective long-term for grammar
姜琳、陈锦（2013）	79名中下级英语水平大学生	1) 间接反馈 2) 元语言反馈 3) 对照	元语言反馈可有效促进英语类指名词短语习得，而间接反馈则不能

6.5.2 对比不同形式直接反馈的效果

目前,共有八项研究对比了不同形式直接反馈的效果(见表6.6),对比主要集中于直接反馈和元语言反馈(即附加口头/书面元语言信息的直接反馈)。例如,Sheen(2007)考察了反馈对于习得冠词两种特指用法(即不定冠词a/an作为第一次指代,定冠词the作为照应指代)的作用,实验结果显示,虽然元语言反馈和直接反馈在短期内的促学效果相当,但从长期看,前者更具优势。然而,Bitchener(2008)却发现,直接反馈比元语言反馈更能促进学习者对于上述两种冠词用法的掌握。可是,当Bitchener & Knock(2008)将Bitchener(2008)的75个受试扩充至144个后,两种反馈效果间的差异就完全消失了。导致上述分歧的主要原因在于:(1)提供元语言解释的方式不同,有些是书面形式,有些口头形式,或者是二者的结合,事实上,口头、书面输入对学习者的注意资源、认知投入程度要求不同(如Sheen 2010),因而学习效果亦会不同;(2)判定反馈作用时采用了不同的测量工具(如看图写作、快速听写、语法判断),然而不同的工具检验不同性质的知识,所以造成了对反馈效果观察时的差异。总之,哪种反馈形式更能促学外语,现有研究尚无定论,值得深入探讨。

近期,笔者开展了一项实验考察元语言反馈和直接反馈对于英语冠词显性、隐性知识发展的影响,实验结果显示,元语言反馈和直接反馈都能有效促进英语冠词显性知识的发展,且二者效果相当;对于隐性知识,元语言反馈比直接反馈更具促学优势。为了充分解释当前的实验结果,笔者通过融合注意假说(如Schmidt 1995)、技能习得理论(如DeKeyser 2007)和频率理论(如Ellis 2012),提出了书面反馈促学路径(以下简称路径),如图6.1所示。

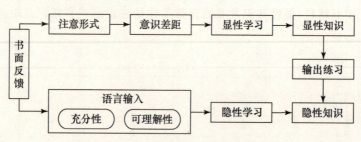

图6.1 书面反馈促学路径

根据路径,一方面,由于书面反馈明确指出错误,故很容易引起学习者注意语言形式(如 Sheen 2010),学习者通过认知比较,意识到差距的存在,从而激发显性学习,产生显性知识后存储于外显记忆。此时,如果外界提供有针对性的言语输出练习,学习者可在反复操练的过程中,有意识地从外显记忆筛选出那些受外界刺激、反复激活的显性知识,将其转化为隐性知识后存储于内隐记忆(Ellis et al. 2006)。另一方面,如果书面反馈提供了充分的可理解性输入,可直接为隐性学习创造条件,学习者通过反复体验正确、恰当的语言输入,最终能够由此及彼,从以项目为基础(item-based)的语言表征转化为以规则为基础(rule-based)的语言表征,实现知识准确、快速地提取和迁移,即产生隐性知识。

笔者以该路径为理论依据,对当前的实验结果进行了深入的剖析。根据路径,显性知识源于显性学习,而显性学习的前提是注意语言形式。Ellis et al. (2006)曾指出,元语言反馈与直接反馈作为显性反馈,其纠错意图(corrective intensions)易为学习者感知,并能激发他们注意语言形式。事实上,当前实验也证实了这一点,通过对三次作文反馈的分析,笔者发现有超过 80%的受试会对作文中的冠词反馈做标记(如画横线、圆圈等),这说明他们注意到了语言形式。由于实验中的两种反馈都提供了正确的冠词用法,受试可通过认知比较,进一步意识到自己对于冠词的掌握程度与目标语之间还存在差距(Ellis 1994)。根据注意假说,意识差距是习得发生的催化剂(Schmidt 1994),会激发学习者有意识地学习目标结构,即显性学习,其结果势必会促进冠词显性知识的发展。

本次实验中,虽然元语言反馈比直接反馈多提供了有关冠词用法的元语言解释,但两种反馈对于冠词显性知识发展的作用相当,这说明元语言解释并没有发挥额外的促学优势,对此结果笔者做了如下分析。根据路径,显性知识发展的充要条件是注意形式和意识差距。由于元语言反馈与直接反馈都指明错误,并提供了正确的冠词形式,这足以引起受试对于形式的注意,并在认知层面进行比较,从而激发显性学习,产生显性知识。此时,尽管元语言反馈还多提供了元语言解释,但这些信息对于显性知识的发展已不具有额外的促学作用了,因此元语言反馈与直接反馈的促学效果相当。

根据路径,隐性知识源自显性知识的程序性转化(proceduralize)或直接来源于隐性学习。前者的实现须有充分的针对性练习和实际使用的机会，而这些条件本次实验没有提供；后者的实现须有充分的可理解性输入作保障，所谓"充分"即指输入的"量"，所谓"可理解性"即指输入的"质"。本次实验针对受试作文中的冠词错误提供元语言反馈和直接反馈，可以说在一定程度上提供了学习者充分的可理解性输入，这必然会激发隐性学习，产生隐性知识。

　　首先，从"量"的角度看，实验中的元语言反馈与直接反馈均称得上是密集型的语言输入。据统计，元语言反馈班与直接反馈班的受试平均每篇作文所能收到的(针对冠词的)反馈次数相当，都在 8—10 次左右，实验共包含了三次写作任务，所以他们就能收到近 30 次的反馈。由于元语言反馈与直接反馈都提供了目标语形式，受试便可以反复接触到正确的冠词用法。根据频率理论，反复体验一个具体语言结构的次数(即实例频率 token frequency)决定了这个结构的固着度(entrenchment)；而反复体验同类语言结构的多种不同表达法(即类型频率 type frequency)决定了这一结构的可生成性(productivity)(Ellis 2012；Tomasello 2003)。在本次实验中，元语言反馈班和直接反馈班都提供了充分的冠词输入量，涵盖了冠词用法的众多实例和类型，这为隐性学习创造了条件，学习者通过反复体验这些语言结构，可加速其大脑表征的固化程度以及使用的创新性，从而有利于流利自如地使用冠词。

　　其次，从"质"的角度看，元语言反馈与直接反馈均提供了可理解性输入，但前者更具优势。一方面，两种反馈所提供的正确形式不是孤立存在的，其背后有着丰富的语境(即作文语篇)支撑，而且这种语境完全是受试自己构建出来的，他们必然会格外关注。所以，针对受试作文中的冠词错误提供反馈，可凸显作文语境的效应，能帮助学习者在语篇层面上学用语言，冠词形式与冠词语境相伴而学，驱动了句法和语用层面认知的自然整合，这不仅能提高语言学习的效率，还能保证受试日后可以流利、正确地使用冠词。

　　另一方面，元语言反馈比直接反馈多提供了元语言解释，这势必更利于隐性学习。隐性学习需要学习者具有较好的规则发现与归纳的能力，而成人外语学习者的隐性学习能力正逐渐退化(DeKeyser 2000)，所以学习效果不理想。本次实验中，元语言反馈提供了冠词用法的详细讲解，这恰好弥补了受试较弱的语言分析及归纳的能力，从而帮助他们高效地隐性学习，产生隐性知识，推动较好的语言产出。与元语言反馈相比，直接反馈仅提供了正确形式，而没有元语言解释，故需要受试在与目标语接触的过程中构建出显性规则,实现对于正确形式的充分理解,从而推动隐性学习,此过程对于受试的语言分析能力及学习自觉性都有一定的要求(Sheen 2007),这势必增加了受试的认知负担。所以对于隐性学习,元语言反馈比直接反馈提供了更为高质的语言输入。

综上所述,尽管元语言反馈与直接反馈在输入"量"上旗鼓相当,但在"质"上,前者更胜一筹,因此其促学效果更明显。

表 6.6　对比不同形式直接反馈的效果

Study	Types of direct written CF	Effectiveness
Bitchener et al. (2005)	1) Direct error correction 2) Direct error correction and oral metalinguistic explanation 3) Control	Group 2 more effective
Bitchener (2008)	1) Direct error correction, written and oral metalinguistic explanation 2) Direct error correction and written metalinguistic explanation 3) Direct error correction 4) Control	Group 1&3 more effective than group 2&4
Bitchener & Knock (2008, 2009a, 2009b, 2010a)	1) Direct error correction, written and oral metalinguisitc explanation 2) Direct error correction and written metalinguistic explanation 3) Direct error correction 4) Control	No difference in types of written CF
Bitchener & Knock (2010b)	1) Direct metalinguistic explanation 2) Indirect circling 3) Direct metalinguistic explanation & oral explanation 4) Control	No difference between the two direct treatment groups (i.e. Group 1 & 3) during both the immediate post-test & delayed post-test pieces of writing
Sheen (2007)	1) Direct error correction 2) Direct error correction with metalinguistic explanation 3) Control	Group 2 more effective

6.5.3 对比不同形式间接反馈的效果

目前,有四个研究(Chandler 2003;Ferris & Roberts 2001;Ferris et al. 2000;Robb et al. 1986)考察了不同形式间接反馈的效果,他们集中探讨了使用代码对间接反馈效果的影响。例如,Chandler(2003)对比了三种不同形式间接反馈的效果:(1) 划出错误并提供错误代码(如图 6.2);(2) 只提供错误代码(如图 6.3);(3) 只划出错误(如图 6.4)。实验结果显示,第三种间接反馈的效果要明显好于前两种,而且前两种反馈间的效果无显著差异。由此可见,使用错误代码并不会提升间接反馈的促学效果。

	"Mayu would you go to the tofu shop and get two pieces of tofu?"
	It was my first try to go to any store by myself.
	"Me? Can I do it? Mmm... it sounds too difficult for me."
ww/art insert	"No, it is easy. The tofu you need to take is called silk tofu. Only thing you need to do is to ask them, 'Could you give me two pieces_ tofu?' That is it."
ww/insert	"O.K. If I say, 'Could you give me two pieces of tofu', do they give me_ ?"
punc	"No, you should say, 'silk tofu'."

图 6.2　间接反馈(1)

wrong form	I crawled back to my sleeping bag and lied down again. I tried to do the method that Skip gave me to focus on my third eye; it did not work so well. I was still wide awake and feeling scared. I looked at my watch and it was almost two o'clock in the morning. Although the method
delete	hadn't worked yet, but I decided to try once more anyhow. I looked up: the moon had just slowly passed a piece of cloud and revealed itself
frag	once more. Just as I was closing my eyes to attempt the method again; suddenly I saw a black spot between my eyes and meanwhile, an
word div	extremely powerful energy as wind squeezed into my body though the black Hole with an ascending "V-Ong" sound... I was unable to make any sound out or move a finger.

图 6.3　间接反馈(2)

> Every day at four-fifty, you would see something magical happened. The building still looked_ ordinary as usual, but it seemed to radiante some kind of incantation_ that the people from all kinds of building in the huge school suddenly spilled out_ their building and flowed to it as natural as the water goes to the lower place. The building just like becoming a magnet in a sudden and the people_ like the spreaded iron sands which attached to it instantly.

图 6.4　间接反馈(3)

6.5.4　对比聚焦与非聚焦反馈的效果

非聚焦反馈即为全面纠错，虽然看似全面，但由于研究目标不明确，因而其结论常常会受到质疑。聚焦反馈即为针对性纠错，虽然可以保证深入细致的实验研究，但无法全面反映学习者的语言水平，更不能满足其语言的个性发展（姜琳 2012b）。目前，二语写作派崇尚全面纠错，而二语习得派则偏向于针对性纠错，逐渐形成各自为政的局面。迄今为止，将两种反馈形式进行对比的实证研究屈指可数。Ellis et al.（2008）对比了两种反馈对冠词习得的影响。49 名日本中级英语水平学习者被分成聚焦与非聚焦反馈两个组，聚焦反馈组只接收冠词方面的反馈，而非聚焦反馈组会收到包括冠词在内的全面反馈。实验结果显示，两种反馈可以同等程度地促进受试对冠词的掌握，但 Ellis 等人同时也指出，由于冠词错误是两组受试最常犯的错误，因此实验中的两种反馈在形式上并没有太大区别。

为了弥补 Ellis et al.（2008）的研究缺陷，Sheen et al.（2009）扩大了考察目标的范围，包括冠词、系动词 be、规则/不规则动词过去式和介词。实验结果显示，聚焦反馈比非聚焦反馈更能促进受试对冠词的掌握；聚焦反馈作为一种集中性（intensive）反馈，易于激发学习者注意形式，加深对于错误原因及本质的认识，同时理解该如何修正错误。但 Sheen 等人承认该实验存在缺陷，即非聚焦反馈组所接收的反馈缺乏系统性，有些错误被纠正，有些则没有，这势必会给受试造成不解，从而影响最终的结果。

陈晓湘等（2013）考察了聚焦与非聚焦反馈对中国学生习得英语非真实条件虚拟语气的作用，实验包含五个组：直接聚焦组、间接聚焦组、直接非聚焦组、间接非聚焦组和对照组。实验结果显示，从短期看,聚焦和非聚焦反馈的效果无明显差异,但直接反馈优于间接反馈;从长期看,聚焦反馈优于非聚焦反馈,间接反馈优于直接反馈;此外,受试的外语水平会影响反馈的效果。虽然上述结果清晰、工整,并证实了聚焦反馈的长效性好于非聚焦反馈,但由于作者没有在文中对目标结构作详细介绍,这在一定程度上削弱了实验结论的可靠性。虚拟语气是一种复杂的语言结构,不仅表现形式多样,在使用时涉及了句法、语义和语用多方面的知识,作者对此没有作任何介绍,因而我们很难想象受试的错误形式,以及教师如何确定并纠正错误。

6.6 错误类型、纠错数量与反馈效果

6.6.1 错误类型与反馈效果

无论是反馈研究者还是外语教师都会问到一个问题:反馈的效果是否会受到错误类型的影响。然而迄今为止,反馈研究主要聚焦于一些规则(rule-based)、独立的(discrete)语法结构错误(如冠词、一般过去式等错误)(如 Bitchener & Knoch 2010;Bitchener et al. 2005;Sheen 2007;Shintani & Ellis 2013),而对于其他语言错误关注较少,这也恰好成为了某些学者批判"纠错有效"的理据之一(如 Xu 2009)。Truscott(1996)认为,单一形式的反馈不可能适用于所有类型的错误,因为句法、形态和词汇知识的习得不仅涉及到对相关形式、意义的理解,还涉及到与其他成分在一起配合使用的问题,甚至还包含了非语言的认知系统。Truscott(2007)进一步指出,反馈仅能帮助学习者修改作文,或者是减少一些相对简单、独立的非句法错误;而对于句法类型的错误,反馈的效果非常有限,因为句法知识是系统性的,不是一个个独立知识点的集合,因此学习者无法通过反馈这种分散提供信息的方式来习得句法知识。

此外,Truscott(2004,2007)认为,由于学习者不可能在写作中使用一些他们没有把握、复杂的语言结构,所以实验人员(或教师)便没有机会针对复杂语言结构的错误提供反馈。同样,Skehan(1998)指出,学习者的注意资源有限,他们必须在语言准确性与复杂性之间做好权衡;当学习者关注语言准确性时,他们就会非常保守地选择所要使用的语言形式,只选取自己有把握的结构,而放弃那些复杂、易出错的结构(Skehan & Foster 2001)。尽管学习者使用复杂语言结构的机

会比较少,但这并不能说明反馈对于复杂结构的错误没有效果。事实上,口头反馈研究已经证实,口头反馈对于复杂结构(如英语问句、双宾结构等)的习得非常有效(Mackey & Oliver 2002;Mackey & Philp 1998;Mackey et al. 2002;McDonough 2006)。由于书面反馈不像口头反馈那样会给学习者造成太多的认知负担,因此我们有理由相信,书面反馈也同样有利于复杂结构的习得,甚至比口头反馈的效果更理想。

目前,只有陈晓湘等(2013)考察了书面反馈对复杂结构习得的效果,该研究考察的目标结构是英语非真实条件虚拟语气。虚拟语气用法比较复杂,涉及到句法、语义和语用多层面知识的集合。在实际应用中,可采用陈述式的一般过去时、过去进行体和过去完成体,也可采用情态助动词的过去式形式加动词不定式或不定式完成体,还可综合使用上述语法手段(章振邦 2004)。该实验的结果显示,反馈可促进学习者对于英语虚拟语气的掌握,而且聚焦反馈的效果好于非聚焦反馈,间接反馈的效果好于直接反馈。

纠错对词汇学习是否有效,无论在理论还是实证层面均存在分歧。理论上,Truscott虽然极力反对语法纠错,但认为纠错可能会对词汇错误有帮助(Truscott 2001),因为词汇错误是不受规则制约、相对独立的简单问题;但Ferris(2006)却认为,恰恰是因为词汇用法在很大程度上无规律可循,所以词汇错误难以纠正。在实证方面,仅有少数几个研究考察了纠错对于词汇学习的作用,而且结论不一。例如,Bitchener et al.(2005)同时考察了纠错对于冠词、一般过去式和介词习得的影响,实验结果表明,纠错对于前两种语法错误(即冠词和一般过去式)的效果比较明显,而对于后一种词汇错误(即介词)的作用却并不理想。对此,Bitchener 等人认为,介词用法常常约定俗成,与具体的语境有关,属于特质型(idiosyncratic)知识,故对于纠错不敏感。van Beuningen et al.(2012)采用全面纠错(comprehensive correction)的方法,考察了纠错对于提升英语写作语言准确性的影响,实验结果表明,纠错有助于学习者减少词汇选择方面的错误,而且间接纠错比直接纠错的效果更明显。

词汇错误中的一大典型错误是搭配(collocation)错误(如 Ferris 2006;Lewis 2000),如*study knowledge(acquire knowledge)、*do/make an operation(perform an operation)等,其产生原因多与母语负迁移、近义词混淆、语义限制重视不够以及词汇学习策略使用不足等

有关。在二语习得领域,搭配知识被视为二语能力的重要体现(如Lewis 2000),Ellis(2004)甚至提出,搭配知识本质上就是隐性知识,是实现流利、正确使用语言的重要保障(Durrant & Schmitt 2010)。目前,搭配研究多为描述性质,即将二语学习者产出的搭配与本族语者语料库数据进行对比,以分析二语搭配的使用规律(参阅 Siyanova & Schmitt 2008)。相比之下,探讨二语学习者如何习得搭配知识的研究却屈指可数(如 Durrant & Schmitt 2010),尤其是纠错反馈对搭配习得的影响,尚无研究见诸报道,但学界已经意识到了此类研究的重要性,因为他们对于认识二语词汇习得机制、发展二语习得理论、提升外语教学质量均至关重要。

近期,笔者开展了一项实验,探讨纠错对英语搭配学习的作用。实验结果表明,纠错可以有效促进中国学生对目标搭配(包括产出性知识和接受性知识)的掌握,而且语境越丰富,纠错效果越好。研究指出,纠错有利于学生注意到中介语与目标语间的差距,从而有意识地学习目标语言形式以弥合差距。丰富的语境信息可以从视觉上加深学习者对于搭配的感官认识和理解,并将搭配形式与对应的语境黏合起来,形成新的组合体,成为一个大脑表征单元。由于组合体各部分之间能够相互启动,因此当学习者日后经历类似的语境时,对应的搭配形式就会被自动激活。

6.6.2　纠错数量与反馈效果

对于一次写作任务,究竟要纠正多少错误才能实现反馈效用的最大化?对此,学界当前主要有三种作法:(1)针对性纠错,即只纠正学习者作文中的一两类语言错误;(2)选择性纠错,即纠正一些比较严重、常犯的语言错误;(3)全面纠错,即纠正每一处语言错误。

全面纠错有以下三个优点。首先,它更接近于实际写作教学(Hartshorn et al. 2010;van Beuningen et al. 2012)。写作教学的目的是帮助学生提高写作语言的整体水平,而不是习得一两类语法结构。其次,它可以满足学生的情感诉求。有调查显示,大多数学生都希望教师可以全面纠错(如 Ferris et al. 2010;Ferris & Roberts 2001;Leki 1991)。最后,它顺应了当下社会对外语学习者的要求。在课堂之外,写作文本的质量会影响到外界对文本作者的印象,无论是升学还是应聘求职,对方都希望看到一份完美或近乎完美的文本,在这种情况下,语言错误会给文本作者带来极大的负面影响,学生要学会全面编辑文本语言的能力,而不仅仅是处理几类语言错误的能力。

但是,全面纠错也存在弊端:(1)实验人员无法保证对每一处语言错误都提供反馈,而这种非系统性的纠错极大地削弱了实验结果的可信度;(2)学习者的注意资源和加工能力有限,很难消化和吸收全部反馈,故容易造成"高耗低效"的尴尬局面;(3)会提升学习者的焦虑感,影响学习效率;(4)不同领域的语言学知识需要通过不同的方式获取,因此以单一形式广泛纠错并不可取(Schwartz 1993;Truscott 1999)。

针对性纠错通过强化学习者的注意力来达到促学的目的,其效果已得到普遍证实。此外,针对性纠错目标明确,能够保证深入细致的实验研究。然而,这种纠错方式也存在缺陷。首先,它无法全面反映学习者的语言水平,更不能满足他们语言的个性发展。其次,从实证研究的角度看,针对性纠错很容易使受试察觉出实验目的,从而对目标结构的使用情况作自我监控,这必然会降低实验结论的有效性(Xu 2009)。最后,从教学的角度看,针对性纠错使写作课变成了语法练习课,背离了写作教学的真正意义(Bruton 2009)。

选择性纠错需要教师对学习者的语言水平有充足的了解,知晓哪些语言错误是危害性较大、易犯的错误,从而有选择地纠正。目前,尚无研究系统地考察选择性纠错的效果,未来研究可对此作深入探讨。

综上所述,三种纠错方式各有利弊,教师可根据学生的实际情况,选择最适合的方法,或者将三者综合利用,使其相互配合、各展所长。例如,对于学生的初稿,教师可针对一些比较突出的错误提供反馈,要求学生在下一稿中将错误改正过来;对于倒数第二稿,教师可要求学生通读全文,尽可能修正每一处错误,随后对学生没有发现的错误提供全面反馈;最后,可要求学生写一份分析报告,总结自己在修改作文语言过程中的收获,以及如何将它们应用于新的写作任务。

6.7 个体和环境因素对反馈效果的影响

6.7.1 个体因素

根据社会文化理论,没有任何一种反馈是万能的,只有当它充分符合学习者的发展能力时,才会最大程度地发挥支架作用(Sheen

2010)。我们在写作教学中也会发现,尽管以同样的方式提供反馈,有的学生受益多,有的受益少。以上从理论到实践的分析说明了反馈的效果很大程度上取决于学习者本人,故关注学习者的个体因素对于解读反馈的促学价值非常有必要。然而,绝大多数反馈研究未将个体因素纳入考察范围,基本上还是属于单变量(反馈形式)因果性研究,这对于外语学习如此复杂的系统而言显然过于简单了,所以研究结论势必存在局限。由于长期受到传统认知观念的影响,反馈研究对于小组表现的关注度远远超过个体表现(Bitchener 2012),他们对于个体因素的探索远不及二语习得领域的其他方向。目前,反馈领域所开展的个体因素研究大致可归分两类:认知视角和社会文化视角。接下来,我们分别概述每类研究的主要发现。

Sheen(2007;2011)从认知视角考察了三种个体因素(即语言分析能力、焦虑和态度)对于口头和书面反馈效果的调节作用。语言分析能力是指通过分析语言输入,归纳出语法规则,并将规则应用到新句子中的能力(Sawyer & Ranta 2001)。Sheen(2007)发现,受试的语言分析能力越高,反馈(包括直接反馈和元语言反馈)对他们的帮助越大,尤其是元语言反馈,效果最为明显。此外,语言分析能力和态度对书面和口头反馈的效果都具有调节作用,但焦虑只影响口头反馈的效果(Sheen 2011)。

根据 Sheen(2007)的实验结果,与直接反馈相比,受试的语言分析能力与元语言反馈的效果更相关,即受试的语言分析能力越高,越容易从元语言反馈中获益。对此结果,我们不免会产生疑问:元语言反馈已经将语言的使用规则提供给了受试,还需要他们再借助语言分析能力来发现和归纳相关规则吗?众所周知,元语言反馈不仅包含正确的语言形式,还有其用法的元语言解释,这些显性语言知识弥补了低语言分析能力者较弱的语言分析和归纳的能力,从而帮助他们高效地获取语言知识。因此,低语言分析能力者可以像高语言分析能力者一样从元语言反馈中获益。相比而言,直接反馈仅提供正确的语言形式,没有相应的元语言解释,故需要学习者依赖语言分析能力推断并概括出目标语用法,进而内化为自己的二语知识。因此,相比低语言分析能力者,高语言分析能力者从直接反馈中的获益会更具优势。综合以上分析,相比元语言反馈,直接反馈的促学效果应该与受试的语言分析能力更加相关,而这显然与 Sheen(2007)的实验结果相悖,因此未来研究可对此做进一步考证。

与认知视角相比,从社会文化视角开展的个体因素研究相对丰富(Goldstein 2006;Hyland 1998,2000,2003;Storch & Wigglesworth 2010;Swain 2006;Swain & Lapkin 2002)。Storch & Wigglesworth(2010)考察了三种情感因素(即信念、目标和态度)对于学习者吸收和内化反馈信息的影响。实验结果显示,当高水平学习者认为某一种反馈与他们内在的信念不一致时,他们就会忽视它;对于低水平学习者,由于信念还未真正形成,所以暂且不会发生这种情况。同样,Swain(2006)和Swain & Lapkin(2002)也发现,当学习者认为某一种反馈违反了他们传统的语言信念,或者改变了他们原本要表达的意思,就会对这种反馈采取抵制的态度,不作任何反应。

此外,Storch & Wigglesworth(2010)还发现,学习目标会影响学习者对于反馈的利用和吸收程度,当学习者渴望提升自己的写作语言时,就会充分利用反馈信息。同样,Hyland(1998,2000,2003)发现,当学习者看重写作语言时,就会对反馈作出非常积极的响应;但如果感觉教师对反馈过程操控得过于严格,或者没有充分考虑学习者的个人目标,他们就会对反馈采取抵制态度。Goldstein(2006)在对两名二语写作者的个案调查中发现,学习动机同样会影响到学习者对反馈的利用程度。最后,学习者的态度也会影响他们对反馈的吸收程度。例如,在Storch & Wigglesworth(2010)的研究中,受试对重述(reformulation)形式的反馈持负面态度,因而就会常常忽视它们。

总之,如果学习者自身不愿意关注反馈,那么反馈对他们的学习发展就起不到任何作用。但由于上述研究多为定性的个案研究,因而还不能充分说明这些个体因素对于更大受试群体的影响。鉴于此,反馈领域可以开展一些纵向的定量研究用以补充个案研究,同时还要加强对于个体因素、反馈形式和错误性质之间交互作用的考察,深入探讨反馈的促学机制和促学效果。

6.7.2 环境因素

二语习得领域对社会环境的研究主要从三个维度展开:(1)宏观与微观;(2)结构(structural)与互动(interactional);(3)主观与客观。反馈研究主要从第一个维度考察社会环境因素的作用;其中,宏观环境是指学习环境(如外语学习环境、二语学习环境等)和教学环境(如传统语法教学、交际教学等)等,微观环境是指写作任务的类型、人与人的社会关系等。目前,反馈研究多集中于宏观环境,而对微观环境的考察比较少见。

学习环境会影响学习者对反馈的关注程度。Hedgcock & Lefkowitz(1994)发现,英语外语和英语二语学习者由于所处学习环境不同,所以学习目的存在差异。英语外语学习者的目的大多是为了获取一个文凭,而不是想从根本上提高英语水平以融入英语社会。不同的学习目的决定了不同的学习动机,并最终影响到学习者对于反馈的关注和利用程度。

此外,教学环境也会影响学习者对反馈的关注程度。如果学习者平时接收的是总结性反馈(summative feedback)而非形成性反馈(formative feedback)①,那么他们对纠正性反馈的关注度就不会太高(Hedgcock & Lefkowitz 1994);如果学习者平时接受的是形式教学,那么他们对于反馈的关注度就会高一些(Ferris 1999;Reid 1998,2005;Roberts 1999)。Bitchener & Knock(2008)考察了教学环境对于反馈效果的影响。实验受试包括国际学生(international students)和移民学生(migrant students);前者处于显性的语法教学环境,经常收到教师(针对语言问题)的反馈;后者则很少参与正规的课堂教学,不常接触到反馈。按照之前的观点(Ferris 1999;Hedgcock & Lefkowitz 1994;Reid 1998,2005;Roberts 1999),国际学生应该比移民学生更容易从反馈中获益。然而实验结果显示,国际学生和移民学生在接收了有关冠词错误的反馈后,他们在后测中的冠词使用情况没有明显区别,究其原因,很可能与受试筛选不严格有关。移民学生也有可能接收了形式教学,因此非常关注语言使用的准确性;国际学生也可能是在自然环境中学习目标语,认为语言交际能力比语法能力重要。

Given & Schallert(2008)考察了师生关系如何影响学习者对反馈的利用程度。实验结果显示,如果学生信任教师,在修改作文时就会充分利用教师的反馈,否则就会不予理睬,从而影响外语学习。该结果表明,学习者与反馈的协同过程与信念和情感有关。王初明(2010)曾指出,人们读鲁迅作品,是因为相信他是伟人,崇敬他,以他为榜样,向他学习。抱有这样信念的人,就会喜欢鲁迅,就会主动找他

---

① 总结性反馈关注学习结果,其目的只是提供一个分数;形成性反馈关注学习过程,其目的是帮助学习者修改作文,提升新作文语言的准确性。

的作品来读,与读物协同的效应自然增大。同样的道理,一位教师的人品和学识受到学生的敬重,就会得到学生的情感认同或协同。这样的教师更能调动学生的学习积极性,他教的课学生爱听,所教的内容易被学生吸收。一旦学生对上课的教师反感,师生情感协同断链,学生就不会跟他学了。近来国外有调查发现,影响外语学得好坏最重要的因素是学生是否喜欢上课的教师。

6.7.3 个体因素与环境因素的交互作用

根据 Coughlan & Duff(1994),个体因素可与环境因素发生交互作用,并影响学习者选择何种方式来完成任务。具体说来,学习者会以不同的方式完成相同的任务,说明了学习者受到了个体因素与环境因素的交叉影响,包括时间、地点、情感状态等。尽管该研究没有特别针对反馈问题,但这些因素在口语活动中的交互影响已经被证实,而且有必要继续考察它们对于写作活动以及反馈效果的调节作用。

6.8 小结

本章介绍了准实验性反馈研究的六个方向。下面,我们对每个方向的研究内容作简要的总结。

第一,反馈能否促进二语语法结构的习得?当前研究主要集中于冠词的两种特指用法,即不定冠词 a/an 作为第一次指代、定冠词 the 作为照应指代,实验结果显示:对于不同学习环境(包括英语二语学习环境、外语学习环境)中的不同水平(包括初、中、高级)的学习者,针对其作文中的冠词错误提供系统性的反馈,可有效增强他们对于上述两种冠词用法的掌握,反馈效果甚至可以长达 10 个月。虽然学习者对冠词的掌握程度是衡量其英语能力的重要标尺,但冠词毕竟不是外语学习的全部,若想为反馈的促学价值提供更充分的证据,需针对多种语法结构进行实验,从研究的深度和广度上求证反馈的效果。

第二,反馈能否帮助学习者提升修改稿语言的准确性?尽管现有研究在反馈形式、错误类型、写作/修改条件,以及学生背景等方面存在诸多差异,但结果非常一致:反馈可以显著提升学习者修改稿语言的准确性。但是,短期进步能否说明语言能力的长期发展?Truscott 认为,修改成功不等于语言能力提升,二者没有相关性;而其他学者

(Ferris 2004;Sachs & Polio 2007)认为,短期进步为实现语言能力长期发展奠定了必要的基础。未来研究可对此问题作深入考察,这不仅有利于解决理论上的纷争,同时对提高外语教学质量具有现实意义。

第三,反馈能否促进学生写作语言的长期发展? 早期研究(Kepner 1991;Robb et al. 1986;Semke 1984;Sheppard 1992)发现,反馈不能提升学习者新作文语言的准确性,但由于这些研究在实验方法上存在缺陷,因而其结论的可信度受到了质疑。近期研究(除 Truscott & Hsu (2008))几乎都证实了反馈对于学生写作语言发展的长期效果,而且语言准确性提升的同时,其复杂性不会降低(Hartshorn et al. 2010)。

第四,反馈的形式是否会影响反馈的效果? 概括起来,(1)直接反馈的效果好于间接反馈;(2)元语言信息会在一定程度上影响直接反馈的效果;(3)使用错误代码不会影响间接反馈的效果;(4)聚焦反馈的效果好于非聚焦反馈。

第五,错误类型和纠错数量是否会影响反馈的效果? 现有反馈研究多集中于规则、独立型的语法结构,并且证实了反馈的有效性,而对于复杂语言结构的效果,相关研究屈指可数,因此还无法全面证实反馈的促学价值。此外,对于全面纠错、针对性纠错和选择性纠错,可视学习者的语言水平与实际教学情况采用适合的纠错方式,或者将三者有机融合,实现反馈效用的最大化。

第六,个体因素和环境因素是否对反馈效果起调节作用? 对于个体因素,学习者的语言分析能力越高,反馈对他们的帮助越大(Sheen 2007);而且,学习者的情感因素(包括信念、目标和态度)决定了他们对反馈的关注和利用情况(Storch & Wigglesworth 2010)。对于环境因素,学习者所处的学习环境、教学方式,以及与教师间的信任关系,都会影响到他们从反馈中的获益程度。

第七章 反馈研究未来展望

7.1 引言

本书在第二、三章分别梳理了不同时期二语习得理论、写作理论的纠错观。虽然这些理论对于纠错的认识逐渐趋于理性,但由于目前缺少系统的反馈促学理论模型,因此一定程度上制约了反馈研究的发展。随后,本书在第四、五、六章分别介绍了观察性、调查性以及准实验性反馈研究,所涉及的研究数量不下百余个,时间跨度长达80年(1930—2013)。在对他们进行分析和评价的过程中,我们看到了反馈研究所取得的成果,同时也注意到了他们的缺陷。最后,如果不能将上述理论和研究成果应用于外语教学,反馈领域的存在和发展就失去了意义。为了推动理论和研究成果向现实教学转化,加强教师培训工作实属必要,而这些都是未来亟待解决的问题。针对上述情况,本章从理论、研究和教学三个层面出发,具体分析反馈领域的未来发展趋势,其中研究部分又分为实验方法和研究内容。

7.2 反馈理论展望

本书在第二章概述了二语习得七大理论流派对于语言纠错的认识。总体上看,我们可以 Krashen 20 世纪 80 年代的监控模型作为分水岭,将之前的理论看作早期理论,其后为近期理论。由于受到 Chomsky 先天论的影响,Krashen 认为纠错的作用是表面性的,它对于改善学习者的二语能力没有任何帮助。而在此之前的早期理论则受行为主义的影响,强调要及时纠错以免妨碍语言发展。近期二语习得理论受认知心理学和社会文化理论的交叉影响,对纠错有了更为理性的认识,即在肯定纠错作用的同时,更加关注纠错的效率问题。

本书在第三章纵观了一语和二语写作理论对错误及纠错的认识。对于一语写作理论,语言错误在早期被认为是性格缺陷的一种反映,应极力消除;随后,它被看成是语言发展过程的必然产物,教师应帮助学生避免犯错;如今,它被视作一种社会观念,不必刻意关注。对于二语写作理论,其早期发展受到了一语写作教学法的影响:上世纪70—80年代,随着过程写作法的推广,二语写作教学的侧重点由传统的篇章结构、语法、词汇,转向了对写作内容及写作过程的关注,语言纠错由此受到了巨大的冲击。但随着应用语言学的发展,人们逐渐意识到,二语写作者的知识结构和经验基础与一语写作者不同,他们除了会犯和一语写作者类似的错误之外,还会犯下更多由于母语负迁移和二语知识缺失所造成的错误,因此适当纠错非常必要,二语写作教学要平衡好培养写作技能与语言水平之间的关系。本章最后还专门介绍了 Truscott 的纠错观,Truscott 于上世纪90年代末相继发表了数篇文章(如 Truscott 1996,1999,2004,2007,2009),批评语言纠错不仅无益、反而有害,建议彻底摒弃;其言论虽受到广泛质疑,却极大地推动了反馈研究的发展,促成了长达15年的黄金发展期。

尽管这些理论从各自的视角分析了反馈促学的理论机制,但他们的分析是碎片化的,尚未形成体系。因此,未来研究有必要构建一个融合认知心理、社会环境因素的综合性理论模型,用以解释反馈促学的内在机制。基于前期研究的成果,笔者拟建了一个反馈促学理论模型(以下简称模型),如图7.1所示。根据模型,所有外在因素会综合作用于学习者,并与学习者的个体因素发生交互作用,从而影响他们对反馈的认知投入,并决定最终的学习效果。该模型表明,学习的过程始终发生在学习者身上,所有影响学习的变量,包括外部的社会环境因素及内部的认知心理因素,都将依托于学习者而发生关联,它们相互作用、相互制约,形成了一个动态的、复杂的交互系统。该模型包含三个关键因素,即个体因素(教师因素、学生因素)、环境因素和投入程度(engagement)。接下来,我们具体分析这些关键因素在模型中的作用。

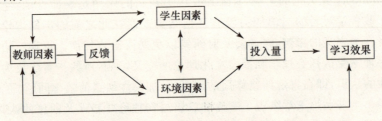

图 7.1　反馈促学理论模型

7.2.1 个体因素

根据模型,个体因素涵盖了学生因素和教师因素。目前,二语习得领域对于学生个体差异的研究主要集中在四个方面:学能(aptitude)、学习风格(learning style)、学习策略和学习动机。

外语学能

外语学能一般是指人们在学习一门第二语言时所表现出来的相对稳定的专业能力倾向(Carroll 1981),它区别于一般智力(general intelligence)(Ellis 1994),是与生俱来、相对稳定的个体因素,它不是二语习得的前提条件,但决定了外语学习的速度和难易程度。Carroll 经过严格的因素分析(factor analysis)统计,进一步归结出构成外语学能的四种重要能力,如表 7.1 所示。

表 7.1 外语学能的四种能力

能力	具体表现
语音编码能力(Phonemic coding ability)	能对新的语音进行编码和记忆
语法敏感度(Grammatical sensitivity)	能辨认出词在句子中的语法功能
语言归纳能力(Inductive language learning ability)	能根据语言输入归纳句法和形态规则
联想记忆能力(Associative memory)	能将一语和二语词汇建立联系,并加以记忆

Skehen(1998:207)将表 7.1 中的语法敏感度和语言归纳能力合称为语言分析能力,并将其定义为"推断语言规则和进行语言总结的能力"。由此,外语学能变为由语音编码能力、语言分析能力和联想记忆能力三种主要能力构成,而其中语言分析能力与联想记忆能力则构成学界所熟悉的语言"双编码系统"(dual-code system),成为从认知角度解释二语习得过程的重要理论(温植胜 2005)。

目前,外语学能与课堂教学、学习环境、交际课堂和学习条件的相关性研究已广泛开展(如 DeGraaf 1997;Ehrman & Oxford 1995;Harley & Hart 2002;Ranta 2002;Reves 1982;Wesche 1981),这里我们重点介绍 DeGraaf(1997)的研究。该研究探讨了外语学能在显性和隐性学习环境下,如何影响学习者学习一种名为 eXperanto 的人工语言(对世界语 Esperanto 稍作修改而成)。实验结果显示,学能分数与显性和隐性学习环境均相关,说明了外语学能不仅作用于显性学习环境,即以规则解释为主导的传统教学环境,也同样适用于隐性学习环境。鉴于此,反馈作为一种显性教学手段,其效果必然会受到外语学能水平的影响,未来研究可对此作深入考察。

学习风格

学习风格是学习心理学、教学心理学等学科关注和探讨的重要课题,但长期以来,人们对它的认识并未达成一致。Grigerenko & Sternberg(1995)区分了学习风格研究的三个流派:认知研究、个性研究和活动研究。认知研究关注认知与感知功能,如 Pask(1976)发现,个体在处理复杂的学习任务时会有两种倾向性,一种是采用整体策略,对有关论题及其关系进行概述;一种是采用逐步处理任务的策略,在形成一个概念的整体图像之前,关注面较窄,集中于细节和程序。Pask 称前一种学习风格为整体思维者,后一种为系列思维者。

个性研究从个性而非认知的角度探讨学习风格。如 Gregorc(1982)根据人们在感知和时间组织方式上的差异,区分了四种类型的学习风格:(1) 具体顺序的学习者(concrete sequential learners)偏好通过系列经验抽取信息,他们是有次序、有逻辑、系列性的学习者;(2) 具体随机的学习者(concrete random learners)喜欢尝试错误式的、直觉、独立的学习方式;(3) 抽象顺序的学习者(abstract sequential learners)偏好采用具体、理性、系列化的学习方式;(4) 抽象随机的学习者(abstract random learners)对人类行为有敏锐意识,有能力评价和解释气氛与情绪。

活动研究认为学习风格是一种学习取向,因此强调学生对教学情景的感知、动机取向及加工方式的重要性。这类研究通常采用因素分析的方法,探讨不同学习活动之间的组合情况。通过因素分析获得的学习活动组合,常常被认为是反映了不同性质但相对稳定的学习风格。

大量研究表明,学习风格直接参与学习活动过程并影响学习成效。学习内容和学习风格匹配,学习效果一般比较好,反之,效果不理想。反馈研究有必要深入探讨学习风格与反馈效果之间的关系。

学习策略

学习策略是指学习者为了理解、学习和记忆信息而进行的某种思考和行动(O'Malley & Chamot 1990),它是认知心理过程和具体行为的结合,是由学习语言的方法手段所构成的动态系统,是为学习语言所采取的具体对策的综合体系(秦建华、王英杰 2007)。文秋芳(1996)提出学习策略具有整体性、开放性和动态性的特点。整体性是指学习策略涵盖了应对语言学习各方面的对策,学习者利用系统内部各要素之间的相互关系,发挥其各自应有的作用。开放性是指学习者能不停地从外界获取新方法、新技巧,从而不断发展、调整、完善和优化自己的学习策略系统。动态性表现在学习者根据自己外语水平的变化和学习任务的不同,对学习策略系统不断地作出调整。

Dörnyei & Skehan(2003)将学习策略分为四类,即认知策略、元认知策略、社交策略和情感策略,如表 7.2 所示。吴本虎(2003)从表现形式、作用方式和意识程度三个维度对学习策略进行了区分。依据表现形式不同,学习策略可分为外显策略和内隐策略;依据作用方式不同,可分为语言学习策略和一般学习策略;依据意识程度的强弱,可分为主动策略和自动策略。

研究学习策略包括三种方法和六种手段。三种方法分别为观察法、内省法和追思法(retrospection);六种手段包括现场记录、有声思维、面谈采访、问卷调查、学习日记和实验检测(吴本虎 2003)。反馈研究应该系统探讨学习者对学习策略的运用情况与反馈效果之间的关系。

表 7.2　四类学习策略

策略类型	功能	具体表现
认知策略	通过对学习材料的直接分析、转换或综合来解决问题	重复、翻译、记笔记、编组、演绎、再结合、关键词、语境化、迁移、推理和详细描述
元认知策略	通过确定学习目标与计划、监控学习过程、评估学习结果等手段来调节外语学习	预先组织机制、集中注意力、自我管理、自我监察、自我评估、延迟表达
社交策略	通过人际互动来增加使用第二语言的机会	发起和本族语者的交流、同伴合作
情感策略	通过调整情感状态,保证学习的主观投入性	

学习动机

学习动机是引起和维持学习活动,并使学习活动朝着一定的目标进行,以满足学习需要的内部动力。从社会心理视角开展的二语动机研究将学习动机分为融入性动机和工具性动机。前者指学习者喜欢目标语社团,希望和目标语社团的成员交往,甚至成为这个社团的成员。后者是指为了实现某一目的而学习,如为了通过考试、找到好工作或提高社会地位等(周颂波等 2011)。

  从教育环境视角开展动机研究的首推 Dörnyei(1994)的外语学习动机框架,该框架将众多动机类型和成分有机整合在一起,从语言层面、学习者层面和学习情境层面对学习动机进行了界定。其中,语言层面包含与二语有关的诸多成分,诸如目标语蕴含的文化、目标语社团以及熟练使用该语言的潜在价值。学习者层面涉及学习者与学习过程有关的个性特征,如成就需求、语言使用焦虑、结果归因模式、自我效能等。学习情境层面由三类动机成分构成。其中与课程有关的动机成分涉及大纲、教材、教学方法以及学习任务;与教师有关的动机成分涉及教师的个性、行为和教学风格;与小组有关的动机成分则包括小组凝聚力、课堂目标结构(合作型、竞争型或个体型)、小组目标倾向、小组规范和奖惩机制等(周颂波等 2011)。基于上述成果,反馈研究可深入探讨学习者的学习动机如何影响他们从反馈中的获益程度。

  事实上,除学能、学习风格、学习策略和学习动机外,可能影响反馈效果的学习者个体因素还包括年龄、外语水平、记忆、性格、语言焦虑和信念等。考察个体差异对反馈效果的调节作用可鼓励外语教师寻找适合自己学生的反馈形式,掌握提供反馈的最佳时机,从而唤起学生对反馈投入足够的心理注意,促进外语学习。这里需要对性格因素做特别说明,性格因素一直未受到二语习得界的关注,但一个人的性格从大的意义上讲,决定了他的人生观和命运,从小的意义上说,决定了他的学习风格、学习策略和学习动机等。因此,将性格因素纳入反馈研究的框架实属必要。本书在附录 3 中给出了 MBTI(Myers-Briggs Type Indicator)性格量表,该量表由美国心理学家 Katharine Cook Briggs 和她的女儿 Isabel Briggs Myers 共同制定,经过半个世纪的使用和完善,已被证明是具有信、效度的人格量表,现已成为具有广泛影响和应用前景的国际著名人格量表(Naomi 2000)。广东外语外贸大学英语语言文化学院 2012 级硕士研究生陈锦在其硕士论文筹备阶段,对该量表的中文版本(罗正学等 2002)进行了调整,增强了其语言表述的准确性和流畅性。

  反馈领域对于学习者个体因素的研究虽刚起步,但至少已经引起了学者们的关注。与之相比,教师个体因素(如培训背景、纠错观、教学任务及方式等)则完全处于被遗忘的角落。然而,教师们对于反馈的认识存在着很大的差异(如 Schulz 2001),包括为什么提供反馈,何时提供反馈,提供多少反馈,针对什么错误提供反馈,如何提供反馈,谁来提供反馈,如何辅助反馈发挥作用,以及如何帮助学生充分利用反馈等,而观念上的差异会导致不同的纠错行为。此外,就同一个教师而言,其纠错方式也不会始终如一,必将会随着时间、对象及环境等因素的变化而发生改变,例如,Nystrom(1983)和 Zamel(1985)发现,教师对错误的态度和方式经常前后不一,而且时常出错。因此,将教师个体因素纳入考察范围不仅可以提高反馈研究的实践价值,还可以扩宽反馈研究的空间。

7.2.2 环境因素

长期以来,反馈研究将环境因素分为宏观环境和微观环境。宏观环境是指学习环境,如浸入环境、二语环境、外语环境等。由于宏观环境比较宽泛,包含了诸多变量因素,故难以控制,因此对宏观环境的考察难度较大,未取得显著成果。目前,反馈领域更多关注微观环境的影响,包括学习活动的性质、师生关系等。反馈研究若想对环境因素的考察取得突破,就需要对环境本体做好区分和界定。王初明(2007)对外语学习语境的论述为反馈研究提供了新的视野,具体内容如下。

根据王初明(2007)的研究成果,外语学习语境分为情景语境(situational context)和语言本体语境(linguistic context)。其中,情景语境可借鉴 Hymes(1974)的语境定义,在这个定义里,语境包含八个要素:情景(situation)、参与者(participants)、目的(ends)、行为顺序(act sequence)、语气(key)、途径(instrumentalities)、规约(norms)和体裁(genres)。由此可见,语境合成于多个变量,每个变量被赋值后便有一种组合,每种组合便构成一个具体的语境。语言本体语境指词、短语、句子本身所构成的语境,如图 7.2 所示。在这个语境层级结构里,上层为下层的语境,范畴大的为范畴小的语境,一个层次是所有下面层次的语境,如语篇是句子的语境,同时也是单词的语境。如此便有句子语境(sentential context)、语篇语境(discoursal context)等等。情景语境可与语言本体语境相互作用、相互渗透。以上对于语境的划分表明,语境不是一个笼统的概念,而是一个层级性的、通达联动的动态系统。未来的反馈研究不仅可以关注一个具体语境变量的影响,也可以考察多个语境变量之间的交互作用。

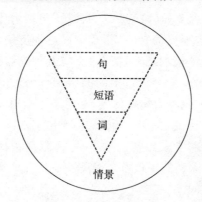

图 7.2　语言本体语境(王初明 2007:192)

7.2.3　投入程度

投入指学习者接收反馈后所作出的回应。反馈的形式、学习者/教师的个体差异及环境因素会综合作用于学习者,影响他们对反馈的投入程度。对投入程度的测量可从认知、行为和情感三个角度开展。

认知角度关注学习者对反馈的注意程度。反馈要想发挥作用,首先需要被学习者所注意。Schmidt(1995,2001)指出,注意(attention)是将输入转化为吸收的必要条件,它包含两个层次,即注意层次(at the level of noticing)和理解层次(at the level of understanding),后者是一个更高的认知层次。口头反馈研究已经通过受激回忆、即时回忆等方法证实了注意与反馈效果之间的关系,而书面反馈研究对此问题的关注还不够。Sheen(2007)对比了直接反馈与元语言反馈对于冠词习得的作用,结果发现后者比前者更具促学优势。Sheen 认为,虽然两种反馈都能引起学习者的注意,但元语言反馈更易激发学习者的理解性意识,因此对外语学习的效果更显著。

行为角度关注学习者如何利用反馈来修改文章。Sachs & Polio(2007)通过出声思考和访谈的方式,发现学习者对反馈的注意程度与作文修改质量显著相关。事实上,已有大量研究证实反馈可以帮助学习者提升修改稿语言的准确性,但短期的进步能否等同于语言能力的长期发展,学者们对此意见不一。Truscott 认为,修改成功不等于语言能力提升,二者没有相关性;而其他学者认为,短期的进步为实现语言能力长期发展奠定了必要的基础(Ferris 2004;Sachs & Polio 2007)。未来研究可对上述争议作进一步的考察。

情感角度关注学习者接受反馈后的情感状态。事实上,有些学者反对纠错的一个重要理由就在于,反馈会提升学习者的焦虑感,因而不利于外语学习(如 Krashen 1982;Truscott 1996)。但遗憾的是,迄今为止,学界尚未对学习者在接受反馈后的情感状态给予必要的关注。目前,只有 Storch & Wigglesworth(2010)对此问题进行了考察,但他们关注的不是学习者的焦虑感,而是喜欢程度;学习者对于不同形式的反馈会产生不同程度的喜好,从而影响他们从反馈中的获益。

以上,我们对拟建的反馈促学理论模型作了详细的分析,理论的价值在于应用,在于解决实际问题,并在实践中得以检验和完善。因此,未来研究可以通过大量的实验,对模型中所涉及的变量因素以及彼此间的交互关系作深入考察,同时根据实验结果和最新的语言学理论,对模型作进一步完善。

7.3 实验方法展望

7.3.1 反馈实验的缺陷

反馈研究发展至今取得了一定的成果,但目前还不能提供没有异议的证据来说明反馈的促学价值,其中一个重要原因在于其实验方法存在缺陷。

首先,缺少完整的"前测-后测-延迟后测"的设计模式。要考察反馈对二语习得的作用,关键要看反馈能否促进学习者二语水平的发展。所以,我们先要确定学习者在接收反馈前的二语水平,这可通过前测来确定;实验干预之后,再通过及时后测和延迟后测来判定学习者语言的发展情况。以上流程构成了一个完整的实验体系。然而,很多反馈研究(如 Ashwell 2000;Fathman & Whalley 1990;Ferris & Roberts 2001)只考察反馈对学习者修改原文的影响,所得结果只能说明反馈对语言发展的短期作用;但若想求证反馈的长期效果,实验设计中至少要包含一次可以用来与前测进行比较的、新的后测任务。

其次,缺少严格控制的对照组。为了说明反馈能促进学习者的语言发展,实验设计必须包含一个没有接收过任何反馈的对照组,通过将实验组与对照组进行比较,从而判定反馈的作用。但很多反馈研究(如 Ferris 1997;Ferris et al. 2000;Kepner 1991;Lalande 1982;Robb et al. 1986)要么根本没有包含对照组,要么对照组控制不严格,例如,对照组虽然没有接收关于写作语言的反馈,但接收了作文内容和结构方面的反馈,而内容与结构问题很多情况下与语言问题紧密相关,因此内容、结构反馈可能会引起学习者关注语言形式。如果反馈实验缺少对照组,那么其本质就变成考察不同反馈形式的效果,而非反馈能否促学外语。

再次,测量工具不统一。有些反馈实验在前测和后测中分别采用了不同类型的写作任务,如前测写日记,后测写论述文。不同类型的写作任务会促使学习者采用不同形式的语言,从而造成长效跟踪语言发展非常困难,并在一定程度上降低了实验结论的可靠性。

最后,没有控制好教师个体差异。近些年来,反馈实验大多由经过培训的实验人员来提供反馈,这样确保了反馈的一致性和系统性。但如果反馈是由写作教师提供,情况则完全不同。Ferris(2006)对三位写作教师进行了一个学期的观察,结果发现:(1)尽管三位教师在实验前都同意给予学生全面、代码式的反馈,但在实际操作中均未遵守该约定;(2)他们所使用的反馈策略存在显著差异;(3)反馈策略不同,学习效果亦不同。此外,还有一些研究(如 Connors & Lunsford 1988;Ferris et al. 2011;Lee 2009;Lunsford & Lunsford 2008;Montgomery & Baker 2007)也发现,写作教师会采取不同的反馈策略,而不同的反馈策略必将导致不同的学习结果。

除了上述典型的实验缺陷外,还有一些比较普遍的实验设计方面的问题,具体归纳如下:(1)没有确保各组受试具有相同的外语水平;(2)没有确保各组受试所参与的实验活动同质、同量;(3)没有确保实验人员(或教师)提供的反馈前后一致;(4)收集数据的过程存在组间差异。

7.3.2 完善实验方法

对于植根自然教学环境中的纵向反馈研究来说,他们面临的最大问题就是如何解决对照组问题。在写作教师看来,这不仅是一个方法问题,更是一个道德问题(ethical questions),因为它意味着有一个班级或一组学生将在很长一段时间内,不能收到作文反馈。由于学生失去了本应属于他们的学习机会,所以教师会感到非常不适应,甚至愧疚。此外,由于没有反馈,学生很容易产生愤怒不满的情绪,从而影响教学任务的有效开展。但另一方面,如果实验缺少对照组,其结论的可靠性就会大打折扣。如何化解这一矛盾,本节提供了三种解决方案。

首先,重新定义对照组。在 Chandler(2003)的研究中,对照组并非没有接收过任何反馈,事实上,他们只是在接收反馈后没有像实验组那样作及时修改,而是在几周之后作修改。因此,实验组与对照组之间的差别即为及时修改与延迟修改的差别,虽然这种差别与接收/未接收反馈的差别不同,但毕竟为解决"对照组"问题提供了一种思路。其次,可通过尾注的方式为对照组提供反馈(Bitchener 2008)。在作文结尾处作简要说明,提示学生在未来写作中要注意的语言问题,这种概括式的尾注反馈完全不同于实验组所接收的文中反馈(text/error-specific feedback)。最后,给对照组作内部划分。实验人员可对他们的某一类错误提供反馈,而对于另一类错误不予反馈,然后对比学习者这两类错误的发展情况(Bitchener & Ferris 2012)。以上三种方法尚不完善,仅供参考。当然,如果教师本身能够接受不反馈的做法,同时也能找到学生愿意成为对照受试,那么"对照组"问题就完全不存在了。

长期以来,反馈研究大多只通过写作任务来检测学习者的语言发展情况,从而判定反馈的作用,例如,通过让受试写修改稿来观察之前的反馈是否帮助他们改正了原文的错误。然而,Truscott(1999)指出,即便学习者修改了原文的错误也不能说明外语学习发生了质的变化,相对保险的做法是写新作文。对此,国际上虽有一些尝试性的研究,但效果不佳,这是因为在实际写作教学中,各种写作任务在类型和题材上的差异造成长效跟踪语言发展非常困难。此外,为了避免再次犯错,学生在新的写作任务中会有意识地采用相对简单的语法结构和单词,从而使得作文语言的准确性有了一定的提高,这造成了反馈促学的假象,因此将写作作为唯一的测试方法存在风险。而且口头反馈研究的经验也告诉我们,通过多种测试来检验反馈的作用非常有必要(如 Ellis 2004;Norris & Ortega 2003)。

目前,书面反馈研究已经意识到了采用多种测量工具的必要性,例如,Sheen(2007)在考察反馈对于冠词习得的作用时,使用了限时写作、快速听写和限时语法改错三种测量工具;陈晓湘等(2013)在考察反馈对于习得英语虚拟语气的作用时,采用了限时写作和不限时语法改错。但同时我们也注意到,这些工具测量的不是学习者的自发性口头产出(spontaneous production)情况,故不能充分反映学习者对语言的实际运用能力。

Norris & Ortega(2000)归纳了测量语言准确性的四种方式：(1)自由式产出(free constructed responses);(2)限制式产出(constrained-constructed responses);(3)选择性产出(selected responses);(4)元语言判断(metalinguistic judgments)。Lyster & Saito(2010)在对口头反馈的元分析研究中,将以上四种测量方式作为一个变量来分析口头反馈的效果,结果发现,通过自由式产出测量到的口头反馈效果要明显好于其他三种方式。由于自由式产出调动的是隐性知识,因此该结果说明了口头反馈可促进学习者隐性知识的发展。

7.3.3　创新实验方法

第一,加强对于个体变异性特征的考察。(1)强调学习环境与条件,主张采用访谈、日记、观察、有声思维、参与体验等定性研究方法收集自然语料,尽量减少使用通过改变环境条件的实验方法来收集"去语境化"的语料;(2)强调语言发展的动态特征,主张通过计算机模拟、纵向跟踪、民族志观察研究等方法全面描述群体或个体发展过程中的变异性特征,进一步探究语言的发展轨迹和发展机制;(3)关注学习者个体差异,主张采用个案研究、叙事语篇分析等可以突显个体感知经验及个体/社会关系的研究方法,摒弃固定的预测因素,关注学习者在具体的社会文化情境中如何发挥主观能动性。

第二,加强对于学习者语言错误的归纳和分析。通过语料库技术对学习者作文中的语言错误做系统评估,对错误的类型和频率展开多维度的分析。例如：哪些是过度使用(overuse),哪些是过少使用(underuse),哪些是误用(misuse)？哪些是失误(mistakes),哪些是错误(errors)？哪些是可医治错误(treatable errors),哪些是不可医治错误(untreatable errors)？哪些是整体错误(global errors),哪些是局部错误(local errors)？通过这些分析评估,一方面可以验证前人的分类模式是否合理,从而建立更加完善的错误分类体系,另一方面可以为反馈研究拓展出新的空间。

第三,充分发挥同伴反馈的作用。在我国,由于受到传统文化氛围的束缚,再加上过程写作法引入较晚以及学习者英语水平偏低等众多因素的影响,教师反馈在英语写作教学与研究中占据着绝对的主导地位。然而,同伴反馈益处颇多(详见莫俊华 2007),因此如何发挥同伴反馈应有的优势是未来研究在方法上需要突破的地方。一方面,我们要尝试调整教师在写作教学中的角色,由从前作文唯一读者和评价者变成同伴互评活动的指导者、促进者。另一方面,利用现代化教育技术开展网络在线评改方法。通过 BBS 平台构建作文评改情境,让学生将作文上传到网上作为主帖,其他同学以跟帖的形式来评改文章。这样,一次评改就完成了交流、评价、修改、展示等四个层面的要求,使得作文评改的形式更趋灵活,减轻学生在传统互评活动中的心理压力和焦虑情绪,有效地提高了作文评改的质量和学生参与的积极性。此外,通过互联网与英美学生开展作文互评,培养学生的英语时代感,使其了解以英语为母语的外国读者对自己作文的感受,从而促进他们在英语能力上潜移默化的进步。

7.4 研究内容展望

7.4.1 反馈目标

反馈研究面临的一个重要的问题是:我们究竟要对哪些错误提供反馈?二语习得研究关注不同知识(如词汇、形态、句法)的习得方式,而反馈研究却忽视了这一点,在他们眼中,漏写的名词复数、介词误用和句子语义错误都是错误,没有本质区别(Truscott 1996)。针对这一情况,Ferris 曾多次建议将学习者的错误分为可医治错误(即规则型错误)和不可医治错误(即特质型/习语型错误),针对不同形式的错误,提供不同形式的反馈(Ferris 1999,2002,2006)。

一直以来,反馈研究多关注独立、规则型的语言错误(如冠词错误),并发现反馈可有效降低此类错误的发生。但实际上,学习者所犯的错误五花八门,这些错误会因人而异、因任务而异(Ferris 2010)。因此,未来研究首先需要从不同维度对错误进行分类,然后有针对性的提供反馈。表 7.3 从八个维度对语言错误进行了分类。其中,全局错误又称"严重错误"(serious error),它与局部错误相对,是指对整个文本理解有干扰的错误;有损形象的错误是指能反映出二语学习背景、会让外界对学习者产出负面印象的错误。

表 7.3 错误分类

维度	错误分类
1	规则型结构错误(rule-based structures)、非规则型结构错误(idiosyncratic structures)
2	独立型(discrete)错误、复杂型(complex)错误
3	词汇错误、句法错误、形态错误、语义错误、语用错误
4	过度使用(overuse)的错误、过少使用(underuse)的错误
5	失误(mistakes)、错误(errors)
6	可医治错误(treatable errors)、不可医治错误(untreatable errors)
7	全局错误(global error)、局部错误(local error)
8	有损形象的错误(stigmatizing errors)

此外，还可以从 Connors & Lunsford(1988)、Ferris(2006)和 Lunsford & Lunsford(2008)的错误列表(见表 5.2)中选取反馈目标，通过对二语教师和本族语者的调查，确认哪些错误比较严重，易于损害学习者的形象，然后确定目标结构和受试群体开展有效的反馈实验。总之，反馈研究应该选择对学习者产生较大影响，而非简单、便于实验操作的错误作为考察目标。

7.4.2 反馈形式

什么形式的反馈利于促学？与其他问题相比，该问题在反馈研究中得到的关注最多，这是因为它与教学质量紧密相关，决定了外语教师在时间和精力上的付出能否得到等价的回报。本书在第六章归纳和分析了对比不同形式反馈效果的实证研究，包括直接反馈与间接反馈、不同形式的直接反馈、不同形式的间接反馈，以及聚焦反馈与非聚焦反馈的对比。

根据常识，间接反馈对于高水平学习者的效果应该好于低水平学习者，因为高水平学习者的语言知识更丰富，认知能力也有了一定的提高，但目前尚无研究见诸报道。此外，对于复杂结构的错误，反馈的形式越显性，效果应该越理想，但由于当前研究考察的均为简单结构的错误，因此无法验证显性反馈的促学优势。对此，未来研究可考察复杂语言结构的错误，将元语言解释从元语言反馈中剥离出来，单独检验其促学作用，可能会有意想不到的发现。

虽然当前研究显示,聚焦反馈的整体效果好于非聚焦反馈,但在现实教学中,学习者需要掌握能够编辑、修改其作文中所有语言错误的能力(Evans et al. 2010;Hartshorn et al. 2010),因此只针对特定的几类错误提供反馈不符合外语教学的长期目标,会误导学习者忽视错误,从而降低对于写作语言准确性的重视程度。有鉴于此,未来研究应加大考察力度,开发出高效的非聚焦反馈模式,关注新模式与反馈形式(如直接、间接反馈等)、个体因素(如年龄、语言水平、学能等)和目标结构的交互作用。

7.4.3 反馈量

大多数反馈实验只持续数周而已,但 Bitchener & Knock(2010a)的实验长达 10 个月,考察的目标结构是冠词,反馈干预只进行了一次,结果显示,反馈的效果可以长达 10 个月。一次反馈就可以如此长效,这样的结果确实令人惊喜。但对于其他语言错误,多少次反馈才能达到促学目的？一次反馈是否足以？未来研究可对此展开深入的探讨。

此外,如果反馈研究采用的是全面纠错,那么几次反馈才能达到比较理想的效果呢？要回答这一问题,我们不仅要考察学习者在每一次写作任务中的语言整体使用情况,还要针对个别语言结构作专门考察,这样可以明确学习者写作语言准确性的整体发展是否与个别语言结构的发展有直接关系。

7.4.4 教辅活动

Ferris(1995c,2002)曾指出,反馈研究应该拓宽视野,跳出纠错的桎梏,看一看其他教学活动对反馈效果的辅助作用,例如,要求学习者根据反馈写修改稿、写错误日志、为学习者提供编辑策略方面的培训或者相关语法教学等等。虽然已有研究建议写作教师在纠错的同时提供这些教辅活动,但迄今为止,有关教辅活动对反馈效果的影响,尚无研究见诸报道。

实际上,考察教辅活动的作用并非难事。例如,实验可包括两组学生,首先确保他们所接收的反馈在质与量上相同;然后,一组学生被要求根据反馈对原文作及时修改,而另一组学生不作修改要求;或者,一组学生接受课内的相关语法教学,而另一组学生不作教学培训;再或者,一组学生作错误日志,而另一组不作;最后,通过后测、延迟后测对两组的学习效果进行比较。此外,还可以作后续的跟踪调查来进一步了解哪些辅助活动更有效,例如,传统的语法教学对比应用型教学活动,记录五种错误类型的日志对比十种错误类型的日志等等。以上研究成果对于提高外语教学质量具有重要的意义,决定了外语教师接下来如何设计和安排自己的教学活动以达到良好的预期成效。

7.4.5 个体因素

长期以来,反馈研究多关注群体的发展特征,而忽视了个体变异性。一方面,根据社会文化理论,没有任何一种反馈是万能的,只有当它的形式充分符合外语学习者所处的发展阶段时,才能最大程度地发挥支架作用(Sheen 2010)。在现实教学中,任何一个有经验的外语教师都知道,尽管提供同样形式的反馈,有些学生受益多,有些受益少。Ferris(2006)就曾发现,虽然小组分数显示学习者的语言准确性随时间的发展有了明显的提高,但是标准差非常大,近乎于小组平均分数的三倍,这说明组内个体差异较大:有些学生取得了明显的进步,有些进步比较小,有些甚至还退步了。

然而,绝大多数反馈研究未将学习者的个体因素纳入考察范围,基本上还属于单变量因果性研究,这对于外语学习如此复杂的系统而言,显然过于简单了。有鉴于此,未来研究应该充分考虑学习者个体因素的影响,本书在附录1—2中分别给出了英语水平量表和语言分析能力量表,并配有答案和说明,希望可以对未来的反馈研究提供参考和借鉴。以下列举了一些具体的研究问题:

- 学习者所处的教学环境(如语法教学、交际教学等)是否会影响到他们从反馈中的获益?
- 学习者对于外语教学、语言准确性及反馈的态度是否与他们的语言发展情况相关?
- 为什么学习者利用或者不利用教师提供的反馈?
- 学习者通过哪些策略来理解和利用反馈?使用策略的成功几率有多大?
- 在学习者眼中,何为最佳的反馈形式?如果反馈是根据学习者的个体特征而量身定制,效果是否会更加理想?
- 哪些个体因素对反馈效果的影响更明显?

另一方面,很多互动研究发现,外语学习者与本族语者的互动不同于他们和外语学习者的互动。例如,Dobao(2012)考察了在学习者—学习者、学习者—本族语者的互动过程中"关于语言形式的话语片段"(language-related episodes,以下简称片段)。片段是指在以意义或交际为核心的互动过程中,"谈论产出的语言、询问语言的使用、纠正自我或他人语言错误的任何对话片段"(Swain & Lapkin 1998:326)。判断学习者是否注意到了某个语言形式主要是通过辨认片断的方式来实现(Swain & Lapkin 1995),而且已有研究证实(如 Swain & Lapkin 1998,2002;Williams 2001),在片段中所学的语法和词汇知识可以保存得更加长久,因此关于语言形式的话语谈论有促学功效。Dobao(2012)研究发现,在学习者—学习者互动中,有23.51%的语言理解或表达困难促成了片段的发生,有80.95%的片段成功将问题解决;在学习者—本族语者的互动中,有43.66%的语言理解或表达困难促成了片段的发生,有92.47%的片段成功将问题解决。

上述结果说明本族语者的出现对互动过程产生了影响。由此推理,教师的个体因素会在一定程度上决定学习者对待反馈的态度和利用程度,从而影响反馈的效果。王初明(2010)曾指出,教师的人品和学识受到学生的敬重,就会得到学生的情感认同或协同,这样的教师更能调动学生的学习积极性,他教的课学生爱听,所教的内容易被学生吸收;一旦学生对上课的教师反感,师生情感协同断链,学生就不会跟他学了。近来国外有调查发现,影响外语学得好坏最重要的因素是学生是否喜欢上课的教师。以上分析告诉我们,考察教师个体因素对反馈效果的影响实属必要,以下列举了一些研究方向:

- 描述教师在实际教学中关注的错误类型、纠错方式等;
- 培训教师如何纠错,然而评估他们的实际纠错行为;
- 比较教师的纠错理念与纠错行为间的差异;
- 教师的纠错行为与其他写作教学条件(如教学大纲、教学材料及评分方式等)的交互作用;
- 学生对教师的信念如何影响反馈效果。

7.4.6 反馈效果

目前,相关研究在检验反馈效果时,没有分别测量显性、隐性知识的习得情况,这影响了对于反馈促学效果的认识。在早期研究中,显性知识被定义为对语言现象的解释,隐性知识是对这些语言现象的运用(如 Hulstijn & Hulstijn 1984;Seliger 1979)。由于该定义比较宽泛,难以保证精准的研究,Ellis(2005)从七个方面入手,对显性、隐性知识作了系统的归纳与区分(见表 7.4)。归结起来,显性知识是有意识的知识,对语言使用起监控作用,隐性知识是潜意识的知识,有助于语言使用自动化,二者相互依存、相互交叉,共同构成了语言学习复杂的动态系统(如 Ellis 2005;Ellis et al. 2009)。因此想全面、客观地反映外语学习的全貌,就需要采用多种测量工具,对两种知识的发展情况分别作考察。Ellis(2005)根据两类知识的不同特质,提出了具体的测量标准:测量显性知识时,受试的关注点在形式且无时间压力,如不限时语法判断、元语言知识测试等;测量隐性知识时,受试的关注点在意义且有时间压力,如口头任务、限时写作等。该测量标准已得到国际二语习得领域的广泛认可。

表 7.4 显性、隐性知识特征

		显性知识	隐性知识
1	意识	有意识的	潜意识的
2	知识类型	陈述性知识	程序性知识
3	稳定性	不稳定的	稳定的
4	可描述性	可用语言描述	难以用语言描述
5	可习得性	在任何年龄都可习得	通常在关键期习得
6	提取方式	受控提取	自动提取
7	使用环境	用于规划性的语言使用	用于自发性的语言使用

当前,学界对于显性、隐性知识学习机制的认识主要包括以下三个方面。第一,注意语言形式是显性知识发展的前提。Schmidt(1994,1995)指出,注意是语言学习的先决条件,学习者对语言形式的注意程度,决定了语言输入能在多大程度上转化为摄入。学习者注意语言形式后,通过分析比较,会意识到自己的语言产出与目标语之间存在差距(Ellis 1994),而这一步对于外语学习至关重要(Schmidt 1994),因为它会激发学习者有意识地学习目标语言形式,即显性学习,其结果会产生显性知识,并存储于外显记忆(Ellis et al. 2006)。

第二,操练,如有意识的言语输出练习(陈亚平 2011),可推进显性知识向隐性知识转化。DeKeyser(2003,2007)指出,语言学习与其他技能(如象棋、钢琴、数学)学习本质相同,都是从最初的改变,不断发展到熟练、自动化行为的过程,而操练是实现自动化的重要保障,它可以减少反应时、降低错误率,推动显性知识向隐形知识转化,实现流利、正确地使用语言。

第三,充分的可理解性输入能保证隐性学习,产生隐性知识。Arthur Reber 作为隐性学习研究的先驱,指出隐性学习的本质,是通过大量接触正确、恰当的语言输入,从而实现对语言结构的理解(Reber 1976)。Ellis(2012)也提出,学习者最初以语块的方式逐一接触语言的具体实例,进而从实例体验中抽绎出带规律性的语言型式,这个由具体到抽象的隐性学习过程取决于语言输入的频率和质量。

综上所述,显性知识来源于显性学习,而显性学习的前提是注意语言形式;隐性知识可由显性知识转化而成,或者直接源自隐性学习。目前,鲜有研究考察反馈对于显性、隐性知识发展的作用,但学界已经意识到了此类研究的重要性(Bitchener 2012;Polio 2012;Williams 2012),因为他们对于认识反馈的促学价值、理解反馈的促学机制大有裨益。

7.5 教师培训

提高反馈效率的关键是加强教师培训。这样做一方面可以充分发挥教师在反馈实验中的作用,提高实验结果的有效性,另一方面有利于提升教学质量,促进外语学习。基于 Bitchener & Ferris(2012) 的研究成果,本节将介绍七个培训步骤以增强外语教师的反馈能力。

7.5.1 了解教师的背景知识

无论是新手教师还是有经验的教师,他们对于错误及纠错都有着自己独到的认识。了解教师的相关背景从而有针对性地制定培训方案,对于提高培训质量起到了决定性的作用。我们可以通过问卷、面谈等方式了解教师对于反馈的运用情况,以及他们所掌握的背景知识。表 7.5 给出了背景知识问卷样例。

表 7.5　背景知识问卷（Bitchener & Ferris 2012：175）

1. Have you taken any courses in English grammar, linguistics, or applied linguistics? What were they (name them)? Where were they taken (name country and institution)? How long were these courses (give months and hours per day)? Did any of them have a focus on written CF? If yes, what information on written CF was covered in the course?
2. On a scale of 1—4 (with 4 being 'very knowledgeable' and 1 being 'not at all knowledgeable'), how would you assess your level of knowledge of the following areas?
   a. Identifying parts of speech (in isolation and within sentences).
   b. Identifying clause structures.
   c. Identifying sentence structures/types.
   d. Identifying learners' written errors.
   e. Correcting learners' written errors.
   f. Explaining the cause of learners' written errors.
   g. Deciding on the most effective ways of giving helpful feedback on learners' written errors.
   h. Determining how effective your written CF has been.
   i. Knowing how to advise learners about their role in the correction process.
   j. Making decisions about the provision of written CF—what to give feedback on, when to give it, how to give it.
3. Have you taken any courses that wholly or partially helped you understand the processes involved in the learning and acquisition of a second language? What were they (name them)? Where were they taken (name country and institution)? What main content areas were covered in them?
4. On a scale of 1—4 (with 4 being 'very comfortable' and 1 being 'not at all comfortable'), how do you feel about your ability to work effectively with second language learners from a range of L1 and general educational backgrounds?
5. Considering your responses to the questions above, please list up to three specific areas or skills where you would like further input or training so that you can work successfully with the grammar issues of second language learners.

7.5.2　帮助教师理解反馈在语言学习中的作用

不同的教育背景、培训经历和教学经验决定了教师们对于反馈有着不同的理解。虽然有些教师经常对学生的语言错误提供反馈，但他们并不清楚为什么以及如何提供反馈。因此在培训开始前，无论是培训者还是受培训者都有必要对反馈问题进行深入思考。表 7.6 是一份反馈知识调查问卷的样例，通过分析问卷结果，培训者可以确定是否有必要让教师作一些有关二语习得方面的补充阅读(如 Lightbown & Spada 2008; Mitchell & Myles 2004),或者进修相关课程,以保证他们对于反馈的作用有一个清楚、客观的认识。

表 7.6 反馈知识问卷(Bitchener & Ferris 2012: 176)

1.	Have you ever learned a second language? Which language(s)? Do you remember receiving written CF on errors you made in your written texts? How did you feel about receiving it (explain)? Do you think it was effective (explain)? How was the feedback given to you? Would you be likely to follow the same approach in giving feedback to learners in your own language classes (explain)?
2.	Have you ever provided written CF to learners in a language class? If yes, describe (a) what areas you tended to focus on and why, (b) how you delivered the feedback and why, (c) whether you would adopt the same approach again and why, (d) how you knew if your approach was effective or not.
3.	What role do you think written CF can play in the language learning process? Do you think it is more effective with certain types of learners (explain)? Why do you think some learners appear to benefit more than other learners from written CF?

7.5.3 强化教师的语法知识

教师只有掌握了扎实的语法知识才能提供有效的反馈,因此在培训之前可以安排他们参加语法测试,了解他们对于语法及语言学知识的掌握情况,从而决定他们是否需要进修语法及语言学基础课程。除语法测试外,还可通过以下途径了解教师们的语法基础:

- 让教师批改两篇不同水平学生的作文,不仅要指出作文中的错误,还要用专业语言说明错误的性质和原因以及如何纠正。
- 把二语学习者常犯的错误列表提供给教师,要求他们分析在何种情况下学生会犯这些错误,以及要提供哪些语法规则和例句来帮助学生理解错误从而避免再次犯错。对于教师不能确定的地方,可允许他们查阅语法书或参考书来予以确认。
- 要求教师根据上述错误列表设计一堂迷你课程,考察他们是否会对不同水平的学习者提供不同形式的语言输入。

以上方法可以帮助培训人员了解教师的语法和语言学基础,判定他们是否适合参加培训,是否需要补充一些相关的语法和语言学知识。

7.5.4 开展学生需求分析

为避免教学内容过难或者过于简单从而损害教学效果,教师有必要在学期之初开展学生需求分析(needs analysis),有效把握学生当前的语言发展水平,有针对性地开展教学活动,提高教学质量。众所周知,二语习得过程会受到学习者认知心理因素和社会环境因素的共同影响,因此需求分析的结果不仅要反映出群体的需求特征,还要彰显少数人群或者个体的需求。需求分析通常在学期之初进行,但由于学习者的语言处于发展之中,故对于知识的需求也会随时发生变化,所以教师有必要在学期之中定期开展需求分析,并根据结果有针对性地调整自己的教学计划和教学内容,真正做到以人为本、因材施教。

需求分析包括以下三个步骤:(1)针对新生做外语背景问卷调查;(2)要求学生在课堂上完成一篇命题作文,教师根据作文材料在班级范围内开展错误分析(Class Error Analysis),具体程序如表7.7所示;(3)通过语法测试来进一步评估学生的语法水平和错误形式。根据需求分析的结果,教师可以全面了解学生的语言水平和对教学内容的需求,从而确定哪些语言错误需要反馈,以及如何反馈。需求分析可避免教学中"一刀切"的做法,使教学有的放矢。

表7.7 班级内错误分析程序

1.	For each student paper, with a highlighter, mark errors in however many categories (and whichever error categories) you would like your analysis to focus.
2.	In class, return the papers to the writers and briefly review the error categories you have marked.
3.	Ask the students to number the highlighted errors consecutively throughout the paper. Use these numbers to complete an analysis chart. For each error the student will indicate its type. (Create a chart based on the categories you have chosen for marking.)
4.	Ask the students to list their 3—4 most prevalent patterns of error and turn in their report form (with chart and list).
5.	Compile the individual forms into a class chart. Go over it with the class later to explain why your in-class grammar work will focus on some error types but not others.

7.5.5 将反馈有效融入课堂教学活动

虽然理解反馈的价值以及学会开展学生需求分析对于有效运用

反馈至关重要,但现实教学中还有很多因素会阻碍反馈发挥作用,其中之一就是教师难以有效地将反馈活动与教学大纲和日常教学任务有机融合在一起。Hartshorn et al. (2010)曾指出,一个典型的过程写作法课堂完全被阅读讨论、写作修辞练习、写作策略分析,以及一些过程型的写作活动(即初稿→同伴反馈→内容修改)所占据,很难找到合适的机会将反馈融入其中。

然而,本书在第三章已经明确指出,二语写作者毕竟在思维模式、所处环境以及语言实践等方面都与一语写作者不同,因此不应把一语写作教学的方法和策略全盘应用于二语写作教学。此外,二语写作者尚处于第二语言习得的过程中,故需要教师对其语言错误给予适当的关注。二语写作教学应该平衡好教授写作技能与语言技能之间的关系,而不是完全置写作语言准确性于不顾(Eskey 1983; Leki 1990a; Raimes 1987; Taylor 1981; Zamel 1982)。有鉴于此,外语写作教师应尽可能地将语言教学与写作教学融合在一起,具体作法包括:(1)要求学生根据反馈对原稿作文的语言至少做一次修改;(2)教师在作文反馈之后,专门利用一节课来分析和讲解学生作文语言的共性问题;(3)对于个别问题,可通过小组辅导或者一对一面谈的方式来解决。

值得注意的是,二语写作教学也存在另一种极端,就是将写作课完全变成了语法改错课,为了便于改错,规定作文词数上限,让学生写短作文,课内限时写。然而,语言的发展不仅包括准确性,还有流利性和复杂性。因此,如果写作任务的目的在于语言的流利性或复杂性,那么将学习者的注意力引向语言准确性则不合时宜。有些写作任务具有多重目的,同时关注语言的流利性和准确性,在这种情况下,教师应先关注流利性,而后为准确性。

在语法教学之后,对写作语言提供反馈可视为一种高效的反馈形式。例如,教师在课堂上讲解了过去完成时的用法,然后给学生布置了相应的写作练习,并对练习中的过去完成时用法错误提供反馈,这种做法可有效提高学习者对于目标结构的掌握。换言之,反馈与显性语法教学相互配合、相互补充可产生极佳的外语学习效应。

7.5.6 个体反馈、小组反馈和班级反馈

二语习得过程会受到学习者内在心理因素和外在环境因素的综合影响,因此学习者的语言错误或具有群体普遍性、或属于少数群体、

或者只是个体错误。所以,教师有必要了解个体反馈、小组反馈与班级反馈之间的异同,掌握相关的反馈技巧。对于个体反馈,培训人员可要求几组教师分别以不同的方式对一篇学生作文给予反馈,然后再进行综合讨论,对每种反馈形式作分析评价,表 7.8 展示了这种工作坊培训的具体步骤。

表 7.8　个体反馈工作坊(Bitchener & Ferris 2012:194)

Prior Reading 　　Bean, J. C. 1996. *Engaging Ideas: The Professor's Guide to Integrating Writing, Critical Thinking, and Active Learning in the Classroom*. San Francisco, CA: Jossey-Bass. 　　Ferris, D. R. & Roberts, B. J. 2001. Error feedback in L2 writing classes: How explicit does it need to be? *Journal of Second Language Writing* 10: 161-184. 　　Haswell, R. H. 1983. Minimal marking. *College English* 45: 600-604.
Your Task 　　You have two copies of an essay by the same student. Assume that the student is going to revise and edit this paper at least one more time before it is finalized. Your job is to give the student feedback about errors that might impact his/her grade if they are not addressed. Complete the following steps to do this.
➣ **Step 1** 　　**Everyone**: Read through the essay. On your first copy, mark (underline, circle, or highlight) all of the errors you see (grammar, punctuation, spelling, other mechanics).
➣ **Step 2** 　　**Group A**: On your second copy of the paper, mark it as if you were going to return it to the student. Use Haswell's (1983) "minimal marking" technique. 　　**Group B**: Look through the errors you marked and identify 2—4 patterns of error—specific problems that are repeated that could be pointed out to the student. Similar to what Ferris & Roberts (2001) did in their study, on your second copy, underline all instances of the 2—4 patterns you want to call the student's attention to. Create an error code for each pattern and mark the underlined errors with the appropriate code. 　　**Group C**: Look through the errors you marked on the first copy. As suggested by Bean (1996, pp. 249—250), write an end comment that might help the student to revise the paper (see example in the middle of p. 250). As also suggested by Bean (bottom of p. 249, top of p. 250), line-edit at least one paragraph and ask the student to work on correcting the rest of the paper.

续表

> **Step 3**
>
> **Get into "mixed" groups (A, B, C) and discuss:**
> - Compare your findings from Step1. Did you find pretty much the same errors?
> - Talk about the method you used to mark errors in Step2. Did you find it hard or easy to do? Could you imagine using this method with your own students' papers? Why or why not?
> - As a group, compare the three approaches to marking grammar that you have tried. Which one do you think would be most helpful to students, and why?
>
> **Step 4**
>
> **Individual Freewrite (5 min.):** Considering the work you did on this exercise as well as the readings for this week, try to articulate a 1—3 sentence philosophy statement about responding to errors in student writing.

通过培训,教师对于何时提供个体反馈、如何反馈等问题有了一定的认识,为开展小组反馈和班级反馈奠定了基础。对于小组反馈,教师可让组内学生先进行同伴互评,然后再作综合性的小组反馈。同样,班级反馈之前可以先开展同伴或小组互评,这种同伴互评与教师反馈有机融合的做法使得反馈形式更趋灵活,调动了学生的学习积极性,同时也减轻了教师的评改负担。

7.5.7 开展教学辅助活动

有学者(Ferris 2002;Hendrickson 1980)指出,反馈研究要跳出"错误→反馈"的桎梏,为了能让反馈最大程度的发挥作用,教师有必要开展一些相应的教学辅助活动,如师生一对一面谈、微型语法课、微型作文编辑技巧课等,这些辅助活动可以增进学习者对于相关问题的理解,强化反馈效果,从而避免再次犯错。

师生一对一面谈可以弥补反馈自身缺少双向互动的局限,通过师生间的问答互动,帮助学习者深入认识自己的错误、充分理解反馈信息,从而促进外语学习。Bitchener et al. (2005)发现,面谈可有效提高学习者新作文语言的准确性。Ferris & Hedgcock(2005)分别针对已批改和未批改作文设计出了相应的面谈程序,如表7.9所示。

表7.9 一对一面谈程序(Ferris & Hedgcock 2005:285)

Preliminary (unmarked) drafts
1. Ask the student to read the paper aloud while you follow along on a separate copy. Instruct the student to stop and verbalize comments about any errors or corrections he/she notices. Note the errors caught by the student and suggest correcitons on your copy of the paper.
2. Then go through the paper again, this time reading it aloud yourself. For any remaining errors not caught by the student during step1, stop and ask an indirect question ("What about this?" or simply repeat the erroneous form or phrase). See if the student can suggest a correction for errors you call to his/her attention. Take notes on your copy using a different color of ink.
3. Show the student your paper, marked with two pen colors—one representing errors he/she found and attemtped to correct independently; the other representing errors you pointed out. Discuss your findings, pointing out (a) what the student did well in terms of finding and correcting errors; and (b) problematic error types that you notice (either frequent or resistant to self-editing). Ask the student to take notes on his/her paper, including correct forms that you provide for him/her.
Revised (marked) drafts
1. Read and provide indirect feedback (underline or highlight all errors you notice, but do not correct them or label them according to error type) on a student's essay draft. Then ask the student, at home or during an in-class revision session, to attempt corrections for all errors that you marked. Ask the student to number each marked error consecutively and complete an error analysis chart. (If you prefer, you can do the charting yourself.) Use the marked and (student) corrected essay draft and the chart for your errror conference.
2. Use the marked essay draft, the chart, and the student corrections as data sources for your conferenece. First, walk through the in-class corrections made by the student, discussing whether the corrections suggested by the student are accurate. Note where the student did/did not make edits and discuss why (lack of understanding, carelessness, etc.) Take notes on your discussion. Ask the student to summarize what he/she learned about his/her patterns of error, points of confusion, and editing strategies.

开展微型语法课可以巩固反馈的效果。将语法教学与写作教学高效融合并非易事,如果过分强调语法内容可能会掩盖写作教学的意义,同时也容易造成学生的厌烦情绪。因此,在写作课中融入语法教学要符合以下五个标准才能发挥语法教学的辅助作用:(1)简明扼

要;(2)中心明确;(3)讲解与例证清晰、准确;(4)与学生的需求紧密相关;(5)包含相应的练习内容。

表 7.10　微型语法课设计步骤(Ferris & Hedgcock 2005: 293-294)

Step 1: Imagine you are teaching a writing course and have selected a particular grammar point on which to present a 20—30 minute mini-lesson to the class. Consult several different sources on this grammar point. After you have examined the sources, consider the following questions:
1. Is one source clearer or more appropriate for the group of students you are working with? Why?
2. What basic information about this grammar point (terms, definitions, rules, examples) will you need to present? Which sources were the most helpful in providing these?
3. What rules and strategies for avoiding errors might you include? Which sources were the most helpful in identifying these?
4. Did you find any discovery activities or practice exercises that might be helpful for your lesson? How might you need to adapt these to accommodate your own students' needs?

Step 2: Now design a 20—30 minute mini-lesson on the same grammar point. Include a discovery (text analysis) activity, deductive explanantions with examples of important terms and rules, and practice/application activities. You may wish to assign some activities as homework to stay within your time constraints. Begin your lesson with a brief overview of the procedures (grouping, timing, materials needed) that you would use to teach this lesson. The overview should specify any prior knowledge or previous instruction assumed as background for the lesson.

除了开展微型语法课外,还可以对学习者的自我编辑能力进行培训。Bitchener & Ferris(2012)在前人研究(Ferris 2002,2008;Ferris & Hedgcock 2005)基础上,提出了一套较为完整的编辑策略培训方案,如表 7.11 所示。

表 7.11　编辑策略培训步骤(Bitchener & Ferris 2012: 160)

1. **Allowing adequate time**: Leave time in the process to put the text away and come back to it with fresh eyes.
2. **Breaking up the task**: It can be hard to maintain focus and attention when editing a longer text. It may be best to break the text into chunks, edit a chunk carefully and take a break before editing the next chunk.

续表

3. **Reading the text aloud**: Reading aloud can help writers notice when a word or a word part is missing or unnecessay, when a word doesn't sound or look right, and when sentences are long or choppy or repetive. Some writers find it helpful to read the text "backwards", meaning to start with the last sentence, then read the next-to-last sentence, and so forth.
4. **Focused editing on specific error patterns**: Some L2 writers make systematic errors, say with verb tense or form, noun plurals, articles, etc. It can be helpful to read through a text focusing only on one issue at a time, for instance identifying all the verbs and analyzing which ones need tense markings.
5. **Studying rules**: While not all errors of grammar or usage have systematic rules behind them, some do, and writers can study those in a handbook or website to understand the terms, the rules, and their exceptions. This knowledge can help writers to make good decisions when eidting their own work.
6. **Using electronic tools effectively**: Word processor or online text-editing tools can be a writer's friend or enemy depending on how they are used.
7. **Another pair of eyes**: Asking a trusted friend or classmate to read over a paper might help writers identify issues that are hard to find in their own writing. However, this person should not replace a writer as the primary editor of his/her work.

7.6 小结

本章从理论、研究和教学三个层面对反馈领域的未来发展趋势提出了具体的意见。理论上，笔者构建了反馈促学理论模型，并对模型中的关键要素进行了剖析。根据该模型，学习过程始终发生在学习者身上，所有影响反馈效果的变量，包括外部的社会环境因素及内部的认知心理因素，都将依托于学习者而发生关联，它们相互作用、相互制约，形成了一个动态、复杂的交互系统。该模型不仅为反馈研究提供了理论支撑，同时拓展出了新的研究空间，未来研究可检验影响反馈效果的潜在因素，不断丰富和完善模型的内容。

研究层面包括两部分：实验方法和研究内容。对于实验方法，本章首先归纳了反馈研究在实验设计上的四点不足，即缺少完整的"前测-后测-延迟后测"的设计模式、缺少严格控制的对照组、测量工具不统一、没有控制好教师个体差异。在此基础上,笔者提出了完善和创新实验方法的具体建议,包括考察个体变异性特征、归纳和分析学习者的语言错误、发挥同伴反馈的作用。在研究内容上,本章从反馈目标、反馈形式、反馈量、教辅活动、个体因素和反馈效果六个方面,提出了未来研究亟待解决的问题,凸显了反馈领域的未来发展动向:(1) 关注个体(学生和教师)差异;(2) 拓宽研究视野,重视教学辅助活动;(3) 关注各研究变量间的交互作用;(4) 注重实证研究的教学现实性。

最后,本章在 Bitchener & Ferris(2012)研究的基础上,提出了培训新手教师有效运用反馈的七个步骤:(1) 通过问卷、面谈等方式了解新手教师对反馈的看法及已掌握的相关知识;(2) 通过推荐阅读或课堂教学的方式帮助他们了解反馈在二语习得和二语写作中的作用;(3) 帮助他们掌握基本的语法及语言学知识;(4) 培训如何开展学生需求分析,让教学有的放矢;(5) 培训如何将反馈有效融入课堂教学活动;(6) 帮助他们掌握个体反馈、小组反馈和班级反馈的方法;(7) 培训如何开展相关教学活动(如师生一对一面谈、微型语法课及微型作文编辑技巧课等)以辅助反馈发挥作用。

总之,上述理论、研究和教学上的展望对于反馈领域的健康发展有着重要的意义。当然,一个章节的论述是有限的,而一个领域的未来发展是无限的,本书旨在抛砖引玉,给读者以启示,激发更多同行的深入思考,愿读者与我们共勉。

附录 1

Quick Placement Test

Oxford University Press and University of Cambridge Local Examinations Syndicate
Version 1

This test is divided into two parts:

Part One (Questions 1—40) — All students.

Part Two (Questions 41—60) — Do not start this part unless told to do so by your test supervisor.

Time: 30 minutes

Part 1

Questions 1—5

- Where can you see these notices?
- For questions 1 to 5, mark one letter A, B or C on your Answer Sheet.

1. Please leave your room key at Reception.
   A. in a shop   B. in a hotel   C. in a taxi

2. Foreign money changed here
   A. in a library   B. in a bank   C. in a police station

3. Afternoon show begins at 2 pm
   A. outside a theatre
   B. outside a supermarket
   C. outside a restaurant

4. Closed for holidays. Lessons start again on the 8th January
   A. at a travel agent's

B. at a music school

C. at a restaurant

5. Price per night: £10 a tent, £5 a person

   A. at a cinema   B. in a hotel   C. on a camp-site

Questions 6—10

- In this section you must choose the word which best fits each space in the text below.
- For questions 6 to 10, mark one letter A, B or C on your Answer Sheet.

Scotland

Scotland is the north part of the island of Great Britain. The Atlantic Ocean is on the west and the North Sea on the east. Some people (6)_____ Scotland speak a different language called Gaelic. There are (7)_____ five million people in Scotland, and Edinburgh is (8)_____ most famous city.

Scotland has many mountains; the highest one is called 'Ben Nevis'. In the south of Scotland, there are a lot of sheep. A long time ago, there (9)_____ many forests, but now there are only a (10) _____. Scotland is only a small country, but it is quite beautiful.

6. A. on   B. in   C. at

7. A. about   B. between   C. among

8. A. his   B. your   C. its

9. A. is   B. were   C. was

10. A. few   B. little   C. lot

Questions 11—20

- In this section you must choose the word which best fits each space in the texts.
- For questions 11 to 20, mark one letter A, B, C or D on your Answer Sheet.

Alice Guy Blaché

Alice Guy Blaché was the first female film director. She first became involved in cinema whilst working for the Gaumont Film Company in the late 1890s. This was a period of great change in the cinema and Alice was the first to use many new inventions, (11)_____ sound and colour.

In 1907 Alice (12)_____ to New York where she started her own film company. She was (13)_____ successful, but, when Hollywood became the centre of the film world, the best days of the independent New York film companies were (14)_____. When Alice died in 1968, hardly anybody (15)_____ her name.

11. A. bringing　　B. including　C. containing　D. supporting
12. A. moved　　　B. ran　　　　C. entered　　　D. transported
13. A. next　　　　B. once　　　 C. immediately　D. recently
14. A. after　　　　B. down　　　C. behind　　　 D. over
15. A. remembered B. realized　　C. reminded　　 D. repeated

UFOs—do they exist?

UFO is short for "unidentified flying object". UFOs are popularly known as flying saucers, (16)_____ that is often the (17)_____ they are reported to be. The (18)_____ "flying saucers" were seen in 1947 by an American pilot, but experts who studied his claim decided it had been a trick of the light.

Even people experienced at watching the sky, (19)_____ as pilots, report seeing UFOs. In 1978 a pilot reported a collection of UFOs off the coast of New Zealand. A television (20)_____ went up with the pilot and filmed the UFOs. Scientists studying this phenomenon later discovered that in this case they were simply lights on boats out fishing.

16. A. because　　B. therefore　C. although　D. so
17. A. look　　　　B. shape　　　C. size　　　D. type
18. A. last　　　　B. next　　　　C. first　　　D. oldest

19. A. like   B. that   C. so   D. such
20. A. cameraman B. director C. actor   D. announcer

Questions 21—40

- In this section you must choose the word or phrase which best completes each sentence.
- For questions 21 to 40, mark one letter A, B, C or D on your Answer Sheet.

21. The teacher encouraged her students _____ to an English pen-friend.
    A. should write   B. write   C. wrote   D. To write
22. They spent a lot of time _____ at the pictures in the museum.
    A. looking   B. for looking   C. to look   D. To looking
23. Shirley enjoys science lessons, but all her experiments seem to _____ wrong.
    A. turn   B. come   C. end   D. Go
24. _____ from Michael, all the group arrived on time.
    A. Except   B. Other   C. Besides   D. Apart
25. She _____ her neighbour's children for the broken window.
    A. accused   B. complained   C. blamed   D. denied
26. As I had missed the history lesson, my friend went _____ the homework with me.
    A. by   B. after   C. over   D. On
27. Whether she's a good actress or not is a _____ of opinion.
    A. matter   B. subject   C. point   D. case
28. The decorated roof of the ancient palace was _____ up by four thin columns.
    A. built   B. carried   C. held   D. supported
29. Would it _____ you if we came on Thursday?
    A. agree   B. suit   C. like   D. Fit
30. This form _____ be handed in until the end of the week.
    A. doesn't need   B. doesn't have
    C. needn't   D. hasn't got
31. If you make a mistake when you are writing, just _____ it out

with your pen.

    A. cross   B. clear   C. do   D. wipe

32. Although our opinions on many things _____, we're good friends.

    A. differ   B. oppose   C. disagree   D. divide

33. This product must be eaten _____ two days of purchase.

    A. by   B. before   C. within   D. under

34. The newspaper report contained _____ important information.

    A. many   B. another   C. an   D. a lot of

35. Have you considered _____ to London?

    A. move   B. to move   C. to be moving   D. moving

36. It can be a good idea for people who lead an active life to increase their _____ of vitamins.

    A. upturn   B. input   C. upkeep   D. intake

37. I thought there was a _____ of jealousy in his reaction to my good fortune.

    A. piece   B. part   C. shadow   D. touch

38. Why didn't you _____ that you were feeling ill?

    A. advise   B. mention   C. remark   D. tell

39. James was not sure exactly where his best interests _____.

    A. stood   B. rested   C. lay   D. centred

40. He's still getting _____ the shock of losing his job.

    A. across   B. by   C. over   D. through

Part 2

Do not start this part unless told to do so by your test supervisor.

Questions 41—50

- In this section you must choose the word or phrase which best fits each space in the texts.
- For questions 41 to 50, mark one letter A, B, C or D on your Answer Sheet.

The tallest buildings—SKYSCRAPERS

Nowadays, skyscrapers can be found in most major cities of the world. A building which was many (41) _____ high was first called a skyscraper in the United States at the end of the 19th century, and New York has perhaps the (42)_____ skyscraper of them all, the Empire State Building. The (43)_____ beneath the streets of New York is rock, (44)_____ enough to take the heaviest load without sinking, and is therefore well-suited to bearing the (45)_____ of tall buildings.

41. A. stages   B. steps   C. storeys   D. levels
42. A. first-rate B. top-class C. well-built D. best-known
43. A. dirt   B. field   C. ground   D. soil
44. A. hard   B. stiff   C. forceful   D. powerful
45. A. weight   B. height   C. size   D. scale

SCRABBLE

Scrabble is the world's most popular word game. For its origins, we have to go back to the 1930s in the USA, when Alfred Butts, an architect, found himself out of (46)_____. He decided that there was a (47)_____ for a board game based on words and (48)_____ To design one. Eventually he made a (49)_____ from it, in spite of the fact that his original (50)_____ was only three cents a game.

46. A. earning   B. work   C. income   D. job
47. A. market   B. purchase   C. commerce   D. sale
48. A. took up   B. set out   C. made for   D. got round
49. A. wealth   B. fund   C. cash   D. fortune
50. A. receipt   B. benefit   C. profit   D. allowance

Questions 51—60

- In this section you must choose the word or phrase which best completes each sentence.
- For questions 51 to 60, mark one letter A, B, C or D on your Answer Sheet.

51. Roger's manager _____ to make him stay late if he hadn't finished the work.

    A. insisted   B. warned   C. threatened D. announced

52. By the time he has finished his week's work, John has hardly

_____ energy left for the weekend.

A. any B. much C. no D. same

53. As the game _____ to a close, disappointed spectators started to leave.

A. led B. neared C. approached D. drew

54. I don't remember _____ the front door when I left home this morning.

A. to lock B. locking
C. locked D. to have locked

55. I _____ to other people borrowing my books: they always forget to return them.

A. disagree B. avoid C. dislike D. object

56. Andrew's attempts to get into the swimming team have not _____ with much success.

A. associated B. concluded C. joined D. met

57. Although Harry had obviously read the newspaper article carefully, he didn't seem to have _____ the main point.

A. grasped B. clutched C. clasped D. gripped

58. A lot of the views put forward in the documentary were open to _____.

A. enquiry B. query C. question D. wonder

59. The new college _____ for the needs of students with a variety of learning backgrounds.

A. deals B. supplies C. furnishes D. caters

60. I find the times of English meals very strange-I'm not used _____ dinner at 6pm.

A. to have B. to having C. having D. have

答案

1	2	3	4	5	6	7	8	9	10	11	12	13	14	15
B	B	A	B	C	B	A	C	B	A	B	A	C	D	A
16	17	18	19	20	21	22	23	24	25	26	27	28	29	30
A	B	C	D	A	A	A	D	D	C	C	A	C	B	C
31	32	33	34	35	36	37	38	39	40	41	42	43	44	45
A	A	C	D	D	D	D	B	C	C	C	D	C	A	A
46	47	48	49	50	51	52	53	54	55	56	57	58	59	60
B	A	B	D	C	C	A	D	B	D	D	A	C	D	B

英语水平等级

Association of Language Testers in Europe		Part 1 Score out of 40	Part 1 & 2 Score out of 60
0	Beginner	0—15	0—17
1	Elementary	16—23	18—29
2	Lower Intermediate	24—30	30—39
3	Upper Intermediate	31—40	40—47
4	Advanced	If a student scores 36 or more it is recommended they complete Part 2 of the test	48—54
5	Very Advanced		55—60

What is the QPT?

The Quick Placement Test (QPT) is a flexible test of English language proficiency. It is quick and easy to administer and is ideal for placement testing and examination screening. It was first published in 2001. Prior to publication the QPT was validated in 20 countries by more than 5000 students. Through two phases of trialling, it is confirmed as both reliable and practical. It's key features include

- There are two parallel versions, to help minimise the risk of cheating.
- It assesses reading, vocabulary and grammar.
- It takes 30 minutes to administer.
- All the questions in the test are in multiple-choice format.
- The test consist of two parts. Part 1 is taken by all students. Part 2 is for higher ability students only.
- The result can be compared with the computer-based result.

附录 2

Language Analytic Ability Test

Time: 20 minutes

The list in the box below contains words/phrases from an imaginary language along with their English translation. Following this, there are 14 English sentences, each with four possible translations into the imaginary language. Based on the information given in the box, please try to work out which of the four options is the correct translation of each English sentence.

Imaginary language	English translation
kau	dog
meu	cat
kau meud bo	The dog is chasing the cat.
kau meud bi	The dog was chasing the cat.
so	watch
ciu	mouse
pa	we, us
xa	you
pasau meud bo	Our dog is chasing the cat.
pa meud bo	We are chasing the cat.
paxbo	We are chasing you.
pa meud bor	We aren't chasing the cat.

1. The dog is watching the cat.
    a. kau meud so   b. kau meud si
    c. meu kaud so   d. meu kaud si

2. The cat was watching the mouse.
   a. meud ciu so
   b. meu ciud so
   c. meud ciu si
   d. meu ciud si
3. You are watching us.
   a. paxbo   b. paxso   c. xapbo   d. xapso
4. You were chasing the dog.
   a. xa kaud bo   b. pa kaud bo   c. pa kaud bi   d. xa kaud bi
5. We were watching you.
   a. xapsi   b. paxso   c. paxsi   d. paxbi
6. You are not watching the cat.
   a. xa meud bor
   b. xa meud sor
   c. xa meud sir
   d. xa meu sor
7. You are not chasing us.
   a. paxbor   b. xapbo   c. xapabor   d. xapbor
8. We were not watching the dog.
   a. pa kaud sir   b. pa kau sir   c. pa kaud sor   d. pa kaud bir
9. We were not chasing you.
   a. xapbir   b. paxbir   c. paxbor   d. xapbor
10. Your cat is chasing the mouse.
    a. xacu meud bo
    b. xaseu ciud bo
    c. meuxa ciud bo
    d. ciuxa meud bo
11. You are not watching our dog.
    a. xa paseud bor
    b. xa pasaud sor
    c. xa pasaud so
    d. xa pasaud bor
12. Our mouse was not chasing the dog.
    a. oasiu kaud bi
    b. xasiu kaud sir
    c. xasiu kaud bi
    d. pasiu kaud bir
13. Your mouse is chasing us.
    a. xa ciu pabo
    b. xasiu pbo
    c. xaciu pa bo
    d. xasiu pabo
14. Our cat was not chasing your dog.
    a. pseu xasaud bir
    b. pseu xsaud bir
    c. paseu xasaud bir
    d. paseu xsaud bir

答案

1	2	3	4	5	6	7	8	9	10	11	12	13	14
a	d	d	d	c	b	d	a	b	b	b	d	b	c

What is the LAAT?

The language analytic ability test (LAAT) was developed by Ottó and used previously by Schmitt, Dönyei, Adolphs, and Durow (2003) and Sheen (2007). The test consisted of 14 multiple choice items. The learners are given a glossary consisting of words and sentences from an artificial language and their English translations. They are then given 14 English sentences and for each sentence are asked to choose the correct translation from the four choices provided. To make the correct choice, the learners need to analyze grammatical markers supplied in the glossary and apply these to the multiple-choice translations. For example, to choose the correct translation in Question 1, the student have to first deduce the rule that "i" is a past (progressive) marker and "o" is a present (progressive) marker and then apply that rule to the translated choices. Because this test is challenging to the students, the researcher should guide them through the first item in the test. This guidance will reduce their anxiety and ensure that they are familiar with the procedure they need to follow. The language analysis test is scored on a discrete item basis with 14 points being the perfect score.

附录 3

MBTI 性格测试

(一) MBTI 性格量表介绍

MBTI(Myers-Briggs Type Indicator)性格量表,是由美国心理学家 Katharine Cook Briggs 和她的女儿 Isabel Briggs Myers 制定的。该量表经过半个世纪的使用和完善,已被证明是具有信、效度的人格量表,现已成为具有广泛影响和应用前景的国际著名人格量表(Naomi 2000)。

罗正学等(2002)将 MBTI 性格量表翻译成了中文。然而,该中文版本在语言表述方面仍有欠缺,有些条目翻译不到位,语言晦涩难懂,不符合中文表达习惯等。对此,广东外语外贸大学英语语言文化学院 2012 级硕士研究生陈锦在其硕士论文筹备阶段,对该中文版量表的语言进行了调整,增强了其语言表述的准确性和流畅性。此外,陈锦将修订后的中文版及英文版 MBTI 在 50 名英语专业研究生中进行了测试,并对结果进行了效标关联效度分析,结果显示:两个版本下的测试结果显著相关,说明该中文版具有较好的效标关联效度。

(二) MBTI 性格量表中文版

量表分四部分,共 93 道题。所有题目没有对错之分,请根据自己的实际情况作选择。

第一部分：哪个选项更能贴切地描绘你一般的感受或行为？

序号	题目描述	选项	E	I	S	N	T	F	J	P
1	当你要外出一整天，你会 A 事先做好计划 B 说去就去	A							○	
		B								○
2	你认为自己是一个 A 较为随兴所至的人 B 较为有条理的人	A								○
		B							○	
3	假如你是一位老师，你会选教 A 以事实为主的课程 B 以理论为主的课程	A			○					
		B				○				
4	你通常 A 容易与他人混熟 B 比较沉静或矜持	A	○							
		B		○						
5	一般来说，你和哪些人比较合得来 A 富于想象力的人 B 较为实际的人	A				○				
		B			○					
6	你经常让 A 情感支配理智 B 理智支配情感	A						○		
		B					○			
7	在处理事情方面，你喜欢 A 凭兴所至行事 B 按照计划行事	A								○
		B							○	
8	你是否 A 容易让人了解 B 难于让人了解	A	○							
		B		○						
9	按照程序表做事 A 合你心意 B 令你感到束缚	A							○	
		B								○
10	当你有一个特别的任务，你会喜欢 A 事先细心计划好 B 边做边找须做什么	A							○	
		B								○

续表

序号	题目描述	选项	E	I	S	N	T	F	J	P
11	在大多数情况下,你会选择 A 顺其自然 B 按程序表做事	A B							○	○
12	大多数人会说你 A 重视隐私 B 坦率开放	A B	○	○						
13	你宁愿被人认为是一个 A 实事求是的人 B 机灵的人	A B			○	○				
14	在一大群人中,通常是 A 你介绍大家互相认识 B 别人向他人介绍你	A B	○	○						
15	你会跟哪些人做朋友 A 常提出新主意的 B 脚踏实地的	A B			○	○				
16	你倾向 A 重视感情多于逻辑 B 重视逻辑多于感情	A B					○	○		
17	你比较喜欢 A 坐观事情发展才作计划 B 很早就作计划	A B							○	○
18	你喜欢花很多时间 A 一人独处 B 和他人相处	A B	○	○						
19	与很多人一起 A 令你活力培增 B 令你心力交瘁	A B	○	○						
20	你比较喜欢 A 很早便把约会、社交聚会等事情安排妥当 B 无拘无束,看当时有什么好玩就做什么	A B							○	○

续表

序号	题目描述	选项	E	I	S	N	T	F	J	P
21	去旅游时,你较喜欢 A 大部分时间跟着当天的感觉决定行程 B 事先计划接下来的日子会做什么	A B							○	○
22	在社交聚会中,你 A 容易感到郁闷 B 常常乐在其中	A B	○	○						
23	你通常 A 和别人容易混熟 B 趋向自我独处	A B	○	○						
24	哪些人会更吸引你 A 思路敏捷、聪明伶俐的人 B 实事求是、常识丰富的人	A B			○	○				
25	在日常工作中,你会 A 喜欢处理分秒必争的突发事件 B 通常预先计划,按部就班	A B							○	○
26	你认为别人一般 A 要花很长时间才认识你 B 用很短的时间便认识你	A B	○	○						

第二部分:下列每一对词语中,哪个更符合你的心意?
请仔细思考每个词语的意思,而非它们的字形和读音。

序号	题目描述	选项	E	I	S	N	T	F	J	P
27	A 注重隐私　　B 坦率开放	A B	○	○						
28	A 预先安排的　B 无计划的	A B							○	○
29	A 抽象　　　　B 具体	A B			○	○				
30	A 温柔　　　　B 坚定	A B					○	○		

续表

序号	题目描述	选项	E	I	S	N	T	F	J	P
31	A 思考　　B 感受	A					○			
		B						○		
32	A 事实　　B 意念	A			○					
		B				○				
33	A 冲动　　B 决定	A								○
		B							○	
34	A 热衷　　B 文静	A	○							
		B		○						
35	A 文静　　B 外向	A		○						
		B	○							
36	A 有系统　B 随意	A							○	
		B								○
37	A 理论　　B 肯定	A				○				
		B			○					
38	A 敏感　　B 公正	A						○		
		B					○			
39	A 令人信服　B 感人的	A				○				
		B						○		
40	A 声明　　B 概念	A			○					
		B				○				
41	A 不受约束　B 预先安排	A								○
		B							○	
42	A 矜持　　B 健谈	A		○						
		B	○							
43	A 有条不紊　B 不拘小节	A							○	
		B								○
44	A 意念　　B 实况	A				○				
		B			○					
45	A 同情怜悯　B 远见	A						○		
		B				○				
46	A 利益　　B 祝福	A					○			
		B						○		
47	A 务实的　B 理论的	A			○					
		B				○				

续表

序号	题目描述	选项	E	I	S	N	T	F	J	P
48	A 朋友不多　B 朋友众多	A		○						
		B	○							
49	A 有系统　B 即兴	A							○	
		B								○
50	A 富想象力的　B 以事论事	A				○				
		B			○					
51	A 亲切的　B 客观的	A						○		
		B					○			
52	A 客观的　B 热情的	A					○			
		B						○		
53	A 建造　B 发明	A				○				
		B			○					
54	A 文静　B 合群	A		○						
		B	○							
55	A 理论　B 事实	A				○				
		B			○					
56	A 富同情心　B 合逻辑	A						○		
		B					○			
57	A 具分析力　B 多愁善感	A					○			
		B						○		
58	A 合情合理　B 令人着迷	A			○					
		B				○				

第三部分：哪个选项更能贴切地描绘你一般的感受或行为

序号	题目描述	选项	E	I	S	N	T	F	J	P
59	当你要在一个星期内完成一项工作，你在开始的时候会 A 依次列出需要完成的工作 B 马上动工	A							○	
		B								○
60	在社交场合中，你经常会感到 A 对某些人很难打开话匣持续交谈 B 与多数人都能从容地长谈	A		○						
		B	○							

续表

序号	题目描述	选项	E	I	S	N	T	F	J	P
61	要做许多人做过的事,你比较喜欢 A 按照传统认可的方法去做 B 构想新的想法去做	A			○					
		B				○				
62	刚认识你的朋友能否说出你的兴趣 A 马上可以 B 要待他们真正了解你之后才可以	A	○							
		B		○						
63	你通常较喜欢的科目是 A 讲授概念和原则的 B 讲授事实和数据的	A				○				
		B			○					
64	哪种描述是较高的赞誉 A 一贯感性的 B 一贯理性的	A						○		
		B					○			
65	你认为按照程序表做事 A 有时是需要的,但一般来说你不大喜欢这样做 B 大多数情况下是有帮助,而且是你喜欢做的	A								○
		B							○	
66	和一群人在一起,你通常会选 A 个别跟你熟悉的人谈话 B 参与大伙的谈话	A		○						
		B	○							
67	在社交聚会上,你会 A 是说话很多的人 B 让别人多说话	A	○							
		B		○						
68	把周末期间要完成的事列成清单,这个主意会 A 合你心意 B 使你提不起劲	A							○	
		B								○

续表

序号	题目描述	选项	E	I	S	N	T	F	J	P
69	哪种描述是较高的赞誉 A 能干的 B 富有同情心的	A B					○	○		
70	你通常喜欢 A 事先安排你的社交约会 B 随兴之所至做事	A B							○	○
71	总的说来,要做一个大型作业时,你会选 A 边做边想该做什么 B 首先把工作按步细分	A B							○	○
72	你滔滔不绝地与人聊天,这种情况 A 只限于跟你有共同兴趣的人 B 几乎跟任何人都可以	A B	○ ○							
73	你会 A 按照被证明有效的方法解决问题 B 尝试新的方法去解决问题	A B			○	○				
74	为乐趣而阅读时,你会 A 喜欢作者奇特或创新的表达方式 B 喜欢作者直话直说	A B			○	○				
75	你比较喜欢为哪一类上司工作 A 天性淳良,但常常前后不一 B 言词尖锐但永远合乎逻辑	A B					○ ○			
76	你做事多数是 A 按当天心情去做 B 照拟好的程序表去做	A B							○	○
77	你是否 A 可以和任何人从容地交谈 B 只是对某些人或在某种情况下才可以畅所欲言	A B	○ ○							
78	要作决定时,你认为比较重要的是 A 据事实衡量 B 考虑他人的感受和意见	A B					○	○		

第四部分：下列每一对词语中，哪个更符合你的心意？

序号	题目描述		选项	E	I	S	N	T	F	J	P
79	A 想象的	B 真实的	A				○				
			B			○					
80	A 仁慈慷慨的	B 意志坚定的	A					○			
			B						○		
81	A 公正	B 关怀	A					○			
			B						○		
82	A 制作	B 设计	A			○					
			B				○				
83	A 可能性	B 必然性	A				○				
			B			○					
84	A 温柔	B 力量	A						○		
			B					○			
85	A 实际	B 多愁善感	A					○			
			B						○		
86	A 制造	B 创造	A			○					
			B				○				
87	A 新颖的	B 已知的	A				○				
			B			○					
88	A 同情	B 分析	A						○		
			B					○			
89	A 坚持己见	B 温柔有爱心	A					○			
			B						○		
90	A 具体的	B 抽象的	A			○					
			B				○				
91	A 全心投入	B 有决心的	A							○	
			B								○
92	A 能干	B 仁慈	A					○			
			B						○		
93	A 实际	B 创新	A			○					
			B				○				
	每项得分										

（三）评分步骤

1. 将每题选中项对应的小圆圈涂黑；

2. 统计 E、I、S、N、T、F、J、P 每项之下涂黑的小圆圈个数；

3. 分别对"E-I""S-N""T-F"和"J-P"进行比较,选取每组中个数多的类型,例如,E＝12,I＝9,则选取 E；如果两个类型同分,则遵循以下选取原则：当 E＝I,选 I；当 S＝N,选 N；当 T＝F,择 F；当 J＝P,选 P；

外向	E			I	内向
实感	S			N	直觉
思考	T			F	情感
判断	J			P	认知

4. 最后,将统计出的结果与 MBTI 十六种性格类型进行匹配,具体性格类型如下：

第一种性格 ISTJ

- 严肃、安静,一旦集中心志,全力投入,即可获得他人信赖,取得成功；
- 对任何事情充满热忱；
- 行事务实、有序、负责任、逻辑性强；
- 在工作、居家、生活方面,均有条不紊；
- 根据目标做出决策,且不畏艰难险阻,坚持到底；
- 重视传统与忠诚；
- 传统的思考者与管理者。

第二种性格 ISFJ

- 安静、和善、负责任；
- 行事尽责投入；
- 稳重,在项目团体工作中,常起稳固团队作用；
- 做事乐于投入,吃苦耐劳,力求精确；
- 注重细节,有耐心；
- 忠诚、考虑周到、知性且关切他人感受；
- 致力于创构有序、和谐的工作环境与家庭氛围。

第三种性格 INFJ

- 坚忍、有创意、目标明确；
- 工作全力以赴；
- 诚挚恳切、默默用心地关切他人；

- 因坚守原则而备受敬重；
- 提出造福大众利益的明确远景，从而为他人所尊敬与拥护；
- 具有洞察力，善于发掘激励他人的方法；
- 为人正直，光明磊落，坚信自身的价值观；
- 果断，有组织地履行自身的愿望。

第四种性格 INTJ
- 为达成目的，动力十足、信念坚定，有创意但固执顽固；
- 愿景宏大，能快速在众多外界事件中找出有意义的模范；
- 对于所承担的职务，具有良好的策划能力且能顺利完成；
- 深思熟虑、吹毛求疵、独立果断，对专业水准及绩效要求高。

第五种性格 ISTP
- 安静、冷静、做事预留余地，会带着好奇心、幽默感观察和分析事物；
- 热衷于探索事物的原因、效果，对技术运作、逻辑使用、组构原理、效能感兴趣；
- 擅长于掌握问题核心并找出解决方式；
- 善于分析成事缘由，能实时从大量资料中找出实际问题的核心。

第六种性格 ISFP
- 羞怯敏感、亲切和善、谦虚安宁；
- 不喜欢争论，不对他人强加已见；
- 是领导身边忠诚的拥护者；
- 办事不急躁，安于现状，非功利型；
- 喜欢有自由的空间，按照自订的计划办事。

第七种性格 INFP
- 忠诚、理想主义、安静的观察者；
- 希望做到表里如一；
- 好奇心强，能快速看出机会所在，常担任开发、创意的触媒者；
- 在价值观不受侵犯的前提下，处事灵活、适应力高、承受力强；
- 善于发掘他人潜能，做事时想法多且能全神贯注；
- 不太在意所处境遇及拥有的东西。

第八种性格 INTP
- 安静、自持、灵活、具有适应力；
- 特别喜爱追求科学理论；

- 习惯以逻辑思维来分析和解决问题；
- 热衷于有创意的事物及特定的工作,对聚会与闲聊不大感兴趣；
- 追求可发挥个人强烈兴趣的职业生涯；
- 喜欢对感兴趣的事务做出逻辑解释。

第九种性格 ESTP
- 擅长现场即时解决问题；
- 做事通常乐在其中,享受其过程；
- 喜好技术事务,热衷运动,乐于结交志同道合的友人；
- 务实、适应力强、能容忍,常投注心力于成效快的工作；
- 不喜欢冗长的概念解释及理论；
- 最擅长可操作、处理、分解或组合的事务。

第十种性格 ESFP
- 外向、和善、接受能力强、乐于和他人分享喜乐；
- 喜欢和他人一起做事,学习；
- 善于知晓事件未来的发展,并积极参与；
- 最擅长人际相处,具备完备的常识,灵活、能快速适应他人与环境；
- 热爱生活,享受物质。

第十一种性格 ENFP
- 充满热忱、聪明活跃、富有想象力,认为生活充满机会,希望得到他人肯定与支持；
- 对于感兴趣的事情,几乎都能达成；
- 对难题很快能做出对策,对有困难的人会施予援手；
- 顺其自然,很少对事情做规划准备；
- 为达到目的,常能找出强制自己为之的理由；
- 即兴执行者。

第十二种性格 ENTP
- 思维敏捷、聪明、多才多艺；
- 善于激励他人,直言不讳；
- 为了有趣,会对问题的对立面加以争辩；
- 富有解决挑战性问题的策略,但会轻忽、厌烦反复出现的任务和细节；
- 兴趣多元,易转移至新的兴趣点；

- 善于看清他人。

第十三种性格 ESTJ
- 务实、真实、尊重事实,具备从事企业管理或技术的天分;
- 不喜欢抽象理论,喜欢便于实践,操作性强的事理;
- 喜好组织与管理活动,高效率行事,以达致成效;
- 判断力强,注重细节,能很快做出决策,是一名优秀的行政者;
- 往往忽略他人的感受;
- 喜作领导者或企业主管。

第十四种性格 ESFJ
- 诚挚善谈、正直磊落、合作性高、备受欢迎,是一名天生的合作者和活跃的组织成员;
- 重视和谐且擅长于创造和谐氛围;
- 常作对他人有益的事务;
- 经常给予他人鼓励、称许,会有更佳的工作成效;
- 热衷于处理会直接影响他人生活的事务;
- 喜欢与他人共事,能按时保质完成工作任务。

第十五种性格 ENFJ
- 热忱敏感,责任感强,具有鼓励他人的领导风格;
- 真正关切他人所想或需求,且用心处理;
- 能自然、巧妙地带领团体讨论或演示文稿提案;
- 爱交际、受欢迎、富有同情心;
- 在意他人对自己的称许和批评;
- 喜欢引导他人,且能使他人或团体发挥潜能。

第十六种性格 ENTJ
- 是一名坦诚、具决策力的活动领导者;
- 最擅长具有内涵、智慧的谈话或公众演讲;
- 乐于吸收新知识,且广开接受信息的渠道;
- 易过度自信,会强加自己的创见于他人身上;
- 喜欢长期规划和设定目标。

参考文献

Ammar, A. 2008. Prompts and recasts: Differential effects on second language morphosyntax. *Language Teaching Research* 12: 183-210.

Ammar, A. & Spada, N. 2006. One size fits all? Recasts, prompts, and L2 learning. *Studies in Second Language Acquisition* 28: 543-574.

Anderson, J. & Fincham, J. 1994. Acquisition of procedural skill from examples. *Journal of Experimental Psychology: Learning, Memory and Cognition* 20: 1322-1340.

Anderson, J. 1983. *The Architecture of Cognition*. Cambridge, MA: Harvard University Press.

Anderson, J. 1985. *Cognitive Psychology and its Implications* (2nd ed.), New York: Freeman.

Anson, C. M. 2000. Response and the social construction of error. *Assessing Writing* 7: 5-21.

Anton, M. 1999. The discourse of a learner-centered classroom: Sociocultural perspectives on teacher-learner interaction in the second-language classroom. *The Modern Language Journal* 83: 303-318.

Arndt, V. 1987. Six writers in search of texts: A protocol-based study of L1 and L2 writing. *ELT Journal* 41: 257-267.

Ashwell, T. 2000. Patterns of teacher response to student writing in a multiple-draft composition classroom: Is content feedback followed by form feedback the best method? *Journal of Second Language Writing* 9: 227-258.

Baldwin, R. G. 1960. Grading freshman essays. *College Composition and Communication* 11: 110-114.

Bartholomae, D. G. 1980. The study of error. *College Composition* and Communication 31: 253-269.

Bates, E. & MacWhinney, B. 1981. Second language acquisition from a functionalist perspective. In H. Winitz (ed.), *Native Language and Foreign Language Acquisition* (pp. 190-214). Annals of the New York Academy of Sciences.

Bean, J. C. 1996. *Engaging ideas: The Professor's Guide to Integrating Writing, Critical Thinking, and Active Learning in the Classroom.* San Francisco, CA: Jossey-Bass.

Beason, L. 2001. Ethos and error: How business people react to errors. *College Composition and Communication* 53: 33-64.

Bitchener, J. 2008. Evidence in support of written corrective feedback. *Journal of Second Language Writing* 17: 102-118.

Bitchener, J. 2012. A reflection on 'the language learning potential' of written CF. *Journal of Second Language Writing* 21: 348-363.

Bitchener, J. & Ferris, D. R. 2012. *Written Corrective Feedback in Second Language Acquisition and Writing.* New York: Routledge.

Bitchener, J. & Knoch, U. 2008. The value of written corrective feedback for migrant and international students. *Language Teaching Research* 12: 409-431.

Bitchener, J. & Knoch, U. 2009a. The relative effectiveness of different types of direct written corrective feedback. *System* 37: 322-329.

Bitchener, J. & Knoch, U. 2009b. The value of a focused approach to written corrective feedback. *ELT Journal* 63: 204-211.

Bitchener, J. & Knock, U. 2010a. The contribution of written corrective feedback to language development: A ten month investigation. *Applied Linguistics* 31: 193-214.

Bitchener, J. & Knock, U. 2010b. Raising the linguistic accuracy level of advanced L2 writers with written corrective feedback. *Journal of Second Language Writing* 19: 207-217.

Bitchener, J., Young, S., & Cameron, D. 2005. The effectiveness of different types of corrective feedback on ESL student writing.

Journal of Second Language Writing 14: 191-205.

Bod, R. 1998. *Beyond Grammar: An Experience-Based Theory of Language.* Stanford, CA: CSLI Publications.

Brannon, L. & Knoblauch, C. H. 1982. On students' rights to their own texts: A model of teacher response. *College Composition and Communication* 33: 157-166.

Brereton, J. C. 1995. *The Origins of Composition Studies in the American College*, 1875—1925. Pittsburgh, PA: University of Pittsburgh Press.

Briggs, J. 1992. *Fractals: The Patterns of Chaos.* New York: Simon and Schuster.

Brooks, N. 1960. *Language and Language Learning.* New York: Harcourt.

Brown, R. 1973. *A First Language: The Early Stages.* Cambridge, MA: Harvard University Press.

Bruton, A. 2009. Improving accuracy is not the only reason for writing, and even if it were… *System* 37: 600-613.

Bruton, A. 2010. Another reply to Truscott on error correction: Improved situated designs over statistics. *System* 38: 491-498.

Bybee, J. 2008. Usage-based grammar and second language acquisition. In P. Robinson & N. Ellis (eds.), *Handbook of Cognitive Linguistics and Second Language Acquisition* (pp. 216-236). New York: Routledge.

Cameron, L. & Deignan, A. 2006. The emergence of metaphor in discourse. *Applied Linguistics* 27: 671-690.

Campbell, C. 1990. Writing with other's words: Using background reading text in academic compositions. In B. Kroll (ed.), *Second Language Writing: Research Insights for the Classroom* (pp. 211-230). Cambridge: Cambridge University Press.

Cardelle, M. & Corno, L. 1981. Effects on second language learning of variations in written feedback on homework assignments. *TESOL Quarterly* 15: 251-261.

Carpenter, H., Jeon, K. S., MacGregor, D., & Mackey, A. 2006. Learners' interpretations of recasts. *Studies in Second*

Language Acquisition 28: 209-236.

Carroll, J. B. 1981. Twenty-five years of research on foreign language aptitude. In K. C. Diller (ed.), *Individual Differences and Universals in Language Learning Aptitude* (pp. 83-118). New York: Newbury House.

Carroll, S. & Swain, M. 1993. Explicit and implicit negative feedback: An empirical study of the learning of linguistic generalizations. *Studies in Second Language Acquisition* 15: 357-386.

Carroll, S. 2001. *Input and Evidence: The Raw Material of Second Language Acquisition*. Amsterdam: Benjamins.

Cazden, C., John, V., & Hymes, D. 1972. *Functions of Language in Classroom*. New York: Teachers College Press.

Chandler, J. 2003. The efficacy of various kinds of error feedback for improvement in the accuracy and fluency of L2 student writing. *Journal of Second Language Writing* 12: 267-296.

Chaudron, C. 1977. A descriptive model of discourse in the corrective treatment of learners' errors. *Language Learning* 27: 29-46.

Chomsky, N. 1957. *Syntactic Structures*. The Hague: Mouton.

Chomsky, N. 1959. A review of B. F. Skinner's verbal behavior. *Language* 35: 26-58.

Christiansen, M. H. & Chater, N. 2001. Connectionist psycholinguistics capturing the empirical data. *Trends in Cognitive Sciences* 5: 82-88.

Cohen, A. D. 1987. Student processing of feedback on their compositions. In A. Wenden & J. Rubin (eds.), *Learner Strategies in Language Learning* (pp. 57-69). New York: Prentice-Hall.

Cohen, A. D. 1989. Reformulation: A technique for providing advanced feedback in writing. *Guidelines* 11: 1-9.

Cohen, A. D. & Cavalcanti, M. C. 1990. Feedback on compositions: Teacher and student verbal reports. In B. Kroll (ed.), *Second Language Writing: Research Insights for the Classroom* (pp. 155-177). Cambridge: Cambridge University Press.

Cohen, A. D. & Robbins, M. 1976. Toward assessing interlanguage performance: The relationship between selected errors, learners' characteristics, and learners' explanations. *Language Learning* 26: 45-66.

Connors, R. 1985. Mechanical correctness as a focus in composition instruction. *College Composition and Communication* 36: 61-72.

Connors, R. 1997. *Composition-Rhetoric: Backgrounds, Theory, and Pedagogy*. Pittsburgh, PA: University of Pittsburgh Press.

Connors, R. 2003. Grammar in American college composition: An historical overview. In L. Ede & A. A. Lunsford (eds.), *Selected Essays of Robert J. Connors* (pp. 117-138). Boston, MA: Bedford/St. Martin's.

Connors, R. & Lunsford, A. A. 1988. Frequency of formal errors in current college writing, or Ma and Pa Kettle do research. *College Composition and Communication* 39: 395-409.

Connors, R. & Lunsford, A. A. 1993. Teachers' rhetorical comments on student papers. *College Composition and Communication* 44: 200-223.

Corder, S. P. 1967. The significance of learner's errors. *International Review of Applied Linguistics* 5: 161-170.

Coughlan, P., & Duff, P. A. 1994. Same task, different activities: Analysis of an SLA task from an activity theory perspective. In J. P. Lantolf & G. Appel (eds.), *Vygotskian Approaches to Second Language Research* (pp. 173-194). Norwood, NJ: Ablex Publishing Corporation.

Davis, A. L. 1972. *Culture, Class, and Language Variety*. Urbana, IL: NCTE.

de Bot, K. 1996. The psycholinguistics of the output hypothesis. *Language Learning* 46: 529-555.

de Bot, K. 2008. Introduction: Second language development as a dynamic process. *The Modern Language Journal* 92: 166-178.

de Bot, K., W. Lowie & Verspoor, M. A. 2005. *Second Language Acquisition: An Advanced Resource Book*. London: Routledge.

DeGraaf, R. 1997. *Differential Effects of Explicit Instruction on Second Language Acquisition*. The Hague: Holland Institute of Generative Linguistics.

DeKeyser, R. M. 1998. Beyond focus on form: Cognitive perspectives on learning and practicing second language grammar. In C. J. Doughty & J. Williams (eds.), *Focus on Form in Classroom Second Language Acquisition* (pp. 42-63). New York: Cambridge University Press.

DeKeyser, R. M. 1997. Beyond explicit rule learning: Automatizing second language morphosyntax. *Studies in Second Language Acquisition* 19: 195-222.

DeKeyser, R. M. 2000. The robustness of critical period effects in second language acquisition. *Studies in Second Language. Acquisition* 22: 499-533.

DeKeyser, R. M. 2001. Automaticity and automatization. In P. Robinson (ed.), *Cognition and Second Language Instruction* (pp. 125-151). Cambridge: Cambridge University Press.

DeKeyser, R. M. 2003. Implicit and explicit learning. In C. G. Doughty & M. H. Long (eds.), *The Handbook of Second Language Acquisition* (pp. 313-348). Oxford: Blackwell Publishing.

DeKeyser, R. M. 2007. *Practice in a Second Language*. Cambridge: Cambridge University Press.

Dobao, A. F. 2012. Collaborative dialogue in learner-learner and learner-native speaker interaction. *Applied Linguistics* 33: 229-256.

Dörnyei, Z. 1994. Motivation and motivating in the foreign language classroom. *The Modern Language Journal* 78: 273-284.

Dörnyei, Z. & Skehan, P. 2003. Individual differences in second language learning. In C. Doughty & M. H. Long (eds.), *The Handbook of Second Language Acquisition* (pp. 256-310). Oxford: Blackwell Publishing.

Doughty, C. & Varela, E. 1998. Communicative focus on form. In C. Doughty & J. Williams (eds.), *Focus on Form in Classroom*

Second Language Acquisition (pp. 114-138). Cambridge: Cambridge University Press.

Dulay, H. & Burt, M. 1973. Should we teach children syntax? *Language Learning* 24: 245-258.

Dulay, H. & Burt, M. 1974. Natural sequences in child second language acquisition. *Language Learning* 24: 37-53.

Dulay, H. & Burt, M. 1975. Creative construction in second language learning and teaching. In M. Burt & H. Dulay (eds.), *New Directions in Second Language Learning, Teaching, and Bilingual Education* (pp. 21-32). Washington, DC: TESOL.

Dulay, H., Burt, M. & Krashen, S. 1982. *Language Two*. New York, NY: Oxford University Press.

Durrant, P. & Schmitt, N. 2010. Adult learners' retention of collocations from exposure. *Second Language Research* 26: 163-188.

Dykema, K. W. 1940. Criteria of correctness. *College English* 1: 616-623.

Edelsky, C. 1982. Development of writing in a bilingual program. Final report. Vols. 1&2. Tempe, Arizona: Arizona State Department of Elementary Education (ERIC Document Reproduction Service No. 221057).

Ehrman, M. & Oxford, R. 1995. Cognition plus: Correlates of language learning success. *The Modern Language Journal* 79: 67-89.

Ellis, N. 2005. At the interface: Dynamic interactions of explicit and implicit language knowledge. *Studies in Second Language Acquisition* 27: 305-352.

Ellis, N. 2006. Selective attention and transfer phenomena in L2 acquisition: Contingency, cue competition, salience, interference, overshadowing, blocking, and perceptual learning. *Applied Linguistics* 27: 164-194.

Ellis, N. 2007. The associative-cognitive CREED. In B. VanPattern & J. Williams (eds.), *Theories in Second Language Acquisition: An Introduction* (pp. 77-96). Mahwah, NJ: Erlbaum.

Ellis, N. 2012. Frequency-based accounts of second language acquisition. In S. Gass & A. Mackey (eds.), *The Routledge Handbook of Second Language Acquisition* (pp. 193-210). New York: Routledge.

Ellis, R. & Sheen, Y. 2006. Reexamining the role of recasts in second language acquisition. *Studies in Second Language Acquisition* 28: 575-600.

Ellis, R. 1988. *Classroom Second Language Development: A Study of Classroom Interaction and Language Acquisition*. London: Prentice Hall.

Ellis, R. 1993. The structural syllabus and second language acquisition. *TESOL Quarterly* 27: 91-113.

Ellis, R. 1994. Implicit/explicit knowledge and language pedagogy. *TESOL Quarterly* 28: 166-172.

Ellis, R. 2004. The definition and measurement of L2 explicit knowledge. *Language Learning* 54: 227-275.

Ellis, R. 2008. Explicit form-focused instruction and second language acquisition. In B. Spolsky & M. Hult (eds.), *The Handbook of Educational Linguistics* (pp. 437-455). Oxford: Blackwell.

Ellis, R. 2009. A typology of written corrective feedback types. *ELT Journal* 63: 97-107.

Ellis, R., Loewen, S., & Erlam, R. 2006. Implicit and explicit corrective feedback and the acquisition of L2 grammar. *Studies in Second Language Acquisition* 28: 339-368.

Ellis, R., Loewen, S., Elder, C., Erlam, R., Philp, J., & Reinders, H. 2009. *Implicit and Explicit Knowledge in Second Language Learning, Testing and Teaching*. Bristol/Buffalo, NY/Toronto: Multilingual Matters.

Ellis, R., Sheen, Y., Murakami, M., & Takashima, H. 2008. The effects of focused and unfocused written corrective feedback in an English as a foreign language context. *System* 36: 353-371.

Elman, J. L., Bates, E. A., Johnson, M. H., Karmiloff-Smith, A., Parisi, D., & Plunkett, K. 1996. *Rethinking Innateness:*

A Connectionist Perspective on Development. Cambridge, MA: MIT Press.

Enginarlar, H. 1993. Student response to teacher feedback in EFL writing. *System* 21: 193-204.

Eskey, D. E. 1983. Meanwhile, back in the real world... Accuracy and fluency in second language teaching. *TESOL Quarterly* 17: 315-323.

Evans, N., Hartshorn, K. J., & Strong-Krause, D. 2011. The efficacy of dynamic written corrective feedback for university-matriculated ESL learners. *System* 39: 229-239.

Evans, N., Hartshorn, J., McCollum, R., & Wolfersberger, M. 2010. Contextualizing corrective feedback in second language writing pedagogy. *Language Teaching Research* 14: 445-463.

Fathman, A. K., & Whalley, E. 1990. Teacher response to student writing: Focus on form versus content. In B. Kroll (ed.), *Second Language Writing: Research Insights for the Classroom* (pp. 178-190). Cambridge: Cambridge University Press.

Felix, S. W. 1981. The effect of formal instruction on second language acquisition. *Language Learning* 31: 87-112.

Ferris, D. R. 1994. Rhetorical strategies in student persuasive writing: Differences between native and non-native speakers. *Research in the Teaching of English* 28: 45-65.

Ferris, D. R. 1995a. Can advanced ESL students be taught to correct their most serious and frequent errors? *CATESOL Journal* 8: 41-62.

Ferris, D. R. 1995b. Student reactions to teacher response in multiple-draft composition classrooms. *TESOL Quarterly* 29: 33-53.

Ferris, D. R. 1995c. Teaching students to teacher response in multiple-draft composition classrooms. *TESOL Journal* 4: 18-22.

Ferris, D. R. 1997. The influence of teacher commentary on student revision. *TESOL Quarterly* 31: 315-339.

Ferris, D. R. 1999. The case for grammar correction in L2 writing classes: A response to Truscott (1996). *Journal of Second Language Writing 8: 1-10.

Ferris, D. R. 2002. *Treatment of Error in Second Language Student Writing*. Ann Arbor, MI: University of Michigan Press.

Ferris, D. R. 2003. *Response to Student Writing: Research Implications for Second Language Students*. Mahwah, NJ: Lawrence Erlbaum.

Ferris, D. R. 2004. The 'grammar correction' debate in L2 writing: Where are we, and where do we go from here? (and what do we do in the meantime…?). *Journal of Second Language Writing* 13: 49-62.

Ferris, D. R. 2006. Does error feedback help student writers? New evidence on the short-and long-term effects of written error correction. In K. Hyland & F. Hyland (eds.), *Feedback in Second Language Writing: Contexts and Issues* (pp. 81-104). Cambridge: Cambridge University Press.

Ferris, D. R. 2008. Myth 5: Students must learn to correct all their writing errors. In J. Reid (ed.), *Writing Myths: Applying Second Language Research to Classroom Teaching* (pp. 90-114). Ann Arbor, MI: University of Michigan Press.

Ferris, D. R. 2010. Second language writing research and written corrective feedback in SLA. *Studies in Second Language Acquisition* 32: 181-201.

Ferris. D. R. 2012. Written corrective feedback in second language acquisition and writing studies. *Language Teaching* 45: 446-458.

Ferris, D. R. & Hedgcock, J. S. 2005. *Teaching ESL Composition: Purpose, Process, and Practice* (2nd ed.). Mahwah, NJ: Erlbaum.

Ferris, D. R. & Roberts, B. J. 2001. Error feedback in L2 writing classes: How explicit does it need to be? *Journal of Second Language Writing* 10: 161-184.

Ferris, D. R., Liu, H., & Rabie, B. 2011. "The job of teaching writing": Teacher views of responding to student writing. *Writ-*

ing and Pedagogy 3: 39-77.

Ferris, D. R., Liu, H., Senna, M., & Sinha, A. 2010. *Written corrective feedback and individual variation in L2 writing*. Paper presented at the CATESOL State Conference, Santa Clara, CA.

Ferris, D. R., Pezone, S., Tade, C., & Tinti, S. 1997. Teacher commentary on student writing: Descriptions and implications. *Journal of Second Language Writing* 6: 155-182.

Ferris, D. R., Chaney, S. J., Komura, K., Roberts, B. J., & McKee, S. 2000. *Perspectives, Problems, and Practices in Treating Written Error*. Colloquium presented at International TESOL Convention, March 14-18, 2000, Vancouver, B. C.

Foin, A. & Lange, E. 2007. Generation 1.5 writers' success in correcting errors marked on an out-of-class paper. *CATESOL Journal* 19: 146-163.

Frantzen, D. & Rissel, D. 1987. Learner self-correction of written compositions: what does it show us? In B. VanPatten, T. R. Dvorak, & J. F. Lee (eds.), *Foreign Language Learning: A Research Perspective* (pp. 92-107). New York: Newbury House.

Frawley, W. & Lantolf, J. 1985. Second language discourse: a Vygotskyan perspective. *Applied Linguistics* 6: 19-44.

Gaskill, W. 1986. *Revising in Spanish and English as a second language: A process oriented study of composition*. Unpublished Ph. D. dissertation, Los Angels: University of California.

Gass, S. 2003. Input and interaction. In C. Doughty & M. H. Long (eds.), *The Handbook of Second Language Acquisition* (pp. 224-255). Oxford: Blackwell Publishing.

Gass, S. & Varonis, E. 1994. Input, interaction, and second language production. *Studies in Second Language Acquisition* 16: 283-302.

Gaudiani, C. 1981. *Teaching Writing in the Foreign Language Curriculum*. Washington, DC: Center for Applied Linguistics/ ERIC Clearing house on Languages and linguistics.

Gilbert, A. H. 1922. What shall we do with freshman themes? *English Journal* 11: 392-403.

Given, L., & Schallert, D. 2008. Meeting in the margins: Effects of the teacher-student relationship on revision processes of EFL college students taking a composition course. *Journal of Second Language Writing* 17: 165-182.

Glenn, C. & Goldthwaite, M. A. 2008. *The St. Martin's Guide to Teaching Writing* (6th ed.). Boston, MA: Bedford/St. Martin's.

Goldberg, A. E. 1995. *Constructions: A Construction Grammar Approach to Argument structure*. Chicago: University Chicago Press.

Goldberg, A. E. 2003. Constructions: A new theoretical approach to language. *Journal of Foreign Languages* 25: 1-11.

Goldstein, L. 2006. Feedback and revision in second language writing: Helping learners become independent writers. In K. Hyland & F. Hyland (eds.), *Feedback in Second Language Writing: Contexts and Issues* (pp. 185-205). Cambridge: Cambridge University Press.

Gregg, K. 1984. Krashen's Monitor and Occam's Razor. *Applied Linguistics* 5: 79-100.

Gregorc, A. R. 1982. *Style Delineator*. Maynard, MA: Gabriel Systems.

Grigerenko, E. L. and Sternberg, R. J. 1995. Thinking styles. In D. H. Saklofske & M. Zeidner (eds.), *International Handbook of Personality and Intelligence* (pp. 205-230). Plenum Press.

Guénette, D. 2007. Is feedback pedagogically correct? Research design issues in studies of feedback in writing. *Journal of Second Language Writing* 16: 40-53.

Guénette, D. & Lyster, R. 2013. Written corrective feedback and its challenges for pre-service ESL teachers. *The Canadian Modern Language Review* 69: 129-153.

Gurzynski-Weiss, L. 2010. Factors influencing oral corrective feedback provision in the Spanish foreign language classroom: Investigating instructor native/nonnative speaker status, second language acquisition education, and teaching experience. Unpublished Ph. D. dissertation, Georgetown University, Washington, DC.

Hairston, M. 1981. Not all errors are created equal: Nonacademic readers in the professions respond to lapses in usage. *College English* 43: 794-806.

Hairston, M. 1986. On not being a composition slave. In C. W. Bridges (ed.), *Training the New Teacher of College Composition* (pp. 117-124). Urbana, IL: NCTE.

Hammer, J. J. & Rice, F. A. 1965. *A Bibliography of Contrastive Linguistics*. Washington, DC: Center for Applied linguistics.

Han, Z. 2002. A study of the impact of recasts on tense consistency in L2 output. *TESOL Quarterly* 36: 543-572.

Harap, H. 1930. The most common grammatical errors. *English Journal* 19: 440-446.

Harley, B. & Hart, D. 2002. Age, aptitude and second language learning on a bilingual exchange. In P. Robinson (ed.), *Individual Differences and Instructed Language Learning* (pp. 301-330). Amsterdam: John Benjamins.

Hartshorn, J. K., Evans, N. W., Merrill, P. F., Sudweeks, R. R., Strong-Krause, D., & Anderson, N. J. 2010. The effects of dynamic corrective feedback on ESL writing accuracy. *TESOL Quarterly* 44: 84-109.

Hartwell, P. 1985. Grammar, grammars, and the teaching of grammar. *College English* 47: 105-127.

Haswell, R. H. 1983. Minimal marking. *College English* 45: 600-604.

Hedgcock, J. & Lefkowitz, N. 1994. Feedback on feedback: Assessing learner receptivity in second language writing. *Journal of Second Language Writing* 3: 141-163.

Hedgcock, J. & Lefkowitz, N. 1996. Some input on input: Two

analyses of student response to expert feedback on L2 writing. *The Modern Language Journal* 80: 287-308.

Hendrickson, J. M. 1978. Error correction in foreign language teaching: Recent theory, research, and practice. *The Modern Language Journal*, 62: 387-398.

Hendrickson, J. M. 1980. The treatment of error in written work. *The Modern Language Journal* 64: 216-221.

Hendrickson, J. M. 1981. *Error Analysis and Error Correction in Language Teaching*. Singapore: SEAMEO Regional Language Centre.

Herron, C. 1981. The treatment of error in written work. *The Modern Language Journal* 64: 216-221.

Herron, C., & Tomasello, M. 1988. Learning grammatical structures in a foreign language: Modeling versus feedback. *French Review* 61: 910-922.

Higgs, T. V., 1979. Coping with composition. *Hispania* 62: 673-678.

Hillocks, G., Jr. 1986. *Research on Written Composition: New Directions for Teaching*. Urbana, IL: NCTE.

Hinkel, E. 2002. *Second Language Writers' Text*. Mahwah, NJ: Lawrence Erlbaum Associates.

Holley, F. M. & King, J. K. 1971. Imitation and correction in foreign language learning. *The Modern Language Journal* 55: 494-498.

Horner, B. 1992. Rethinking the "sociality" of error: Teaching editing as negotiation. *Rhetoric Review* 11: 172-199.

Horner, B. 1994. Mapping errors and expectations for basic writing: From the "frontier field" to the "border country". *English Education* 26: 29-51.

Horowitz, D. 1986. Process not product: Less than meets the eye. *TESOL Quarterly* 20: 141-144.

Huitt, W. & Hummel, J. 2006. An overview of the behavioral perspective. Educational Psychology InteractiveValdosta, GA: Valdosta State University. Retrieved [date], from http: //chiron.

valdosta. edu / whuitt / col /behsys / behsys. html.

Hulstijin, J. H. 1995. Not all grammar rules are equal: Giving grammar instruction its proper place in foreign language teaching. In R. Schmidt (ed.), *Attention and Awareness in Foreign Language Learning* (pp. 359-386). Honolulu: University of Hawaii Press.

Hulstijn, J. H. & Hulstijn, W. 1984. Grammatical errors as a function of processing constraints and explicit knowledge. *Language Learning* 34: 23-43.

Hyland, F. 1998. The impact of teacher written feedback on individual writers. *Journal of Second Language Writing* 7: 255-286.

Hyland, F. 2000. ESL writers and feedback: Giving more autonomy to students. *Language Teaching Research* 4: 33-54.

Hyland, F. 2003. Focusing on form: Student engagement with teacher feedback. *System* 31: 217-230.

Hyland, F. & Hyland, K. 2001. Sugaring the pill: Praise and criticism in written feedback. *Journal of Second Language Writing* 19: 185-212.

Hyland, K. 2002. *Teaching and Researching Writing*. London: Longman.

Hyland, K. & Hyland, F. 2006. Feedback on second language students' writing. *Language Teaching* 39: 83-101.

Hyltenstam, K. 1977. Implicational patterns in interlanguage syntax variation. *Language Learning* 27: 383-411.

Hymes, D. 1974. *Foundations in Sociolinguistics: An Ethno Graphic Approach*. Philadelphia: University of Pennsylvania Press.

Inagaki, S., & Long, M. H. 1999. The effects of implicit negative feedback on the acquisition of Japanese as a second language. In K. Kanno (ed.), *Studies on the Acquisition of Japanese as a Second Language* (pp. 9-30). Amsterdam: Benjamins.

Iwashita, N. 2003. Negative feedback and positive evidence in task-based interaction: Differential effects on L2 development. *Studies in Second Language Acquisition* 25: 1-36.

Jacobs, G. M., Curtis, A., Braine, G., & Huang, S. 1998. Feedback on student writing: Talking the middle path. *Journal of Second Language Writing* 7: 307-318.

Johns, A. M. 1990. L1 composition theories: Implications for developing theories of L2 composition. In Kroll, B. (ed.), *Second Language Writing: Research Insights for the Classroom* (pp. 24-36). Cambridge: Cambridge University Press.

Johns, A. M. 1995. Not all grammar rules are equal: Giving grammar instruction its proper place in foreign language teaching. In R. Schmidt (ed.), *Attention and Awareness in Foreign Language Learning* (pp. 359-386). Honolulu: University of Hawaii.

Kadia, K. 1988. The effect of formal instruction on monitored and spontaneous naturalistic interlanguage performance: A case study. *TESOL Quarterly* 22: 509-515.

Kaplan, R. M. & Bresnan, J. 1982. Lexical functional grammar: A formal system for grammatical representation. In J. Bresnan (ed.), *The Mental Representation of Grammatical Relations* (pp. 173-281). Cambridge, MA: The MIT Press.

Keck, C., Iberri-Shea, G., Tracy-Ventura, N., & Wa-Mbaleka, S. 2006. Investigating the empirical link between task-based interaction and acquisition. In J. Norris & L. Ortega (eds.), *Synthesizing Research on Language Learning and Teaching* (pp. 91-131). Amsterdam: Benjamins.

Keh, C. 1990. Feedback in the writing process: A model and methods for implementation. *ELT Journal* 4: 329-344.

Kepner, C. G. 1991. An experiment in the relationship of types of written feedback to the development of second-language writing skills. *The Modern Language Journal* 75: 305-313.

Knoblauch, C. H. & Brannon, L. 1981. Teacher commentary on student writing: The state of the art. *Freshman English News* 10: 1-4.

Krashen, S. D. 1981. *Second Language Acquisition and Second Language Learning*. Oxford: Pergamon Press.

Krashen, S. D. 1982. *Principles and Practice in Second Language Acquisition*. Oxford: Pergamon.

Krashen, S. D. 1984. *Writing: Research, Theory, and Application*. Oxford: Pergamon Press.

Krashen, S. D. 1985. *The Input Hypothesis: Issues and Implications*. London: Longman.

Krashen, S. D. 1987. *Principles and Practice in Second Language Acquisition*. Englewood Cliffs, NJ: Prentice-Hall.

Krashen, S. D. 1998. Comprehensible Output? *System* 26: 175-182.

Kroll, B. M. & Schafer, J. C. 1978. Error-analysis and the teaching of composition. *College Composition and Communication* 29: 242-248.

Labov, W. 1972. *Language in the Inner City: Studies in the Black English Vernacular*. Philadelphia, PA: University of Philadelphia Press.

Lado, R. 1957. *Linguistics across Cultures: Applied Linguistics for Language Teachers*. University of Michigan Press: Ann Arbor.

Lalande, J. F., II. 1982. Reducing composition errors: An experiment. *The Modern Language Journal* 66: 140-149.

Langacker, R. W. 1987. *Foundations of Cognitive Grammar. Vol. 1: Theoretical Prerequisites*. Stanford, CA: Stanford University Press.

Langacker, R. W. 1991. *Foundations of Cognitive Grammar. Vol. 2: Descriptive Application*. Stanford, CA: Stanford University Press.

Lantolf, J. P. & Appel, G. 1994. Theoretical frameworks: An introduction to Vygotskian perspectives on second language research. In J. Lantolf, & G. Appel (eds.), *Vygotskian Approaches to Second Language Research* (pp. 1-5). Norwood, NJ: Ablex.

Lantolf, J. P. & Thorne, S. 2006. *Sociocultural Theory and the Genesis of Second Language Development*. Oxford: Oxford University Press.

Larsen-Freeman, D. 1997. Chaos/ Complexity science and second language acquisition. *Applied Linguistics* 18: 141-165.

Larsen-Freeman, D. & Long, M. H. 1991. *An Introduction to Second Language Acquisition Research*. New York: Longman.

Lee, I. 1997. ESL learners' performance in error correction in writing. *System* 25: 465-477.

Lee, I. 2004. Error correction in L2 secondary writing classrooms: the case of Hong Kong. *Journal of Second Language Writing* 13: 285-312.

Lee, I. 2008. Understanding teachers' written feedback practices in Hong Kong secondary classrooms. *Journal of Second Language Writing* 17: 69-85.

Lee, I. 2009. Ten Mismatches between teachers' beliefs and written feedback practice. *ELT Journal* 63: 13-22.

Lee, I. 2013. Research into practice: Written corrective feedback. *Language Teaching* 46: 108-119.

Leki, I. 1990a. Coaching from the margins: Issues in written response. In B. Kroll (ed.), *Second Language Writing: Research Insights for the Classroom* (pp. 57-68). Cambridge: Cambridge University Press.

Leki, I. 1990b. Potential problems with peer responding in ESL writing classes. *CATESOL Journal* 3: 5-19.

Leki, I. 1991. The preferences of ESL students for error correction in college-level writing classes. *Foreign Language Annals* 24: 203-218.

Leki, I. 2000. Writing, literacy, and applied linguistics. *Annual Review of Applied Linguistics* 20: 99-115.

Leonard, S. A. & Moffett, H. Y. 1927. Current definitions of levels in English usage. *English Journal* 16: 345-359.

Lewis, M. (2000). *Teaching collocation: Further developments in the lexical approach*. Hove: Language Teaching Publications.

Li, S.-F. 2010. The effectiveness of corrective feedback in SLA: A meta-analysis. *Language Learning* 60: 309-365.

Lightbown, P. M. 1983. Acquiring English L2 in Quebec classrooms. In S. W. Felix & H. Wode (eds.), *Language Development at the Crossroads: Papers from the Interdisciplinary Conference on Language Acquisition at Passau* (pp. 101-120). Tübingen, Germany: Gunter Narr.

Lightbown, P. M. 1985. Input and acquisition for second-language learners in and out of classrooms. *Applied Linguistics* 6: 263-273.

Lightbown, P. M. & Spada, N. 2008. *How Languages are Learned*. New York, NY: Oxford University Press.

Linnell, J. 1995. *Negotiation as a context for learning syntax in a second language*. Unpublished Ph. D. dissertation, University of Pennsylvania, Philadelphia.

Loewen, S. 2004. Uptake in incidental focus on form in meaning-based ESL lessons. *Language Learning* 54: 153-188.

Loewen, S. & Philp, J. 2006. Recasts in the adult English L2 classroom: Characteristics, explicitness, and effectiveness. *The Modern Language Journal* 90: 536-556.

Long, M. H. 1983. Linguistic and conversational adjustments to non-native speakers. *Studies in Second Language Acquisition* 2: 177-193.

Long, M. H. 1985. Input and second language acquisition theory. In S. Gass & C. Madden (eds.), *Input in Second Language Acquisition* (377-393). New York: Newbury House.

Long, M. H. 1991. Focus on form: A design feature in language teaching methodology. In K. de Bot, R. Ginsberg, & C. Kramsch (eds.), *Foreign Language Research in cross-cultural Perspective* (pp. 39-52). Amsterdam: Benjamin.

Long, M. H. 1996. The role of the linguistic environment in second language acquisition. In W. C. Ritchie & T. K. Bhatia (eds.), *Handbook of Second Language Acquisition* (413-468). San Diego, CA: Academic Press.

Long, M. H. 2007. *Problems in SLA*. Mahwah: Lawrence Erlbaum Association.

Long, M. H., Inagaki, s., & Ortega, L. 1998. The role of implicit negative evidence in SLA: Models and recasts in Japanese and Spanish. *The Modern Language Journal* 82: 357-371.

Loschky, L. 1994. Comprehensible input and second language acquisition: What is the relationship? *Studies in Second Language Acquisition* 16: 303-323.

Lunsford, A. A. & Lunsford, K. J. 2008. "Mistakes are a fact of life": A national comparative study. *College Composition and Communication* 59: 781-806.

Luria, A. R. 1961. Study of the abnormal child. *American Journal of Orthopsychiatry. A Journal of Human Behavior* 31: 1-16.

Lyons, J. 1977. *Semantics*. (2 vols.). Cambridge: Cambridge University Press.

Lyster, R. 1998. Recasts, repetition, and ambiguity in L2 classroom discourse. *Studies in Second Language Acquisition* 20: 51-81.

Lyster, R. 2001. Negotiation of form, recasts, and explicit correction in relation to error types and learner repair in immersion classrooms. *Language Learning* 48: 183-218.

Lyster, R. 2004. Different effects of prompts and effects in form-focused instruction. *Studies in Second Language Acquisition* 26: 399-432.

Lyster, R. & Mori, H. 2006. Interactional feedback and instructional counterbalance. *Studies in Second Language Acquisition* 28: 269-300.

Lyster, R. & Ranta, L. 1997. Corrective feedback and learner uptake. *Studies in Second Language Acquisition* 19: 37-66.

Lyster, R. & Saito, K. 2010. Oral feedback in classroom SLA: A meta-analysis. *Studies in Second Language Acquisition* 32: 265-302.

Mackey, A. & Goo, J. 2007. Interaction research in SLA: A meta-analysis and research synthesis. In A. Mackey (ed.), *Conversational Interaction in SLA: A Collection of Empirical Studies* (pp. 408-452). New York: Oxford University Press.

Mackey, A. & Oliver, R. 2002. Interactional feedback and children's L2 development. *System* 30: 459-477.

Mackey, A. & Philp, J. 1998. Conversational interaction and second language development: Recasts, responses, and red herrings? *The Modern Language Journal* 82: 338-356.

Mackey, A., Gass, S., & McDonough, K. 2000. How do learners perceive interactional feedback? *Studies in Second Language Acquisition* 22: 471-497.

Mackey, A., Oliver, R., & Leeman, J. 2003. Interactional input and the incorporation of feedback: An exploration of NS-NNS and NNS-NNS adult and child dyads. *Language Learning* 53: 35-66.

Mackey, A., Philp, J., Egi, T., Fujii, A., & Tatsumi, T. 2002. Individual differences in working memory, noticing of interactional feedback and L2 development. In P. Robinson (ed.), *Individual Differences and Instructed Language learning* (pp. 181-210). Amsterdam: John Benjamins.

MacWhinney, B. & Anderson, J. 1986. The Acquisition of grammar. In I. Gopnik & M. Gopnik (eds.), *From Models to Modules* (pp. 3-23). Norwood, NJ: Ablex.

Manchon, R. 2011. *Learning-to-Write and Writing-to-Learn in an Additional Language*. Amsterdam: John Benjamins.

Manchon, R. 2012. *L2 Writing Development: Multiple Perspectives*. Boston: Walter de Gruyter.

Matsuda, P. K. 2003. Process and post-process: A discursive history. *Journal of Second Language Writing* 12: 65-83.

McCrimmon, J. M. 1939. Commas and conformity. *College English* 1: 68-70.

McDonough, K. 2005. Identifying the impact of negative feedback and learners' response on ESL question development. *Studies in Second Language Acquisition* 27: 79-103.

McDonough, K. 2006. Interaction and syntactic priming: English L2 speakers' production of dative constructions. *Studies in Second Language Acquisition* 28: 179-207.

McDonough, K. & Mackey, A. 2006. Responses to recasts: repetitions, primed production, and linguistic development. *Language Learning* 56: 693-720.

McLaughlin, B. 1978. The Monitor Model: Some methodological considerations. *Language Learning* 28: 309-322.

McLaughlin, B. 1980. Theory and research in second language learning: An emerging paradigm. *Language Learning* 30: 331-350.

McLaughlin, B. 1987. *Theories of Second Language Learning*. London: Edward Arnold.

McLaughlin, B. 1990. Restructuring. *Applied Linguistics* 11: 113-128.

McLaughlin, B. & Heredia, R. 1996. Information-processing approaches to research on second language acquisition and use. In W. Ritchie & T. Bhatia (eds.), *Handbook of Second Language Acquisition* (pp. 213-228). San Diego, CA: Academic Press.

Meara, P. 2006. Emergent properties of multilingual lexicons. *Applied Linguistics* 27: 620-644.

Mellow, J. D. 2006. The emergence of second language syntax: A case study of the acquisition of relative clauses. *Applied Linguistics* 27: 645-670.

Mergel, B. 1998. Instruction Design and Learning Theory. http://www.usask.ca/education/oursework/8-2/papers/mergel/brenda.htm.

Milton, J. 2006. Resource-rich web-based feedback: Helping learners become independent writers. In K. Hyland & F. Hyland (eds.), *Feedback in Second Language Writing: Contexts and Issues* (pp. 129-139). Cambridge: Cambridge University Press.

Mitchell, R. & Myles, F. 2004. *Second Language Learning Theories* (2nd ed.). New York, NY: Oxford University Press.

Mito, K. 1993. *The effects of modeling and recasting on the acquisition of L2 grammar rules*. Unpublished manuscript. University of Hawai'i at Manoa.

Montgomery, J. L. & Baker, W. 2007. Teacher-written feedback: Student perceptions, teacher self-assessment, and actual teacher performance. *Journal of Second Language Writing* 16: 82-99.

Nabei, T. & Swain, M. 2002. Learner awareness of recasts in classroom interaction: A case study of an adult EFL student's second language learning. *Language Awareness* 11: 43-63.

Naomi, L. Q. 2000. *Essentials of Myers-Briggs Type Indicator Assessment*. New York: Consulting Psychologists Press.

Nicholas, H., Lightbown, P., & Spada, N. 2001. Recasts as feedback to language learners. *Language Learning* 51: 719-758.

Nobuyoshi, J., & Ellis, R. 1993. Focused communication tasks and second language acquisition. *ELT Journal* 47: 203-210.

Norris, J. M. & Ortega, L. 2003. Defining and measuring SLA. In C. G. Doughty & M. H. Long (eds.), *Handbook of Second Language Acquisition* (pp. 717-761). Oxford: Blackwell Publishing.

Nystrom, N. 1983. Teacher-student interaction in bilingual classrooms: Four approaches to error feedback. In H. Seliger & M. H. Long (eds.), *Classroom-Oriented Research in Second Language Acquisition* (pp. 169-189). New York: Newbury House.

O'Grady, W. 2003. The radical middle: Nativism without University Grammar. In C. J. Doughty & M. H. Long (eds.), *The Handbook of Second Language Acquisition* (pp. 43-62). Malden, MA: Blackwell.

O'Grady, W. 2008a. The emergentist program. *Lingua* 118: 447-464.

O'Grady, W. 2008b. Innateness, universal grammar, and emergentism. *Lingua* 118: 620-631.

Oliver, R. 1995. Negative feedback in child NS-NNS conversation. *Studies in Second Language Acquisition* 17: 459-481.

Oliver, R. 1998. Negotiation of meaning in child interactions. *The Modern Language Journal* 82: 372-386.

Oliver, R. & Mackey, A. 2003. Interactional context and feedback in child ESL classrooms. *The Modern Language Journal* 87: 519-533.

Oller, J. W. & Ziahosseiny, S. M. 1970. The contrastive analysis hypothesis and spelling errors. *Language Learning* 20: 183-189.

O'Malley, J. M. & Chamot, A. U. 1990. *Learning Strategy in Second Language Acquisition*. Cambridge: Cambridge University Press.

Ortega, L. & Long, M. H. 1997. The effects of models and recasts on the acquisition of object topicalization and adverb placement in L2 Spanish. *Spanish Applied Linguistics* 1: 65-86.

Panova, I. & Lyster, R. 2002. Patterns of corrective feedback and uptake in an adult ESL classroom. *TESOL Quarterly* 36: 573-595.

Pask, G. 1976. Styles and Strategies of Learning. *British Journal of Educational Psychology* 46: 128-148.

Patthey-Chavez, G. G. & Ferris, D. R. 1997. Writing conferences and the weaving of multi-voiced texts in college composition. *Research in the Teaching of English* 31: 51-90.

Philp, J. 1999. *Interaction, noticing and second language acquisition: an examination of learner's noticing of recasts in task-based interaction*. Unpublished Ph. D. dissertation. University of Tasmania.

Philp, J. 2003. Constraints on 'noticing the gap': Nonnative speakers' noting of recasts in NS-NNS interaction. *Studies in Second Language Acquisition* 25: 99-126.

Piaget, J. 1970. *Genetic Epistemology*. Columbia, OH: Columbia University Press.

Piaget, J. & Inhelder, B. 1966. *The Psychology of the Child* (H. Weaver, Trans.). New York: Basic Books.

Pica, T. 1988. Interlanguage adjustments as an outcome of NS-NNS negotiated interaction. *Language Learning* 38: 45-73.

Pica, T., Young, R., & Doughty, C. 1987. The Impact of Interaction on Comprehension. *TESOL Quarterly* 21: 737-758.

Pica, T., Holliday, L., Lewis, N., & Morgenthaler, L. 1989. Comprehensible output as an outcome of linguistic demands on the learner. *Studies in Second Language Acquisition* 11: 63-90.

Pienemann, M. 1981. Der Zweitsprachenerwerb ausl? ndischer Arbeitskinder. Bonn: Bouvier.

Pienemann, M. 1987. Determining the influence of instruction on L2 speech processing. *Australian Review of Applied Linguistics* 10: 83-113.

Pienemann, M. 1989. Is language teachable? Psycholinguistic experiments and hypotheses. *Applied Linguistics* 10: 52-79.

Pienemann, M. 1998. *Language Processing and Second Language Development: Processability Theory*. Amsterdam: John Benjamins.

Pienemann, M. 2003. Language processing capacity. In C. G. Doughty & M. H. Long (eds.), *The Handbook of Second Language of Second Language Acquisition* (pp. 679-715). Oxford: Blackwell Publishing.

Plann, S. 1977. Acquiring a second language in an immersion classroom. In H. D. Brown, C. A. Yorio, & R. H. Crymes (eds.), *On TESOL 77: Teaching and Learning English as a Second Language: Trends in Research and Practice* (pp. 213-225). Washington, DC: TESOL.

Polio, C. 2012. The relevance of second language acquisition theory to the written error correction debate. *Journal of Second Language Writing* 21: 375-389.

Polio, C. Fleck, C, & Leder, N. 1998. "If only I had more time": ESL learners' changes in linguistic accuracy on essay revisions. *Journal of Second Language Writing* 7: 43-68.

Quirk, R., Sidney, G., Geoffrey, L., & Jan. S. 1985. *A Comprehensive Grammar of the English Language*. London: Longman.

Radecki, P. M., & Swales, J. M. 1988. ESL student reaction to written comments on their written work. *System* 16: 355-365.

Raimes, A. 1979. *Problems and Teaching Strategies in ESL Composition*. Arlington, Center for Applied Linguistics.

Raimes, A. 1983. *Techniques in Teaching Writing*. London: Oxford University Press.

Raimes, A. 1985. What unskilled ESL students do as they write: A classroom study of composing. *TESOL Quarterly* 19: 229-258.

Raimes, A. 1987. Language proficiency, writing ability, and composing strategies: A study of ESL college student writers. *Language Learning* 37: 439-468.

Ramirez, A. G. & Stromquist, N. P. 1979. ESL methodology and student language learning in bilingual elementary schools. *TESOL Quarterly*, 13: 145-158.

Ranta, L. 2002. The role of learners' language analytic ability in the communicative classroom. In P. Robinson (ed.), *Individual Differences and Instructed Language Learning* (pp. 159-180). Amsterdam: John Benjamins.

Reber, A. S. 1976. Implicit learning of synthetic languages: The role of the instructional set. *Journal of Experimental Psychology: Human Learning and Memory* 2: 88-94.

Reid, J. 1994. Responding to ESL students' texts: The myths of appropriation. *TESOL Quarterly* 28: 273-292.

Reid, J. 1998. "Eye" learners and "ear" learners: Identifying the language needs of international students and U.S. resident writers. In P. Byrd & J. M. Reid (eds.), *Grammar in the Composition Classroom: Essays on Teaching ESL for College-Bound Students* (pp. 3-17). Boston: Heinle & Heinle.

Reid, J. 2005. "Ear" learners and error in US college writing. In P. Bruthiaux, D. Atkinson, W. Eggington, W. Crabbe & V. Ramanathan (eds.), *Directions in Applied Linguistics* (pp. 117-278). Toronto: Multilingual Matters.

Reves, T. 1982. What Makes a Good Language Learner?. Unpublished Ph. D. dissertation, Hebrew University of Jerusalem.

Révész, A. 2009. Task complexity, focus on form, and second language development. *Studies in Second Language Acquisition* 31: 437-470.

Révész, A. & Han, Z-H. 2006. Task content familiarity, task type, and efficacy of recasts. *Language Awareness* 3: 160-179.

Riazantseva, A. 2012. Outcome measure of L2 writing as a mediator of the effects of corrective feedback on students' ability to write accurately. *System* 40: 421-430.

Robb, T., Ross, S. & Shortreed, I. 1986. Salience of feedback on error and its effect on EFL writing quality. *TESOL Quarterly* 20: 83-95.

Roberts, B. 1999. *Can Error Logs Raise More Than Consciousness? The Effects of Error Logs and Grammar Feedback on ESL Students' Final Drafts*. Unpublished master's thesis, California State University, Sacramento.

Russell, J. & Spada, N. 2006. The effectiveness of corrective feedback for second language acquisition: A meta-analysis of the research. In J. Norris & L. Ortega (eds.), *Synthesizing Research on Language Learning and Teaching* (pp. 131-164). Amsterdam: Benjamins.

Sachs, R. & Polio, C. 2007. Learners' uses of two types of written feedback on a L2 writing revision task. *Studies in Second Language Acquisition* 29: 67-100.

Saito, H. 1994. Teachers' practices and students' preferences for feedback on second language writing: A case study of adult ESL learners. *TESL Canada Journal* 11: 46-70.

Santa, T. 2006. *Dead Letters: Error in Composition*, 1873-2004. Cresskill, NJ: Hampton Press.

Sawyer, M., & Ranta, L. 2001. Aptitude, individual differences, and instructional design. In P. Robinson (ed.), *Cognition and Second Language Acquisition* (pp. 319-353). Cambridge: Cambridge University Press.

Schmidt, R. & Frota, S. 1986. Developing basic conversational ability in a second language: A case of an adult learner of Portuguese. In R. R. Day (ed.), *Talking to Learn: Conversation in Second Language Acquisition* (pp. 237-322). New York: Newbury House.

Schmidt, R. 1990. The role of consciousness in second language learning. *Applied Linguistics* 11: 129-158.

Schmidt, R. 1994. Deconstructing consciousness in search of useful definitions for applied linguistics. *Aila Review* 11: 11-26.

Schmidt, R. 1995. *Attention and Awareness in Foreign Language*

Learning. Honolulu: University of Hawaii Press.

Schmidt, R. 2001. Attention. In P. Robinson (ed.), *Cognition and Second Language Instruction* (pp. 3-32). Cambridge: Cambridge University Press.

Schmitt, N., D? rnyei, Z., Adolphs, S., & Durow, V. 2003. Knowledge and acquisition of formulaic sequences: A longitudinal study. In Schmitt, N. (ed.), *The Acquisition, Processing, and Use of Formulaic Sequences* (pp. 55-86). Amsterdam: John Benjamins.

Schulz, R. 2001. Cultural differences in student and teacher perceptions concerning the role of grammar instruction. *The Modern Language Journal* 85: 244-258.

Schumann, J. H. 1978a. *The Pidginization Process: A Model for Second Language Acquisition.* New York: Newbury House.

Schumann, J. H. 1978b. Second language acquisition: The pidginization hypothesis. In E. M. Hatch (ed.), *Second Language Acquisition: A Book of Readings* (pp. 256-271). New York: Newbury House.

Schwartz, B. D. 1993. On explicit and negative data effecting and affecting competence and 'linguistic behavior'. *Studies in Second Language Acquisition* 15: 147-163.

Schwartz, B. D. & Sprouse, R. 1994. Word order and nominative case in nonnative language acquisition: a longitudinal study of (L1 Turkish) German interlanguage. In T. Hoekstra & B. Schwartz (eds.), *Language Acquisition Studies in Generative Grammar: Papers in Honor of Kenneth Wexler from the GLOW 1991 Workshops* (pp. 317-368). Amsterdam: John Benjamins.

Schwartz, B. D. & Sprouse, R. 1996. L2 cognitive states and the Full Transfer/Full Access model. *Second Language Research* 12: 40-72.

Searle, D. & Dillon, D. 1980. The message of marking: Teacher written responses to student writing at intermediate grade levels. *Research in the Teaching of English* 14: 233-242.

Seliger, H. 1979. On the nature and function of language rules in language teaching. *TESOL Quarterly* 13: 359-369.

Selinker, L. F. 1972. Interlanguage. *International Review of Applied Linguistics* 10: 209-241.

Semke, H. D. 1984. Effects of the red pen. *Foreign Language Annals* 17: 195-202.

Sharwood Smith, M. 1981. Consciousness raising and the second language learner. *Applied Linguistics* 2: 159-169.

Sharwood Smith, M. 1993. Input enhancement in instructed SLA: Theoretical bases. *Studies in Second Language Acquisition* 15: 165-179.

Shaughnessy, M. P. 1977. *Errors and Expectations*. New York: Oxford University Press.

Sheen, Y. 2004. Corrective feedback and learner uptake in communicative classrooms across instructional settings. *Language Teaching Research* 8: 263-300.

Sheen, Y. 2007. The effect of focused written corrective feedback and language aptitude on ESL learners' acquisition of articles. *TESOL Quarterly* 41: 255-283.

Sheen, Y. 2010. Differential effects of oral and written corrective feedback in the ESL classroom. *Studies in Second Language Acquisition* 32: 201-234.

Sheen, Y. 2011. *Corrective Feedback, Individual Differences and Second Language Learning*. Springer Publishing.

Sheen, Y., Wright, D., & Moldawa, A. 2009. Differential effects of focused and unfocused written correction on the accurate use of grammatical forms by adult ESL learners. *System* 37: 556-569.

Sheppard, K. 1992. Two feedback types: Do they make a difference? *RELC Journal* 23: 103-110.

Silva, T. 1988. Comments on Vivian Zamel's "Recent research on writing pedagogy". *TESOL Quarterly* 22: 517-519.

Silva, T. 1990. Second language composition instruction: Developments, issues, and directions in ESL. In B. Kroll (ed.), *Second Language Writing: Research Insights for the Classroom* (pp. 11-23). Cambridge: Cambridge University Press.

Silva, T. 1993. Toward an understanding of the distinct nature of L2 writing: The ESL research and its implications. *TESOL Quarterly* 27: 657-677.

Silva, T. 1997. On the ethical treatment of ESL writers. *TESOL Quarterly* 31: 359-363.

Siyanova, A. & Schmitt, N. 2008. L2 learner production and processing of collocation: A multi-study perspective. *Canadian Modern Language Review* 64: 429-458.

Skehan, P. & Forster, P. 2001. Cognition and tasks. In P. Robinson (ed.), *Cognition and Second Language Instruction* (pp. 183-205). Cambridge: Cambridge University Press.

Skehan, P. 1998. *A Cognitive Approach to Language Learning*. Oxford: Oxford University Press.

Skinner, B. F. 1957. *Verbal Behavior*. Eaglewood, Cliff, NJ: Prentice Hall.

Sommers, N. 1980. Revision strategies of student writers and experienced adult writers. *College Composition and Communication* 31: 378-388.

Sommers, N. 1982. Responding to student writing. *College Composition and Communication* 33: 148-156.

Storch, N. 2010. Critical feedback on written corrective feedback research. *International Journal of English Studies* 10: 29-46.

Storch, N. & Wigglesworth, G. 2010. Learners' processing, uptake, and retention of corrective feedback on writing: Case studies. *Studies in Second Language Acquisition* 32: 303-334.

Straub, R. 2000. *The Practice of Response: Strategies for Commenting on Student Writing*. Cresskill, NJ: Hampton Press.

Straub, R. & Lunsford, R. F. 1995. *Twelve Readers Reading: Responding to College Student Writing*. Creskill, NJ: Hampton Press.

Swain, M. 1985. Communicative competence: Some roles of comprehensible input and comprehensible output in its development. In S. M. Gass & C. G. Madden (eds.), *Input in Second Language Acquisition* (pp. 235-253). New York: Newbury House.

Swain, M. 1995. Three functions of output in second language learning. In G. Cook & B. Seidlhofer (eds.), *Principles and Practice in the Study of Language* (pp. 125-144). Oxford: Oxford University Press.

Swain, M. 2005. The output hypothesis: Theory and research. In E. Hinkel (ed.), *Handbook of Research in Second Language Teaching and Learning* (pp. 471-483). Mahwah, NJ: Erlbaum.

Swain, M. 2006. Languaging, agency and collaboration in advanced language proficiency. In H. Byrnes (ed.), *Advanced Language Learning: The Contribution of Halliday and Vygotsky* (pp. 95-108). New York: Continuum.

Swain, M. & Lapkin, S. 1995. Problems in output and the cognitive processes they generate: A step towards second language learning. *Applied Linguistics* 16: 371-391.

Swain, M. & Lapkin, S. 1998. Interaction and second language learning: Two adolescent French immersion students working together. *The Modern Language Journal* 82: 320-337.

Swain, M. & Lapkin, S. 2002. Talking it through: Two French immersion learners' response to reformulation. *International Journal of Educational Research* 37: 285-304.

Swain, M. & Lapkin, S. 2007. 'Oh, I get it now!' From production to comprehension in second language learning. In D. M. Brinton & O. Kagan (eds.), *Heritage Language Acquisition: A New Field Emerging* (pp. 301-319). Mahwah, NJ: Lawrence Erlbaum.

Taylor, B. P. 1981. Content and written form: A two-way street. *TESOL Quarterly* 15: 5-13.

Terrell, T. D., Baycroft, B., & Perrone, C. 1987. The subjunctive in Spanish interlanguage: Accuracy and comprehensibility. In B. VanPatten, T. R. Dvorak, & J. F. Lee (eds.), *Foreign Language Learning: A Research Perspective* (pp. 19-32). New York: Newbury House.

Tomasello, M. 2003. *Constructing a Language: A Usage-based Theory of Language Acquisition*. Cambridge, Mass.: Harvard

Unviersity Press.

Tomasello, M. & Herron, C. 1988. Down the garden path: Including and correcting overgeneralization errors in the foreign language classroom. *Applied Psycholinguistics* 9: 237-246.

Tomasello, M. & Herron, C. 1989. Feedback for language transfer errors: The garden path technique. *Studies in Second Language Acquisition* 11: 385-395.

Trahey, M. 1996. Positive evidence in second language acquisition: some long term effects. *Second Language Research* 12: 111-139.

Trahey, M. & White, L. 1993. Positive evidence and preemption in the second language classroom. *Studies in Second Language Acquisition* 15: 181-204.

Truscott, J. 1996. The case against grammar correction in L2 writing classes. *Language learning* 46: 327-369.

Truscott, J. 1999. The case for "The case against grammar correction in L2 writing classes": A response to Ferris. *Journal of Second Language Writing* 8: 111-122.

Truscott, J. 2001. Selecting errors for selective error correction. *Concentric: Studies in English Literature and Linguistics* 27: 93-108.

Truscott, J. 2004. Evidence and conjecture on the effects of correction: A response to Chandler. *Journal of Second Language Writing* 13: 337-343.

Truscott, J. 2007. The effect of error correction on learners' ability to write accurately. *Journal of Second Language Writing* 16: 255-272.

Truscott, J. 2009. Arguments and appearances: A response to Chandler. *Journal of Second Language Writing* 18: 59-60.

Truscott, J. 2010. Some thoughts on Anthony Bruton's critique of the correction debate. *System*, 38: 329-335.

Truscott, J. & Hsu, A. Y. P. 2008. Error correction, revision, and learning. *Journal of Second Language Writing* 17: 292-305.

Vainikka, A. & Young-Scholten, M. 1996. The early stages in adult L2 syntax: additional evidence from Romance speakers. *Second Language Research* 12: 140-176.

van Beuningen, C., de Jong, N. H., & Kuiken, F. 2008. The effect of direct and indirect corrective feedback on L2 learners' written accuracy. *ITL International Journal of Applied Linguistics* 156: 279-296.

van Beuningen, C., de Jong, N. H., & Kuiken, F. 2012. Evidence on the effectiveness of comprehensive error correction in second language writing. *Language Learning* 62: 1-41.

VanPatten, B. 1990. Attending to content and form in the input: An experiment in consciousness. *Studies in Second Language Acquisition* 12: 287-301.

VanPatten, B. & Williams, J. 2007. Introduction: The nature of theories. In B. VanPatten & J. Williams (eds.), *Theories in Second Language Acquisition: An Introduction* (pp. 1-6). Mahwah, NJ: Erlbaum.

Varonis, E. & Gass, S. 1985a. Non-native/non-native conversations: A model for negotiation of meaning. *Applied Linguistics* 6: 71-90.

Varonis, E. & Gass, S. 1985b. Miscommunication in native/non-native conversation. *Language in Society* 14: 327-343.

Vygotsky, L. S. 1962. *Thought and Language*. Cambridge, MA: MIT Press.

Vygotsky, L. S. 1978. *Mind in Society: The Development of Higher Psychological Processes*. Cambridge, MA: Harvard University Press.

Wall, S. & Hull, G. 1989. The semantics of error: What do teachers know? In C. M. Anson (ed.), *Writing and Response: Theory, Practice, and Research* (pp. 261-292). Urbana, IL: NCTE.

Wang, C. M. & M. Wang. (in press). Effect of alignment on L2 written production. *Applied Linguistics*.

Wardhaugh, R. 1970. The contrastive analysis hypothesis. *TESOL Quarterly* 4: 123-130.

Wesche, M. B. 1981. Language aptitude measures in streaming, matching students with methods, and diagnosis of learning problems. In K. C. Diller (ed.), *Individual Differences and Universals in Language Learning Aptitude* (pp. 119-154). New York: Newbury House.

White, L. 1990/1991. The verb-movement parameter in second language acquisition. *Language Acquisition* 1: 337-360.

White, L. 1991. Adverb placement in second language acquisition: some effects of positive nad negative evidence in the classroom. *Second Language Research* 7: 133-161.

White, L. 1992. Long and short verb movement in second language acquisition. *Canadian Journal of Linguistics* 37: 273-286.

White, L. 2003. *Second Language Acquisition and Universal Grammar*. Cambridge: Cambridge University Press.

White, L., Spada, N., Lightbown, P. & Ranta, L. 1991. Input enhancement and L2 question formation. *Applied Linguistics* 12: 416-432.

Williams, F. 1970. *Language and Poverty*. Chicago: Markham Publishing Co.

Williams, J. 2012. The potential role(s) of writing in second language development. *Journal of Second Language Writing* 21: 321-331.

Williams, J. M. 1981. The phenomenology of error. *College Composition and Communication* 32: 152-168.

Wolfram, W. & Fasold, R. W. 1974. *The Study of Social Dialects in American English*. Englewood Cliffs, NJ: Prentice-Hall.

Wykoff, G. S. 1939. An open letter to the educational experts on teaching composition. *College English* 1: 140-146.

Xu, C.-Q. 2009. Overgeneralization from a narrow focus: A response to Ellis et al. (2008) and Bitchener (2008). *Journal of Second Language Writing* 18: 270-275.

Yeh, S.-W. & Lo, J.-J. 2009. Using online annotations to support error correction and corrective feedback. *Computers & Education* 52: 882-892.

Zamel, V. 1976. Teaching composition in the ESL classroom: What we can learn from research in the teaching of English. *TESOL Quarterly* 10: 67-76.

Zamel, V. 1982. Writing: The process of discovering meaning. *TESOL Quarterly* 16: 195-209.

Zamel, V. 1983. The composing process of advanced ESL students. Six case studies. *TESOL Quarterly* 19: 79-102.

Zamel, V. 1985. Responding to student writing. *TESOL Quarterly* 19: 79-102.

Zamel, V. 1987. Recent research on writing pedagogy. *TESOL Quarterly* 31: 697-715.

Zhang, S. 1995. Reexaming the affective advantage of peer feedback in the ESL Writing class. *Journal of Second Language Writing* 4: 209-222.

Zhang, S. 1999. Thoughts on some recent evidence concerning the affective advantage of peer feedback. *Journal of Second Language Writing* 8: 321-326.

陈平. 1987. 释汉语中与名词性成分相关的四组概念.《中国语文》第 4 期,81-92.

陈晓湘、彭丽娜、郭兴荣、张姣、刘星. 2013. 聚焦和非聚焦书面反馈对英语非真实条件虚拟语气习得的影响.《外语与外语教学》第 2 期,31-40.

陈亚平. 2011. 有意识的言语输出——显性知识作用于隐性知识发展的途径.《解放军外国语学院学报》第 4 期,61-65.

戴曼纯. 2007. 二语习得研究的生成语法新范式——中介语特征理论评介.《外语教学与研究》第 6 期,444-450.

戴曼纯、魏淑兰. 2007. Michael Long 论二语习得研究中的问题.《外语电化教学》第 5 期,76-80.

邓云华、石毓智. 2007. 论构式语法理论的进步与局限.《外语教学与研究》第 5 期,323-330.

范晔. 2009. 有关问题在二语习得研究中的作用研究综述.《外语界》第 2 期,56-65.

顾伟勤. 2008. 关于不同学习环境对二语词汇习得的影响的一项对比实验研究.《外语电化教学》第 5 期,45-50.

顾伟勤. 2010. 论"互动假说"的发展与局限.《外语学刊》第 5 期,

94-97.

胡壮麟. 2008. 行为主义学习理论为何批而不倒.《英语教师》第4期,4-7.

贾光茂. 2011. 语言知识有多少是先天的?——二语习得涌现论与先天论之辩述评.《当代语言学》第4期,361-368.

姜琳. 2009. 双宾结构和介词与格结构启动中的语义启动.《现代外语》第1期,59-67.

姜琳. 2011. 互动对第二语言发展的影响.《英语教师》第4期,2-7.

姜琳. 2012a. 被动结构跨语言启动及其机制.《现代外语》第1期,54-61.

姜琳. 2012b. 书面纠正性反馈研究的现状与未来.《英语教师》第11期,60-64.

姜琳、陈锦. 2013. 书面纠正性反馈与二语习得——针对英语类指名词短语用法的实证研究.《当代外语研究》第11期,31-35.

姜琳、易慧文. 2013. 正面证据、负面反馈与二语习得——英语动词第三人称单数形式习得的实证研究.《英语教师》第12期,50-55.

姜孟. 2012. 从社会文化理论透视二语习得.《英语研究》第3期,53-58.

李兰霞. 2011. 动态系统理论与第二语言发展.《外语教学与研究》第3期,409-421.

李俏. 2005. 二语习得和外语教学的认知心理学探讨.《课程、教材、教法》第11期,39-45.

罗正学、苗丹民、皇甫恩、陈足怀. 2002. MBTI-G人格类型量表中文版的修订.《心理科学》第3期,361-362.

莫俊华. 2007. 同伴互评:提高大学生写作自主性.《解放军外国语学院学报》第3期,35-39.

牛瑞英. 2007.《社会文化理论和第二语言发展的起源》述介.《外语教学与研究》第4期,314-316.

秦建华、王英杰. 2007. 大学生英语学习策略的个案研究.《外语界》第2期,73-81.

束定芳、庄智象. 1996.《现代外语教学—理论、实践与方法》. 上海外语教育出版社.

王初明、牛瑞英、郑小湘. 2000. 以写促学——一项英语写作教学改革的试验.《外语教学与研究》第3期,207-212.

王初明. 2003. 补缺假设与外语学习.《外语学刊》第1期,1-5。

王初明. 2006. 从补缺假说看外语听说读写.《外语学刊》第1期, 79-84.

王初明. 2007. 论外语学习的语境.《外语教学与研究》第3期, 190-197。

王初明. 2009. 学相伴用相随——外语学习的学伴用随原则.《中国外语》第5期,53-59。

王初明. 2010. 互动协同与外语教学.《外语教学与研究》第4期,297-299.

王初明. 2011a. 基于使用的语言习得观.《中国外语》第5期。

王初明. 2011b. 外语教学三大情节与语言习得有效路径.《外语教学与研究》第4期,540-549。

王初明. 2012. 读后续写——提高外语学习效率的一种有效方法.《外语界》第5期,2-7。

王初明. 2013. 哪类练习促学外语.《当代外语研究》第2期,28-31.

王启. 2012. 二语交互中的隐性正面证据———一项探讨交互促学机理的实证研究.《现代外语》第1期,62-69.

王颖、刘振前. 2013. 教师反馈对英语写作准确性、流利性、复杂性和总体质量作用的研究.《外语教学》第6期,49-53.

王月平. 1999. 对比分析、错误分析、中介语与1998年高考英语试题书面表达题典型错误分析.《首都师范大学学报》(社会科学版)增刊.

温植胜. 2005. 对外语学能研究的重新思考.《现代外语》第4期,383-392.

文秋芳. 1996. 英语学习策略论. 上海:上海外语教育出版社.

吴本虎. 2003.《英语学习策略》. 北京/合肥:人民教育出版社,安徽教育出版社.

肖婷. 2013. 协同对提高二语写作准确性的影响. 广东外语外贸大学硕士论文.

薛慧航. 2013. 浅析"读后续写"中趣味性对协同的影响. 广东外语外贸大学硕士论文.

杨梅. 2009. 基于处理器的语言涌现观——William O'Grady访谈.《现代外语》第4期,421-426.

余震球. 2004.《维果茨基教育论著选》. 北京:人民教育出版社.

袁野. 2010. 构式语法的语言习得观.《解放军外国语学院学报》第 1 期, 35-40.

张莹. 2006. 成品写作法向过程写作法的嬗变.《外语教学》第 6 期, 51-54.

章振邦. 2004.《新编英语语法教程》. 上海外语教育出版社.

赵芳. 2009.《建构一种语言: 一种基于使用的语言习得理论》简介.《当代语言学》第 1 期, 89-91.

周颂波、何莲珍、闵尚超. 2011. 教育环境下非英教育环境下非英语专业大学生英语学习动机结构的建模与验证.《现代外语》第 3 期, 287-295.